2004

ACADEMIC LIBRARIES AS HIGH-TECH GATEWAYS

A Guide to Design & Space Decisions

SECOND EDITION

RICHARD J. BAZILLION

CONNIE L. BRAUN

AMERICAN LIBRARY ASSOCIATION
Chicago and London
2001

Composition by the dotted i in Caslon and Avant Garde using QuarkXpress 4.1 for the Macintosh.

Printed on 50-pound white offset, a pH-neutral stock, and bound in 10-point Bristol cover stock by Data Reproductions

The paper used in this publication meets the minimum requirements of American National Standard for Information Sciences—Permanence of Paper for Printed Library Materials, ANSI Z39.48-1992. ∞

Library of Congress Cataloging-in-Publication Data

Bazillion, Richard J., 1943-
　　Academic libraries as high-tech gateways : a guide to design and space decisions / Richard J. Bazillion, Connie L. Braun.—2nd ed.
　　　　p.　　cm.
　　Includes bibliographical references and index.
　　ISBN 0-8389-0792-X (alk. paper)
　　1. Library architecture—United States.　2. Libraries—United States—Automation.　3. Academic libraries—United States.　I. Braun, Connie.　II. Title.
　　Z679.2.U54 B39　　2000
　　727'.8'0973—dc21　　　　　　　　　　　　　　　　　　00-059424

Printed in the United States of America.

05　04　03　02　01　　　　5　4　3　2　1

CONTENTS

When the first edition of this book appeared more than five years ago, Web browsing with the aid of Netscape was so new that it failed to merit a single reference. We mention the World Wide Web frequently in the pages that follow. Here is one simple measure of how dramatically the world of information technology changed in a few years. Innovation's pace shows no signs of flagging, which creates a challenge for writers of books such as this. "Regrettably," wrote one of our reviewers, "there is much about this book that will go out of date quickly." This observation certainly applies to the details of particular technologies, though, we hope, not to the planning and features of modern library buildings themselves. As long as designers strive for and achieve the greatest possible flexibility of space, infrastructure, and functionality, their buildings should be able to accommodate successive generations of technology. If we cannot accomplish this much, then perhaps the library as a physical entity indeed will be superseded by the Web.

We referred to academic libraries in 1995 as "high-tech" gateways. A volume of essays published two years later by the MIT Press ramified this idea.[1] "The gateway library," wrote Richard C. Rockwell, "provides a simple integrated electronic interface between the inquirer and the resource—and the interface is the same no matter which resource the inquirer is seeking."[2] This is the sort of library whose form and function we describe in this book. Our basic assumption, in this world of information technology, is that *access* has superseded *ownership* with respect to library resources of all types. If seamless access is available, then the size of locally held collections is irrelevant both to the research function and to the accreditation process. Notwithstanding this emphasis on access, our second principle is the library's survival as an institution. As the editor of *Gateways to Knowledge* puts it, "[s]tudents still need places to study," places that exist only within a physical structure.[3] With respect to information access, however, the library is not so much a discrete location as an electronic gateway to resources within or beyond its own walls. This duality may confuse those who seek to define libraries *either* as physical entities *or* solely as virtual ones. Today's academic libraries in fact are *hybrids:* physical space combined with cyberspace. They are and will remain citadels for books. As Rockwell says, "What happens to our books matters to the future of our cultures."[4]

Our belief, strengthened by the large number of building projects begun since 1995, is that libraries remain tangible, robust social institutions. In many ways, they symbolize the information revolution itself. Libraries always have been early adopters of technology as well as advocates for technology's social utility. Because no evidence exists that books are an endangered knowledge medium, libraries of a hybrid sort are likely to survive in the decades ahead. New buildings consequently will continue to be erected on campuses that welcome technological innovation.

Buildings created from now on must be flexible enough to integrate new technology while performing their traditional role as repositories for printed material. Although electronic means of storing and disseminating information are improving rapidly, books remain the most elegant and satisfactory way to present a substantial intellectual product. Despite the fragility of modern acidic papers, large book collections will survive for the foreseeable future. But they will have to share building space with new information technologies that claim a growing portion of scarce institutional resources.

Building design is the embodiment of certain ideas about the relationship between print and electronic media drawn from past experience, and the extrapolation of these ideas. Because new buildings are expected to operate efficiently for several decades, basic principles should be tested for soundness before the concrete is poured.[5] That is why it is best to be clear about the role that the new library will play within the university, and about the contribution of information technology to that mission. Even if a library does not aspire to occupy the cutting edge of change, its planners have to understand the direction of technological and economic trends in the publishing and computing industries. The manner in which scholarly research is conducted and its results disseminated in the years ahead has a direct bearing on academic-library design.

Planning a library building involves more than trying to express information-science theories in bricks and mortar. Selection of furniture, shelving, and equipment requires close attention to ergonomics. Because of the variety of computer activities that can be carried on in the library, people may spend longer periods in the building. A pleasant working environment and comfortable study space, therefore, are important considerations. Carpets, color schemes, upholstery fabrics, shelving finishes, and artwork are a few aspects of interior design that cannot be overlooked nor left entirely to the architect's discretion. Librarians are justified in insisting that design factors must complement efficient operation of the building. There is no reason why a functional library cannot also be an attractive building.

Academic libraries of all types face the same constellation of issues: how to balance their collections between print and electronic resources, and how to provide seamless access to both formats. Library-based information services are still the answer for every academic library. A good example of new construction on a community college campus is the Paul A. Elsner Library at Mesa Community College in Arizona. This 95,000-square-foot structure, which supports a student body of 23,000, contains the same electronic facilities found in the newest university libraries.[6] Scope and depth of collections will differ, because community college resources are more closely aligned with the curriculum.

During the past five years, we lived through another library-building project, this time at Winona State University in southeastern Minnesota. We tried to take our own advice, as offered in the following pages. Success sometimes eluded us, as evidenced by the drain spout strategically situated above the book drop, or the impressive octagonal foyer whose hard surfaces and glass enclosure create a gigantic megaphone. Each project teaches its own lessons, from which this new edition tries to profit. There are a few eternal verities among the shifting technological and architectural sands: one is that new libraries must always be designed to be people places; another is that technology, although pervasive, should always be unobtrusive. Pursuit of these goals usually produces interesting experiences. One such experience was to watch a talented owner's representative, Ken Anderson (of Armlin, North and Associates in Minneapolis), forge a building team and hold it together until the job was done. Another was to see a cross-campus move flawlessly executed by Bester Bros. of St. Paul, Minnesota. Our thanks to Paul and Ed Lentz for exceeding all expectations. Many of the vendors with whom we worked supplied quality products and service. By and large, things unfolded as they should.

We hope this book will contribute to the success of other building projects undertaken in a world of constant technological change. The most important piece of advice we can offer is this: Choose your architect with care and become a full partner in the entire construction process. A corollary is: When you know you are right and the architect is not, recall that function must rule over form and have it your way. The only way to get the building you want is to accept personal responsibility for the outcome. This is best accomplished through the process of "building commissioning," which we describe in chapter 5. Many pitfalls can be avoided, if the entire project team recognizes that collaboration will produce a better building.

Richard J. Bazillion
Connie L. Braun

Notes

1. Lawrence Dowler, ed., *Gateways to Knowledge: The Role of Academic Libraries in Teaching, Learning, and Research* (Cambridge, Mass.: MIT Press, 1997).

2. Richard C. Rockwell, "Using electronic social science data in the age of the Internet," in *Gateways to Knowledge*, ed. Dowler, 67.

3. Lawrence Dowler, "Gateways to knowledge: A new direction for the Harvard College Library," in *Gateways to Knowledge*, ed. Dowler, 103.

4. Rockwell, "Using electronic social science data," 120.

5. David Leroy Michaels, "Technology's impact on library interior planning," *Library Hi Tech* 5 (4): 59 (winter 1987).

6. See Website at <http://www.mcc.maricopa.edu>.

ACKNOWLEDGMENTS

Several individuals and institutions assisted us in the course of preparing this second, revised edition. We are pleased to acknowledge their contribution:

- Paul Willis and Judy Sackett of the University of Kentucky in Lexington
- Don Craig of Middle Tennessee State University Library
- Tom Simon, Sheehy Construction Company, Saint Paul, Minnesota
- Ken Anderson, Armlin, North and Associates, Minneapolis, Minnesota
- Special thanks to Tom Grier, Public Information Office, WSU, for his photographic work.

Academic Libraries and the Information-Technology Landscape

*The buildings which house our libraries today are not bad buildings or inade-
quate buildings because the men who planned them and who built them were fools.
They are bad buildings because what goes on inside them now is different from
what was planned to go on inside them. . . . They are akin to the dinosaur and the
mammoth. . . . Feel sorry for them, if you will . . . but do not condemn them, or
their Builders—and above all, do not copy them.*[1]

Where Technology Is Taking Us

In responding to rapid technological change, library designers face a
challenge: the need to plan buildings that are flexible enough to accommodate a future governed by information technology. Electronic publication, full-text databases, worldwide interactive interlibrary loan,
hypertext, and broadband networking now define the world of academic
libraries. Since 1994, the World Wide Web has become the means most
libraries use to gain access to digitized information sources. The Internet
is now a ubiquitous presence and print materials are disappearing from
reference collections.[2] Commercial publishers and university presses are
moving "cautiously" into the realm of electronic publishing.[3] Scholarly
journals are migrating in growing numbers to the Web. A number of universities now require their students to own or lease notebook computers.
How will these developments affect the physical and intellectual structure of library buildings in the decades ahead? Can buildings intended to
house book collections continue to serve in coming years, as they have

1

done in the past, as gateways to human knowledge? Is the library losing its fancied identity as "the heart of the university"? Cynics predict that "ready access [to digitized libraries] obviates the need for all but a small reference division on campus, staffed by a few information specialists."[4]

Designers cannot ignore questions of this sort, which affect all their decisions on architectural, mechanical, electrical, and layout matters. Often the answers are tentative at best; sometimes they represent only a vague sense of the direction in which new technologies are taking us. Occasionally an architect experienced in library design will boldly assert that "it is extremely important that the center of the academic campus maintain as its focus a library with books."[5] Library planning today is an exercise in futurology, as space and resources are refocused on new kinds of services. One thing, however, is certain: The future lies in high-speed networking and ever more nimble access to digitized words, images, and sounds. Academic libraries, moreover, will become community resources that serve a wider public than a university's enrolled students.

Asynchronous learning through the Internet is perhaps the most significant educational innovation of the late 1990s. Web-based and -enhanced courses have proliferated; the University of Texas World Lecture Hall lists hundreds of courses in seventy disciplines.[6] On-campus use of Web-enhanced courses is growing as faculty discover the advantages of interactivity and electronic delivery of course materials. Course electronic discussion groups, e-mail, and threaded-discussion forums enhance and supplement traditional classroom teaching. Programs to offer students universal access to computers, such as the "ThinkPad University" idea pioneered at the University of Minnesota–Crookston, are sprouting around North America. One of the chief advantages of laptop computers is their value as communication devices. They consequently have stimulated faculty interest in collaborative learning, a development with special implications for librarians and libraries. New buildings must now accommodate group studies, electronic classrooms, "information galleries," and space for faculty to create Web-enhanced courses. Computers in these areas will require a high-speed network connection (e.g., ATM or ATM/IP) to allow for transmission of full-motion video. Other software solutions are available for streaming media files (e.g., Real Player). Libraries, in other words, are becoming the communications hubs of their campuses and, thus, centers of expertise in a variety of fields, both informational and pedagogical. Far from losing status as their custodial role declines, libraries are achieving new prominence as educational institutions.[7] A case can be made that librarians, and their buildings, are moving toward the center of the academic enterprise.

If the library is to involve itself in teaching electronic research skills (ERS), then space must be provided for this activity. Almost ten years ago, the University of Iowa installed an Information Arcade in its main library that brings together a variety of hardware and software to encourage "the integration of electronic information resources" into the teaching and learning process (fig. 1). Multimedia and hypertext "electronic manuscripts" can be created by using source material that comprises a large selection of full-text databases. Included in the Arcade is a 1,400-square-foot electronic classroom used by librarians and university faculty to teach courses in art, education, engineering, English, and history.[8] The university has established a second Arcade in the library of the Faculty of Medicine. Other libraries are trying similar experiments. The Leavey Library at the University of Southern California has two learning rooms and a fifty-seat auditorium in its Electronic Information Commons. Similar spaces are features of the new libraries at Middle Tennessee State University and Winona State University in Minnesota. An electronic classroom belongs in every academic library built from now on. This is a place in which librarians may teach electronic research skills in the context of particular courses. Students learn best when they are able to repeat a demonstration on their own computer and obtain advice from the instructor as they go. Information technology may be part of the building's fabric, but its use still has to be taught if the investment in infrastructure is to pay off.

FIGURE 1
Information Arcade, University of Iowa

As student access to portable computers becomes ubiquitous, faculty will feel the pressure to use information technology in their teaching. Many are using such programs as FrontPage, Authorware, and Asymetrix Learning Systems Click2Learn to migrate their courses to the Web. These early efforts amount, in many cases, to little more than "shovel-ware," which merely converts lecture notes to HTML. In other cases, student learning benefits from clever animations used to illustrate such concepts as the Coriolis effect in meteorology.[9]

The explosive growth in campus networking, accompanied by faculty enthusiasm for information technology, suggests a need for facilities in which to develop new kinds of course materials. Libraries, as central places on campus, are good locations for development laboratories. Winona State's new library, for example, contains a 2,500-square-foot Academic Technologies Center (ATC), where faculty are able to engage in discussion and development of new curricular resources that cultivate an innovative learning and teaching environment. Users of the ATC have access to high-end computers, top-of-the-line peripherals (e.g., flatbed and slide scanners, digital still and video cameras), and the latest versions of selected software applications for their course-development work. Expert assistance is available from staff members who report to the library administration. Given the library's own reliance on information technology, it makes sense to include faculty development in its mandate. Acceptance of this role, however, imposes another demand on library space.

Instruction in the use of computer utilities is part of the library's educational mission, which is to provide access to the information sources and knowledge available on campus and elsewhere. Students in all disciplines need to be comfortable doing bibliographic research in the electronic indexes to literature in their particular field. Harold B. Schill warns that "[i]f librarians do not apply their bibliographic and instructional skills to training for electronic era information retrieval, their institutions and patrons will suffer."[10] Patricia Battin pursues this theme, arguing, "A university supported capacity to develop and maintain a variety of software tools for its students and scholars would be both cost-effective and enable the scholarly community to retain control over its information costs."[11] Decisions then have to be made on which computer utilities will be supported and who will assume responsibility for teaching their use. The challenge of learning and teaching new technologies may seem overwhelming, but it is only by embracing the reality of ever-changing information technology that we can understand its evolution and its influence on library design.

If libraries now being built are no longer exclusively places to which seekers of information must come to retrieve printed sources from the shelves, what are they? Will seamless electronic access to vast arrays of information sources destroy the library as a physical entity? Information technology is powerful and pervasive enough to raise such basic questions. For reasons cited earlier, we reply that the library, as a building, will continue to be a central place on campus, to which people will come in search of information or simply a quiet place to study. They will arrive either in person or through an electronic link from a remote terminal. Students enrolled in distance-education courses, for example, may do their own bibliographic research using the online catalog and may consult a reference librarian by means of telephone, electronic mail, video-conference, or fax.[12] Requests for material are met in the usual way by the library department responsible for supporting off-campus courses through document delivery. Physical items need not be transported when digital facsimile is easily available. Faculty may search the catalog from home or office, as may any member of the public who uses the resources of a local university library, although license agreements restrict access to full-text databases. These same licenses, by limiting access to terminals located in a specific place (e.g., the library) actually strengthen the library's physical presence.[13] A publicly accessible online catalog lets the wider community know what types of information are available. Those who teach and study on campus will find that the library is becoming a rather different sort of place, one where information technology assumes a human face.

For some time to come, and maybe forever, library users who are confused by the variety of information systems will require assistance. One way around this problem is to reduce the number of search protocols that a researcher has to learn in order to assemble relevant sources. Almost universal adoption of a Web interface has eliminated an earlier profusion of search engines offered by hundreds of database vendors. The North American (now international) Z39.50 standard is being used to create an interface between the local OPAC (online public access catalog) and such databases as CD-ROMs, OCLC, and other online catalogs. Library catalogs are themselves increasingly Web-based. The Z39.50 standard "allows users to search other systems without having to learn the native search languages of these other systems."[14] This standard offers the means to create a "virtual" electronic library by allowing systems with different search protocols to communicate transparently with one another. Each one, using client/server architecture, translates its searching program into the Z39.50 standard language. With Z39.50 operating on each end, two different systems can interact without the user knowing that translation is being carried out. Familiar searching techniques, therefore, may be used on "foreign" OPACs or on any CD-ROM product. As more and more libraries and computing centers adopt the standard, information seekers are able to locate documents efficiently wherever they are to be found. With Z39.50 in operation, each study space can support a scholar's workstation that offers access both to bibliographic data and to full-text resources in abundance.[15]

Web access to servers operated by database vendors now dominates the information universe. JStor, which offers page-facsimile backruns of important journals in the humanities and social sciences, is a prime example. Like CARL UnCover, Project Muse, and many online catalogs, JStor has a Web front end that simplifies searching and retrieval. Almost instantly, Web formats and protocols have become the standard for locating information and publishing research projects. No innovation since the microcomputer almost twenty years ago has so influenced the practices of higher education and the mission of academic libraries. Demand for Web connections is universal in a modern library, whose role is that of gateway to information resources in all forms.

Library users expect to find a network port anywhere in the building they may choose to work. From a "wired" study carrel they may access the campus information network, consult the local online catalog, or search for resources on the Internet. No longer confined to on-campus information sources, library users can extend their reach around the world. As access to information replaces the ownership of limited collections of print materials, libraries can concentrate on improving interlibrary loan services and negotiating consortial access to electronic databases. Paper-based sources, as many scholars have noted, are becoming adjunct to digitized text and multimedia. Until ISDN (Integrated Services Digital Network), cable modems, or ADSL (Asymmetric Digital Subscriber Line) telephone lines are widely available, the library is where information networking can best be exploited.[16]

Information technology adds a new dimension to the educational process, namely the teaching of what commonly is called "information literacy." "To be information literate," according to the American Library Association, "a person must be able to recognize when information is needed and have the ability to locate, evaluate, and use effectively the needed information."[17] Implicit in this definition is an ability to use the technology that permits access to electronic information sources. The world of information technology is so complex that a library's clientele, faculty and students alike, cannot be expected to navigate it unassisted. Librarians, of course, have a long-standing interest in all matters concerning the research process and the tools used to gather information. Electronic sources, and the equipment needed to access them, pose a different set of challenges. Yet the overall mission is unchanged: to establish intellectual control over electronic texts and images, and to make information available to those who need it. An understanding of information technology and the ability to teach information literacy are essential to librarians.

So bountiful is the cornucopia of Internet resources that the National Science Foundation and other federal agencies are spending $24.4 million to impose order on the chaos spilling from it. There were 3.2 million host computers on the Internet late in 1994, 81 percent more than the year before.[18] The number today is well over 43 million, an increase of almost 1,000 percent.[19] Students and faculty alike face the challenge of learning how best to use the Web's research and presentation resources. Existing demand already taxes the ability of academic libraries to respond adequately. Information technology—its application, study, and interpretation—requires that higher education invent a new way to do business. Libraries can be part of the solution, but only if they contain the equipment, tools, and expertise to make information technology of use to those who need it.

Information technology embraces the computerized systems and software used in the research process, as well as the tools and techniques of Webpage creation. Its main purpose is to enable fast and comprehensive access to electronic information sources consisting of literature citations of the sort normally found in traditional indexes or abstracts, or to the full text of a particular document. Full-motion video, along with audio and voice transmission, is now available. Well-known search engines, such as Hot-Bot, Lycos, and Excite, though cruder than most online catalogs, are becoming more effective. An online library catalog is an "information base" composed of several "databases": author, subject, and title files; bibliographic records; circulation information; holdings information.[20] In the recent past, there have been many kinds of information bases, including:

- online electronic utilities, such as JStor, FirstSearch, or InfoTrac
- CD-ROM, which is currently the favored means of publishing large data collections, but which has inherent limitations related to (a) the variety of search protocols used by such systems and (b) the difficulty and expense of providing access to multiple users
- online catalogs of most of the world's major research libraries accessible via the Internet
- GIS workstations
- assorted document-delivery services, such as CARL UnCover or *Current Contents*, which allow subscribers to identify and order specific publications
- government-produced information bases, such as the *Statistical Abstract of the United States* published by the Bureau of the Census or the census series published by Statistics Canada
- full-text and multimedia sources on CD-ROM or other storage media

Each information base has an associated search protocol, which must be learned by those who wish to examine its contents. Familiarity with one or more products does make the learning process somewhat easier, but the great variety of systems remains an obstacle to access. Z39.50, which governs how one machine communicates with another, now operates over TCP/IP, thus making possible worldwide intercommunication among computers. Convenient access to large data collections, once restricted to CD-ROM products, is now available over the Internet. Web-based resources are, of course, quite user-friendly in their own right.

CD-ROM, omnipresent in today's libraries, will be replaced shortly by Web-accessible files; for the time being it remains a formidable storage medium. Bibliographic data, indexes and abstracts, encyclopedias, and any large collection of print or graphic data are candidates for publication on CD-ROM. There is no doubt that CD-ROM is an excellent medium for large or multimedia databases. It is both cost-effective and increasingly user-friendly. The main advantage of laser-readable disks is that they "are a form of permanent publication and they share many of the characteristics of print on paper." [21] It may well be that, "as hardware costs decrease, CDs will increasingly be used to manage archival and low-demand information." [22] They can also store visual images and, thus, potentially act as an archival storage medium for photographic collections. [23] Be cautious, however, because CDs are susceptible to delamination and are not to be trusted for long-term storage of important data. Digital-imaging systems store documents that may be retrieved and printed in facsimile copy. Each system comes with its own search software, and publishers often assume that each CD-ROM product deserves its dedicated PC. Space vacated by retired card catalogs often is filled with CD-ROM workstations. The heyday of CD-ROM has passed; it and "locally loaded databases may not yet be dead, but they are at the beginning stages of failing to thrive." [24] The World Wide Web is pushing CD-ROM out of tomorrow's library.

Demand for library access to CD-ROM databases is nevertheless strong as these products replace such traditional print abstracts as *America: History and Life, Historical Abstracts,* and *Psychological Abstracts.* Stand-alone workstations can rapidly consume floor space unless library planners adopt a different strategy. CD-ROM "towers" can make a large selection available on the campus information network, but even these devices will give way to direct Web access. When licensed access to the vendor's Website is available, the space problem ceases to exist. In essence, the library user's portable computer becomes the gateway. That is why ubiquitous network connectivity is mandatory in all academic library buildings constructed henceforth. Institutions pondering renovation need to ensure that this kind of connectivity is included, too.

Information technology encompasses more than the Web's search engines, vendor-supplied resources, and locally held electronic titles.

There is a wide range of analytical and production software that runs the gamut from common word-processing packages to Webpage creation tools (e.g., Microsoft's FrontPage, WBT's TopClass, ULT's WebCT, Blackboard's CourseInfo) to management systems, such as Lotus Notes and LearningSpace. Because the products are legion and every campus has different needs, most institutions will identify a few standard packages for e-mail, Web browsing, page creation, and course management. The mix will always be dynamic, because technology evolves ceaselessly. Discipline-specific software, introduced by departments for use by their majors, complicates things, though perhaps not much longer. The Web has quickly imposed its own standards on what had threatened to become an utterly chaotic marketplace. Information technology now values transparency and common user interfaces. Learning to use the technology thus is becoming a manageable goal, to be superseded in importance by the need to acquire and apply analytical skills to networked sources of information. Some years ago these higher-order skills acquired the label "computer literacy." With the advent of the Web came an emphasis on "information literacy," a still more sophisticated idea that has more to do with intellectual activity than with the manipulation of computers and their associated software.

Computer literacy is related to the idea of information technology, but is not synonymous with it. Dartmouth College, in the mid-1970s, defined "computing literacy" as the ability to write a computer program.[25] Carnegie-Mellon University's Task Force for the Future of Computing on Campus offered a broader definition in its 1982 report:

> Computer literacy is not equivalent to learning to program, but is different in at least the following ways: First, using a computer often means not programming, but using available tools—editors, electronic mail, statistical packages, simulators, computer-aided design systems, data base systems, and so on. . . . Second, using a computer effectively involves more than just local skills for using particular languages or tools. It requires understanding the fundamental nature of the computer, what kinds of things it can and cannot do. Third, if the role of computation is to increase . . . , computer literacy must include competence in the local computational facilities. This part of computer literacy is in fact an important part of good access.[26]

Carnegie-Mellon's conception of computer literacy recognizes the evolutionary direction of campus automation and is as valid today as it was almost two decades ago. The university's vice provost for computers and planning, Douglas Van Houweling, said at the time: "We don't believe that all students should know how to program. . . . It's more important that people are able to use the computing tools that are directly relevant to their fields." [27] This comment parallels a definition of computer literacy proposed in 1980 by the Duke University Personal Computing Project: "an awareness of computing capabilities within a discipline or profession, and an ability to recognize and articulate problems that can be solved with the aid of computing technology. The definition does not necessarily imply an ability to program or operate computers." [28] The goal of information literacy is "not to make liberal arts students technologists, but rather, to make them capable, thinking people who can make use of technological tools in their everyday lives." [29]

Peter Lyman even denies that computer literacy has anything to do with computers, which ought to be designed for ease of use in the first place. In Lyman's estimation, a computer-literate person is one who can "evaluate the truth value of digital information and images which simulate realities which have never existed, in a manner fully satisfactory to the senses." [30] There has to be enough understanding of information technology to enable one to evaluate the knowledge value of its products. For that reason, "the history of science and technology . . . is a fundamental part of liberal education." [31] That is why the acquisition of electronic research skills is perfectly compatible with the liberal arts.

Now that a wide variety of information-technology software is easily obtainable, those who wish to be computer literate must know how to "operate" a machine. For most, the need to write special-application programs will never arise. Either the particular situation has been addressed already, or else expert assistance is available in the university's support departments. In any event, programming knowledge no longer is the sine qua non of computer literacy. Facility with word-processing and computational software, along with the ability to search and evaluate electronic information bases, is today's imperative. Access to proper computing equipment, therefore, is an indispensable part of the university experience.

Ten years ago, about one-half million microcomputers populated American college campuses. Ernest Boyer, then president of the Carnegie Foundation for the Advancement of Teaching, reported in 1987 that "more than a dozen colleges now ask their students to buy personal computers along with textbooks." [32] Schools such as Drew University have made computers available to all freshmen since 1984, with satisfying results both for enrollment levels and academic performance. As the Carnegie Foundation discovered, a "revolution is under way" in the use of information technology. Ubiquitous campus computing is the essence of this revolution. In 1999, at least one hundred higher-education institutions required their students to own or lease a portable computer. [33] In no case has mandatory leasing or purchasing of computers caused enrollment to decline.

Information literacy has been at the top of higher education's agenda since the early 1990s, when Internet access became widespread. By mid-decade, the World Wide Web had created a global computer network dedicated to self-publication and, within months, electronic commerce and advertising. Exponential growth of host computers overwhelmed the Internet's original focus on education and research, though academics continued to enjoy "a more informal, immediate kind of exchange than traditional scholarly exchange through print."[34] To preserve the educational and scientific potential of the Internet, a more advanced network had to be built. Currently under development, the National Research and Education Network (NREN, or Internet2) is sponsored by NASA and a number of research universities throughout the country. This next-generation Internet "will propel the present Internet into the future with orders of magnitude greater speed, bandwidth, and reliability."[35]

Libraries will be among the prime users of NREN, created by an act of the Congress of the United States and signed into law in December 1992. NREN, which gave rise to Internet2 and the research universities' Abilene project, became the high-speed, broadband backbone of the Internet in the United States; its Canadian equivalent is CANARIE (Canadian Network for the Advancement of Research, Industry, and Education) and CA*net 3, which became active in mid-1999 and is considerably faster than Abilene.[36] NREN has been described as "the vehicle through which research libraries will realize the virtual library" and as "the primary technical resource for providing the new information infrastructure."[37] Internet2 aims to enhance the Internet applications available to scholars and researchers, whose work is impeded by today's highly commercialized Web. Electronic distribution of ideas, information, and data sources has wrought a basic change in the nature of scholarly activity. Although print publication, especially of books, undoubtedly will survive for some time to come, digital resources have achieved equal billing. As information technology becomes part of the curriculum, teaching will occur in different ways. Other innovations are bound to follow, and each has implications for library design.

Turn-of-the-century academic libraries will accommodate technology in different, sometimes idiosyncratic ways. Recent influences on library design include: laptop-computer leasing programs for both students and faculty, electronic classrooms, information galleries equipped with high-end computers, and faculty-development centers whose purpose is to promote innovative teaching via integration of technology. Each function belongs in the library, which is a central location on campus. Together, they affect building architecture and internal geography in several important respects.

Seen from the outside, new academic libraries still present monumental façades to visitors, features that proclaim the library's enduring role in higher education (fig. 2). Inside the building, one hopes, functionality rules. If the building team has done its work properly, architectural statements are confined to the building's exterior or periphery, so that functional relationships remain uncompromised. Interior layouts naturally reflect particular operating philosophies as applied both to user services and to staff working conditions. Some libraries, for example, offer private offices; others (like the new University of Kentucky library) equip large open areas with modular workstations. Campus culture, a taste for experimentation, or fondness for traditional environments may all influence internal geography, which is mainly the province of librarians and not of architects. The greatest challenge is to define the functional relationships among several new purposes in ways that enhance library service to an entire campus community. Information technology is the common theme in the design development of every new academic library built from now on.

Seamless integration of computer networks into a building's infrastructure is the overarching goal. Technology must be part of a building's fabric if it is to serve library users effectively. Unobtrusive yet pervasive technology supports them best. If they arrive with a portable computer,

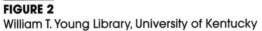

FIGURE 2
William T. Young Library, University of Kentucky

network access must be universal. If they come in search of large-scale computing power, it must be available. Above all, if they come to find someone who can mediate between information seekers and the technology, such expertise cannot be far away. Nowhere else on campus is the convergence between technology and education more obvious than in a well-designed academic library. Before such a building can take form, the design team needs to be clear about the changing character of library services. What the library seeks to do determines its shape.

Today's academic library may be characterized as a local hub on a global information network. That role will grow immensely with the arrival of Internet2, which will enable streaming audio and video over a national backbone and not simply over an individual campus's high-speed network.[38] The network offers connectivity, services, and research support that are not available to individuals working at remote computers, regardless of modem speed. Although print materials are unlikely to disappear, certain reference sources, scholarly journals, and monographs will be published digitally; codex books will continue to be produced and collected in the years ahead. The library's curatorial function therefore will not disappear, and buildings will have to integrate seamlessly both traditional services and electronic ones.

During the life span of today's new buildings, the five-century reign of print will come to an end. Paper will cease to be the primary medium of scholarly communication; "eventually paper will be obsolete."[39] A different publishing economy will arise to serve the needs of academic research, and libraries will be transformed as a result. This change will occur over several decades, but certainly while libraries built at the turn of the century are still in service. Designers, therefore, are obliged to create buildings that can make a graceful transition from their traditional role to one that cannot yet be clearly perceived.

How We Respond to Change

Computers influence library design by virtue of their ability to bring researchers together with their sources. Broad access to bibliographic citations came first, as Internet resources multiplied; now full-text material is commonly available. Cornell University uses a broad definition of "electronic formats," one that includes "the full range of optical, magnetic, and digital technologies as used in the dissemination of published information."[40] Although electronic publishing constitutes, at the moment, an insignificant proportion of the total, its importance will grow as journal literature migrates to this medium for economic and other reasons. FirstSearch, JStor, and Project Muse are but three examples of this obvious trend. Computers, especially small, easily portable ones, make electronic publications accessible anywhere there is a telephone line or a network connection. One of those places is the library, where advice and assistance are also available. Buildings, therefore, must be designed to encourage research in electronic media by providing suitable study facilities, learning opportunities, and knowledgeable staff. Information technology and computer literacy converge in libraries, where the economics of scholarly publication is helping to redefine their mission.

Theoretical physicists, to cite one example, find themselves on the leading edge of changes in information transfer partly as a result of economic pressures on library budgets. As subscriptions are canceled, "some journals may reconfigure in electronic form, but the termination of the revenue stream will mean most of them will just die."[41] Electronic preprints and citation databases will take over, propelled by hypertext links among many e-documents. One sign that physics is in the vanguard of a larger movement is the appearance of the *Harvard Business Review* in electronic format. "In two decades," writes Gregory J. E. Rawlins, "paper technical books will be the equivalent of phonograph records today; they will exist for historical, sentimental, or ceremonial reasons."[42] Over a somewhat longer time span, the same fate may befall all codex books. "Books, after all," as George Landow points out, "are teaching and communication machines."[43] They, like the computer, are a form of information technology, and not cultural icons. How text is presented to a reader—as words on paper or as images on a screen—is less important than the message conveyed. Networked text is always available and is infinitely malleable (provided that the original version is carefully archived). Hypertext ignores the linearity of printed books, with as yet unknown consequences for the education of readers. When space limitations disappear, the potential of a hypertext document as a learning tool grows mightily. Knowledge can be pursued in other than strictly linear ways. As the Web becomes a more polished medium, its ability to present text, data, sound, and images will improve, along with its power to integrate these elements of information. Be that as it may, the Web will shortly achieve the capacity to offer seamlessly integrated electronic documents of high resolution.

Academic libraries have expanded their traditional role as storehouses for the printed word while at the same time becoming gateways to the world of information beyond their walls. The whipsaw effect on library budgets of declining support from their universities, together with rising materials prices, is an important accelerator of this process. Double-digit inflation has boosted the cost of journal subscriptions.[44] Between 1986 and 1996, subscription prices increased 147 percent, while respected university presses slipped into the red as sales hovered between 250 and 300 copies per title.[45] Limited press runs of scholarly works have forced up the price of monographs. Meanwhile, institutional support for the acquisitions budgets of academic libraries in the United States and Canada has fallen some 25 percent over the past two decades.[46] In just a few years, "the combined impact of inflation and the growth of information would result in our libraries' being able to purchase only 2 percent of the 'total' information acquired only two decades before."[47] Collections in academic libraries are tending to resemble each other because shrinking resources are forcing "more and more duplicative information" to be bought. With all hope lost of possessing more than a fraction of published scholarly output, librarians are turning more and more to such devices as resource-sharing and interlibrary consortia to serve their clientele. Digital libraries are yet another option. In 1998, it cost about 20 cents to store one megabyte of information, or $2 per book; book storage costs closer to $40.[48] Under such conditions, electronic access to bibliographic data and to full-text documents is indispensable to a modern library, which is then under pressure to make electronic texts available on the local computer network. Print journals have proliferated and subscription costs escalated to the point at which libraries can no longer afford to buy a broad range of paper-journal subscriptions. Electronic publication is emerging as the solution, because its cost is only 25 percent that of paper, and because it is the best way to direct "esoteric" material toward its sole audience: academic specialists.[49] The "journal" may survive as a taxonomic device to impose order on the stream of scholarly output, but the medium is likely to be electronic rather than paper. As Bernard Naylor writes:

> Libraries have been hostages in the Faustian bargain scholars have had to make with paper publishers in order to reach the eyes and minds of fellow scholars. Libraries are now much better advised to ally themselves with those scholars, forming consortia to help pay in advance the much reduced per-page costs of electronic publication, with the product then available for free to all. . . .[50]

A debate among Naylor (then library director, University of Southampton), Stevan Harnad (then of Princeton University), and Andrew Odlyzko (Bell Laboratories), during the summer of 1994, explored issues involved in electronic scholarly publishing.[51] Pointing to "the exponential growth in the mathematical literature" as but one genre of scientific publication in general, Odlyzko declared that "traditional paper journals will become irrelevant to mathematicians' needs within 10 years."[52] Harnad argued that the lower costs and peer-review guarantees offered by e-journals make them an acceptable alternative to paper journals whose existence is subsidized by libraries. Because of their esoteric (i.e., highly specialized) nature, Harnad characterized "the vast bulk of the scholarly corpus [as] . . . a no-market literature." [53] Odlyzko agreed that "the average published scientific article has fewer than 10 readers and no citers." He speculated that "the same is true for the average piece of scholarship in the humanities." Not only can e-journals "demonstrate that they can be as rigorous as refereed paper journals," but they are also searchable and interactive. Others experienced in electronic publishing point out that "the authoring process . . . can realistically be completed within no more than three months against a current norm of six months." [54] Efficiency of scholarly communication is well served by the electronic medium. For these reasons, electronic scholarly publication quickly became a significant library resource. Even though the migration to digital is taking longer than originally expected, Odlyzko expects to see it in his lifetime. [55] He pointed out in 1998 that the cost of publishing an article in electronic format was only 25 percent or less of print publication; economics therefore clearly favors the e-journal. [56] As retrospective digitizing and archiving of journal backruns proceeds, the disappearance of bound-periodicals collections is imminent. Storage space will find other uses in buildings intentionally constructed or retrofitted for information-technology purposes. The same fate awaits printed indexes, bibliographies, concordances, and all other reference works that can be used most effectively in electronic format.

E-journals, such as Harnad's *Psycholoquy* and the *Journal of Postmodern Culture*, demonstrate that scholarly integrity will survive in the electronic medium. By the spring of 1994, fifty active e-journal titles (half of them refereed) existed on the Internet. [57] In 1999, the number rose to over 1,050 refereed e-journals and e-newsletters, most of which charge for a subscription. [58] According to Harnad, "interactive publication in the form of open peer commentary on published work" is the key to effective validation, and peer review, in turn, will make e-journals legitimate and respectable within the scholarly community. [59] Naylor, Harnad, and Odlyzko accurately forecast the future of scholarly publishing, and new academic library buildings, therefore, will need to devote much less space to the storage of print journals. (The current stock of backruns, of course, will need to be accommodated for the time being, but the space they occupy should be easily convertible to other uses in the future.) Scholarly communication clearly has found a congenial medium in the Internet and the World Wide Web.

Eldred Smith, writing on the implications of electronic publishing for libraries, refers to a "transition from a print-based system of scholarly communication to an electronic-based system." [60] Scholars who belong to a particular electronic-information network may receive articles of interest in a timely manner, and more economically than if the library had to own a range of paper-journal subscriptions. [61] An article in *Nature* acknowledged that costly, little-read print journals in fact may impede scientific communication and incur "overheads [that] are economically unsustainable."[62] Major publishers, such as Reed/Elsevier, have moved their titles online. "A journal without a web version is now rare," according to *Nature,* "and may even be endangered."[63] The outcome of this revolutionary process will be a fully indexed database comprising an electronic record of "authenticated scholarship." Smith predicts that publication in such a system soon will be a completely accepted form of communication within the scholarly community. In Britain, for example, the SuperJANET project will provide access to electronic journals over a high-speed fiber optic network linking the country's universities.[64] Smith points out that the comprehensiveness and accessibility of research collections will be greatly enhanced if published materials and their bibliographic apparatus are in electronic format:

> They would be accessible anywhere, using the worldwide communications structure that presently exists. Desired portions could be retrieved on computer screens, transferred to local data stores, and even printed out on printers. Although much work would certainly be required to plan and implement such a collection and apparatus, no substantial technical problem lies in the way of its accomplishment.[65]

Some proponents of electronic publication argue that, because scholars provide articles to commercial publishers free of charge, universities should take control of the process by sponsoring electronic journals. From the authors' point of view, copyright ownership is not an issue because they routinely assign it to the journal that publishes their work and "[c]ommercial publications . . . sell it back to academia at exorbitant prices."[66] A solution may be to make electronic journals available free within the university community on the same principle of resource-sharing that underlies interlibrary loan. "[W]hy not," asks the director of the Pennsylvania State University Press, "let academic editors . . . handle distribution directly in electronic form over the Internet, as the new experimental electronic journals are already doing . . . ?"[67] The challenge is to convince scholars that Internet publication will be recognized and rewarded in the traditional manner, and to ensure the integrity of the peer-review process. Large obstacles remain, as the National Institutes of Health e-journal project illustrates.

When the NIH director proposed early in 1999 to create an electronic archive of research papers in biomedicine, controversy erupted. Even proponents of e-journals, such as Stevan Harnad, complained that a project and funding agency should not control which research studies are published. Commercial publishers predictably criticized "E-biomed" on financial grounds, as did the scholarly societies who publish journals. Several thorny issues need to be resolved before e-journals supplant traditional print media, as the disputes over E-biomed confirm.[68] Yet, there exists the definite potential for a radical transformation of scholarly communication, for which libraries must prepare themselves. There are success stories.

The *Chicago Journal of Theoretical Computer Science*, a peer-reviewed e-journal published by the MIT Press and available by subscription on the Internet, may be downloaded to a library's computer and distributed on the campus information network. Printing-out, copying, and lending through interlibrary loan would be permitted according to existing American copyright law. Libraries at the University of Chicago and MIT will maintain the journal's electronic archives. In the field of physics, as noted earlier, "the paper pre-print is well on its way to extinction, supplanted in the information ecosystem by the electronic pre-print, or e-print."[69] Berkeley's Project SCAN (Scholarship from CAlifornia on the Net) is another example of innovation in scholarly publishing. It "represents an early experiment to develop an economically viable publishing model for humanities scholarship that integrates electronic publishing, library access, and scholarly use."[70] Other publications, distributed in similar fashion, are on the way. As leading academic publishers commit to an electronic format, the volume of literature will grow. Librarians inherit the task of imposing intellectual control over these electronic publications as they add them to their databases and provide access to them. This task, efficiently performed, may help to persuade scholars to accept the new format; at the moment, opinion on the merits of electronic publishing is sharply divided.

Problems, primarily legal and custodial, will arise as electronic publication on the Internet continues to expand. Who, for example, owns material distributed on a network, and who is responsible for preserving the integrity of the original version (or *Urtext*)? How is copyright to be enforced if recipients of an HTML document then disseminate it in an altered form? One solution is Portable Document Format (PDF) encoding, which preserves the look of the original but which excludes hyperlinks. There is as yet no way to assure that electronic documents will remain accessible over time, given the certainty of technological change and the advent of different storage media. Equally intractable at present are the intellectual property issues surrounding electronic publication. How are the legitimate property rights of authors and publishers to be protected as "the distinction between the medium (the book) and the content (information) disappears with the dematerialization of the medium and the disembodiment of information"?[71]

Progress on the copyright front is slow, because lawmakers are having great difficulty applying an industrial age notion of intellectual property to digital products. "The most significant difference between print and digital publications," writes Peter Lyman, "is a consequence of the facticity of print, its form as a fixed material commodity, compared to the immaterial and therefore malleable quality of digital information."[72] Hypertext documents have no fixed physical reality, because they can be altered by any recipient; the information they contain, rather than their form, defines their essence. Evanescence complicates any effort to create a market in digital documents, which typically appear "free" on the Internet and without the guarantees of quality offered by the traditional editorial process that yields printed books. Lyman suggests that "the Internet may well fail as a public institution because it is entirely a gift culture and therefore suffers from poor quality information."[73] How to protect an information marketplace while preserving freedom of speech on the Internet is the great legal dilemma of today's electronic environment.

Because a way has to be found to respect copyright as it applies to digital products, institutional site licenses are common. Universities protect themselves by purchasing these licenses, which permit free use of the electronic medium within the campus. "The increasing reliance on license agreements as replacements for copyright," as Kenneth D. Crews points out, "creates inconsistent rules and many times leads to new restrictions that exceed the law's requirements."[74] Sections 107 and 108 of the Copyright Act of 1976 confer some latitude for the "fair use" of computer software, rights that licenses may seek to abridge. The Digital Millennium Copyright Act of 1998, while acknowledging the notion of fair use, also ensures that licensing will be more widely used by publishers of digital media. Experts in copyright law generally agree that the ease with which electronic information sources may be copied and distributed frustrates efforts by publishers to defend their monopoly position.[75] They see licenses as a contractual means of enforcing their copyrights. Users of this licensed material argue for liberality. A draft statement on "lawful uses of copyrighted works," circulated by the Coalition for Networked Information, recommends that the "fair use" clause (Sec. 108) be extended to cover electronic reserves and interlibrary loan.[76] It remains to be seen whether this will happen. Copyright law has not yet succeeded in reconciling the competing claims of ownership and access under changed circumstances, although the National Information Infrastructure (NII) is now tackling the issue.[77] Most guidelines advise that the safest course is to make sure that one's Web product falls under the "fair use" dispensation for criticism, comment, teaching, scholarship, and research.

A site-licensed CD-ROM product, moreover, may not be owned by the library, which typically loses access to it when its subscription ends.[78] The electronic medium is volatile by nature and, as the case of CD-ROM illustrates, by the choice of commercial publishers. Because electronic documents are easily shared, "it is understandable that information producers are reluctant to place documents in an electronic library without strict agreements governing use." [79] Although electronic publishing represents at present a small sector of the market, it is expanding steadily. Libraries, therefore, have to consider their archival role in the years ahead. The immediate task is to reap the benefits of both the electronic and the paper cultures, because both probably will coexist for some time to come.

Whether book-length publications will abandon the printed page is still an open question. In 1993, university authorities in Britain concluded: "It is very unlikely that books, periodicals, and other traditional media will be superseded in the foreseeable future." [80] Even strong advocates of the electronic book concede that "paper will be with us for decades to come because of the hundreds of years of technological development behind simple, cheap, light, detachable pieces of paper." [81] The Association of American Universities and Colleges expects that, "in the area of scientific, technical, and medical publishing, only 20 percent of this information will be available in a fully electronic mode by the year 2015." [82] Paper is expected to dominate 50 percent of this market, although this prediction already is proving to be too timid. Failure to agree on a pricing model for electronic journals is one reason for their slow appearance. Another is the reluctance of scholars to accept the electronic format. [83] There is reason to believe, however, that highly specialized scholarly monographs may be published in electronic format before long. One reason for this shift is the fact most manuscripts are now prepared on a computer and can be produced in camera-ready copy by laser printers. Electronically created text is easily edited; font technology has progressed to the point at which laser-printed copy, at 600 dpi, is virtually indistinguishable from typeset. Two simultaneous forms of publication therefore are possible: electronic and hard-copy. According to Paul J. Korshin, an expert in the field of scholarly publishing, "[P]ublishers can surely explore the possibility of a limited edition on paper . . . to satisfy the hidebound. Such a publishing strategy—a limited edition of a monograph in book form, with all other copies available on diskettes—would succeed in persuading the academic world that a book issued in this manner deserves to be taken seriously." [84]

The incentive to move beyond Gutenberg is the efficiency with which the whole review and editorial process can be managed through electronic file transfer. [85] Texts can pass from author to potential publisher to reviewer and back again over the Internet. [86] Publishers, who retain an electronic copy of the final version, can produce copies on demand in either format. Libraries, of course, may purchase books in one or both, and may even produce a printed copy themselves should they wish to do so. Officials at Brown University predicted that "the 1990s will probably see a steady progress towards an information distribution system where most incoming information arrives electronically and is printed locally." [87] This prophecy has come true in some market sectors, though not yet for book-length publications. Copyright naturally subsists in the work, regardless of the format(s) in which it appears. Royalties presumably would have to be paid in order to acquire duplication rights to an entire work; partial copying would be licensed according to the contract between the institution (or group of institutions) and the national copyright collective. This is how JStor, for example, provides access to its backrun files.

Electronic publishing is not likely to be an unmitigated blessing, even though it does not necessarily threaten the library as an institution. As critics of the medium warn, entrusting the scholarly record to volatile electronic storage may well endanger it. "Would an electronic society, relying primarily on computer-based electronic systems for the storage and distribution of recorded information," asks Gordon B. Neavill, "be able to retain contact with its accumulated stock of recorded knowledge?" [88] If information is stored and disseminated only in electronic format, its integrity is imperiled in several ways. Economics, lax standards, and informal editing all may conspire against the survival and reliability of a cumulative scholarly record. Information as a commodity, highly specialized and sold to micro-audiences, easily can disappear if not archived and preserved somewhere. Access in perpetuity is the real issue. Information retrieval that depends entirely on technology troubles those who prefer not to rely solely on electric power and particular access software.[89] Clifford Lynch argues that "a reasonable number of independently controlled archive sites for certain material are necessary to provide confidence in the continued integrity and accessibility of our scholarly, historical, and cultural record." [90] Computer scientists and scholars, such as Lynch, who work on the frontiers of information technology, grant an essential role to libraries in the research process. Unless printed or archival copies on CD-ROM or in digital image are preserved in their original form and are accessible to researchers, scholarly inquiry could cease to evolve.

Neavill's warning, therefore, is a cogent one for librarians, to whom he assigns "the primary responsibility for defining and shaping a society's stock of recorded knowledge." [91] Librarians and scholars share a vested interest in ensuring that information continues to be preserved in hard copy and in many locations, so that the danger of irretrievable loss is controlled. As Lynch writes: "[T]he role of libraries as trustees for society as a whole in preserving, organizing, and providing access to the record needs to be maintained as we enter the networked information environment." [92] The "limited editions on paper," which Korshin grudgingly concedes to "the hidebound," serve an essentially archival purpose. Hard copy may survive for this very reason. As the historian Robert

Darnton suggests, "concentrated long-term reading would take place by means of the conventional book or downloaded text." Darnton predicts that "the Gutenberg galaxy will expand, thanks to a new source of energy, the electronic book, which will act as a supplement to, not a substitute for, Gutenberg's great machine."[93] Worth keeping in mind is that the availability of electronic artifacts depends on their producer, who is driven by economic advantage and commercial success. If the publisher goes under, the resource disappears.[94] Who has responsibility for its preservation? Human pleasure and comfort, moreover, are *not* trivial concerns. As Jacques Barzun and Henry Graff tartly remark in the latest edition of their classic work, *The Modern Researcher:* "Anybody who prefers Shakespeare's dialogue flickering in blue or brown on a curved screen is in need of special care and compassion."[95]

Such considerations as legibility, transportability, and the convenience of following an extended discussion through a succession of pages mean that "print continues to be the preferred medium for certain purposes."[96] There is also the financial aspect. With estimated conversion costs running at about twelve cents per page, existing book stocks are likely to remain as they are until they disintegrate.[97] Only the most historically valuable works are likely to be digitized, although there is no guarantee that digital media, over time, are any more stable or permanent than acid-free paper. "Notwithstanding the vision of the disincarnated digital library," observes Geoffrey Nunberg, ". . . it's clear that local, brick-and-mortar libraries will have a continuing role to play, not just for the immediate present but for any period we can reasonably foresee."[98] Libraries will continue to collect books, though perhaps not as comprehensively as in the past. Resource-sharing consortia, to which many academic libraries belong, shift the emphasis from ownership to access. Electronic communications offer an efficient means of transmitting text from a distant repository or database to a local researcher. As these trends develop, they certainly will influence the mission and design of library buildings.

Advocates of electronic publishing argue, not altogether persuasively, that there are no insurmountable technical or legal obstacles.[99] If this indeed is the case, then, from a librarian's perspective, the main questions are: How will building design be affected by the revolution in scholarly publishing? How will computerized access to a multitude of information sources change the organization and delivery of library services? What sort of building is needed to house the automated library of the present and the foreseeable future? No library designer can answer these questions with certainty, because too many variables are at work. The best that can be done is to extrapolate on the basis of current developments, while realizing that technology has forever changed the traditional means of knowledge transfer. Storage of, arrangement of, and intellectual control over large collections of printed paper will occupy librarians less and less in the years ahead. To be sure, current stocks of print materials will have to be managed until chemical reactions within their own pages finally destroy them. Physical books (now printed on acid-free paper) will continue to exist in a world of electronic publishing, simply because of their convenience. The library itself "will be home to resources that are too new, expensive, complex, or arcane to be used outside its walls." [100] Scholarly research will come to depend increasingly on access to a wide variety of electronic sources, access facilitated by librarians who are masters of the bibliographic apparatus of a new age.

Librarians traditionally are the custodians of books and other forms of published material, whether bound or in microcopy, owned by a particular institution. Electronic publication has altered that mission, though without nullifying it. "The new research library," says William Y. Arms, "will no longer be a passive repository, but will provide instantaneous and interactive access to information, with the ability to sift, sort, rearrange, and reformat that information." [101] Machine-readable text has become an established part of the library's inventory. Powerful online systems permit intellectual control over all types of collections and provide researchers with ever more efficient means of gaining access to information. Systems already are available in which it is possible to move from citation to full-text to keyword searching within a document by using hypertext. Networks allow researchers to move beyond the confines of their own library and to consult online catalogs around the world. Thanks to the World Wide Web, there now exists a global virtual library, described as "a system by which a user may connect transparently to remote libraries and databases using the local library's online catalog or a university or network computer as a gateway." [102] Hyperlinks to full-text documents from their catalog record point the way toward the "virtual book." [103]

Carnegie-Mellon University in Pittsburgh currently is applying these principles in its long-term strategy to develop an electronic library (Project Mercury). [104] The intent is "to build an entire electronic-library collection across the board. Within disciplines, you could do all your work online." [105] Planners predict a transitional period lasting some twenty-five years before the traditional paper-based library is superseded by a fully electronic one. The University of California at Berkeley foresees two libraries on its campus, one of them a "new online library . . . [that] will deliver an increasing percentage of its collections and services, and provide a wider array of service options." [106] Carried further, the process may result in libraries that are no longer "independent parts of larger organizations" but are "part of the technical infrastructure of [their] parent organization." [107] Libraries built in the meantime will have to accommodate both old and new formats, with the balance shifting perceptibly toward the latter as time passes. That is why flexibility of space and extensiveness of the electric power and communications infrastructure are important considerations. The pace of technological change requires buildings to provide electronic environments capable of meeting demands that can be foreseen in general outline, if not in specific detail.

The Changing Role of Librarians

These developments portend a transformation in the librarian's role and workplace. Although the custodial function will continue, mediating electronic access to a broadening array of knowledge systems will become the librarian's chief concern. As for the local library itself, "the stand-alone collection is a starting point rather than a self-contained environment." [108] Librarians find themselves working in different circumstances. "Librarians will be called upon," in Deanna Marcum's words, "to do an even better job of integrating the physical collections on campuses with access to information contained on remote electronic and optical file servers." [109] At Cornell University, "reference staff have expanded their technical knowledge in order to respond effectively to other types of questions from electronic library users." [110] Librarians who staff the information "galleries," "arcades," and "commons" found in many recently constructed libraries also will need some hardware expertise. The ability to connect peripherals, install hardware, and resolve device conflicts without recourse to technicians is very helpful. Ergonomic aspects of workstation design and arrangement are also within the librarian's purview. How the new workplace is designed and built depends, in large part, on the activities librarians and patrons will pursue within its walls and in the "virtual library" that exists in telecommunications networks. Richard De Gennaro may be correct in saying that "the concept of the library without walls is a pipedream." [111] Inside the building, though, basic changes already are under way.

Technological innovation has "created an ascendant class of librarians and nonlibrarians with technological mastery, while librarians with traditional skills have suffered a relative loss of status." [112] Most Web-based information systems provide reasonably transparent retrieval protocols, thus facilitating their use. The "professional" role reserved to librarians is narrowing as technology expands and library assistants assume greater responsibilities. How librarians should be educated, and for which tasks, poses a challenge to library schools and library administrators. What qualifications ought those who work in tomorrow's academic libraries possess? Architects need a clear idea of roles and responsibilities in order to create functional buildings. Their task is complicated by uncertainty over the future of the academic librarian as a professional.

As electronic-information access becomes pervasive, some observers see the librarian's role evolving into that of "knowledge manager."[113] Locating, exploiting, indexing, and cataloging sources thus become the focus of attention, rather than the custodial care of local print and CD-ROM collections. The library building itself is a service center for information seekers, and thus will remain a physical presence on campus where professional assistance is always available. In a learning institution, as opposed to a business enterprise, there needs to be a place in which students convert information into knowledge under the guidance of those who understand how this process occurs. The need for qualified library staff will grow, along with the importance of the Web as an information resource.[114]

With access to the campus information network available to all library users, instruction in its use is a necessity. Academic librarians with faculty status, who may have puzzled over their proper role in the teaching function of the university, now have the essential task of teaching information access, retrieval, and delivery systems. Another responsibility is the creation of online interfaces simple enough to enable technologically unsophisticated users to locate information inside a myriad of different systems. Librarians have a vital role in the design of such interfaces.[115] The library itself "is important because it satisfies users' desires to browse—to establish human contact with sources of knowledge."[116] According to Susan J. Barnes of Cornell University, "electronic libraries . . . are designed to use with librarians serving not as intermediaries but as consultants."[117] This view, though partly true, is perhaps too sanguine. As resource-sharing and institutional networking evolve, the librarian's contribution to research activity will increase. Although easily accessible, the bibliographic record and attendant full-text databases will never be perfectly transparent to their users. "Because of the inevitable idiosyncrasy of the bibliographic apparatus' terminology," writes Eldred Smith, "it will be very difficult for scholars to use the electronic record. . . . Can [they] be rescued from this dilemma? Yes, but only by the intervention of the research librarian."[118] This is the person who is most familiar with the organization and operation of the electronic (or hybrid) research library now coming into being.

"The research librarian's primary role," Smith continues, "will be intermediation between the information needs of the scholar and the information structure of the scholarly record."[119] Once researchers establish their agenda, which is a matter of far greater importance to them than literature searching, librarians contribute their expertise in locating materials.[120] "Managing currently available information," according to

Chodorow and Lyman, "will become their principal function." [121] They may in fact become "intermediaries between their clients and the array of meta-information tolls [i.e., 'knowbots,' or simply 'bots'] with which users can themselves develop an interface with the information available through the Internet." [122] Active support of research implies less emphasis on ownership, organization, and custody of materials, and more on facilitating access to information sources wherever they are found. "[T]he critical issue for research librarians," argue Eldred Smith and Peggy Johnson, "is to design and demonstrate a system that will make prompt and reliable access possible, irrespective of ownership." [123] Physical location and format are ceasing to be barriers to access, as electronic systems become more competent. Because knowledge about and manipulation of these systems now comprise the essence of what research librarians do, building design should reflect this reality. Libraries are gateways to the entire range of documentation, in whatever form it exists.

Many observers do agree with Barnes that "librarians will increasingly assume the roles of consultants and teachers" as information systems become more prominent. [124] "For many years," as David W. Lewis notes, "the library has been the primary teaching tool outside of the classroom, and except for faculty, librarians have been the only university staff to assist large numbers of students in the academic process." [125] Librarians "will become teachers, offering bibliographic instruction . . . , interpreters of the information scene . . . [and] professors, teaching classes in information theory and information retrieval to college students." [126] In broad perspective, "the future of libraries may rest upon our [librarians'] ability to collaborate in the creation, management, and distribution of knowledge in a networked system of publication." [127] Should this fail to happen, Clifford Lynch anticipates that libraries "will end up competing with commercial services to support their primary clienteles" and may not prevail against the profit-motivated information merchants. [128] An important survival technique is acceptance of a very significant teaching role with respect to information technology.

Richard A. Lanham, a humanities scholar who has pondered the implications of electronic texts for librarians and their buildings, offers the following wisdom:

> Librarians of electronic information find their job now a radically rhetorical one—they must consciously construct human attention-structures rather than assemble a collection of books according to commonly accepted rules. They have, perhaps unwillingly, found themselves transported from the ancillary margin of the human sciences to their center. [129]

Given the present state of library-science education, and the status of librarians in their institutions, Lanham's prediction is sanguine indeed.

Yet, James J. O'Donnell, a classicist with professional involvements in information technology, goes even farther. "Can we imagine a time in our universities," he asks, "when librarians are the well-paid principals and teachers their mere acolytes? I do not think we can or should rule out that possibility."[130] The education of librarians will have to change in its essentials before these prophecies come true. One critic observes that "IS [information science] education needs to (finally) decouple itself from the 'library' concept so as 'to address new information problems.'"[131] As information technology pervades academe, the demand for new kinds of library facilities and a different philosophy of public service will drive the transformation of the librarian's role. That much is clear from recent campus developments, including "Laptop University" and the construction of new library buildings.

Academic libraries now feature such unique facilities as information arcades, electronic classrooms, and development centers for faculty who are applying technology to their teaching. It is entirely appropriate that these new spaces be located in the library, which, as a building, remains the campus's learning center for all university constituencies. As a consequence, staff will be working in the library who are neither librarians nor involved in "traditional" library activities. Yet there is bound to be, indeed should be, a close professional relationship among all who assist library users in their quest for information resources regardless of format. From that interaction will come mutual changes in service orientation and levels of technological expertise. Librarians and computer-information specialists are on converging paths, a fact recognized by those institutions that employ chief information officers (CIOs) or that seek to merge libraries and computer centers. In the process, elements of one group's skill set may well transfer to the other, meaning that librarians become more technologically adept as computer people absorb more of the service ethic.

This confluence requires that librarians become more familiar with machines: not only with a computer's capabilities, but also with its inner workings. June Lester writes that "technological competence" currently "includes being able to design and maintain a web site, but tomorrow who knows?"[132] We believe that librarians need to know something about the hardware they work with every day, although "it is unreasonable to expect every librarian to become a digital technology expert."[133] Some argue, on the other hand, that "librarians need deep technical proficiency."[134] They need to be able to resolve common problems, such as IRQ conflicts, unrecognized new hardware, software that refuses to load, replacement of "accidentally" deleted operating files, and so on. They should be able to diagnose equipment failures, insert memory upgrades, and install additional cards and associated driver files for peripherals.

Scanners, printers, external drives, and modems are within the library's purview, especially if the building contains an information arcade and electronic classroom. There are not enough technicians (either staff or students) to react to every emergency; troubleshooting activities necessarily devolve to the librarian on the scene.

Current practice calls for the intervention of a technician whenever hardware problems arise. If minor troubles can be attended to on the spot, that solution is much more efficient. Librarians consequently need to possess some technical expertise, perhaps acquired during their degree programs, but certainly on the job. A quick survey of library school curricula reveals only a limited inclusion of such matters. Most programs are too short to accommodate anything beyond standard library-school fare. Yet the job demands frequent mediation between library user and machine, in the course of which a bit of technical knowledge can be very helpful.

Identification and procurement of relevant source materials in support of research are, and will remain, the librarian's primary task. Because many of these will be multimedia resources, a knowledge of delivery systems, such as RealPlayer, or ATM media servers is useful. Faculty will embed links to such materials in their electronic syllabi, and the library's servers will make them available. This is why, in a digital future, "the skills and competence of librarians will be highly valued" even if librarians themselves lose their institutional role, but only if they develop expertise in other areas.[135] Successful performance depends on familiarity with existing and emerging information technologies and on the ability to distinguish innovations from what Raymond Kurzweil called "false pretenders," or analog technologies, such as the cassette tape, that turned out to be evolutionary dead ends.[136] This knowledge then can be brought to bear on several specific duties for which librarians are typically responsible: (1) the organization of information delivery systems, such as citation and full-text databases; (2) instruction in the operation of the campus network and the standard campus information system; (3) instruction in research techniques appropriate to various disciplines and in the use of specialized information sources; (4) management of collections, the main purpose of which increasingly will become support of the curriculum on a particular campus; and (5) liaison with teaching faculty on such matters as collection development, instruction of students in research techniques, and provision of new informational databases.

Teaching is a large component of every librarian's job, especially in an electronic environment such as that of the modern academic library. Some training in the techniques of teaching could become part of an expanded or revised MLS degree program, along with the technical skills suggested earlier.[137] As industrial-age library buildings give way to structures with embedded technology, librarians will find their professional horizons broadening as their range of competencies increases. The buildings themselves, with their networked teaching and learning facilities, demand highly skilled staff who understand and can explain information technology. They will work in a "Gateway library" that emphasizes teaching, learning, and an ongoing dialog between students and librarians.[138] As librarians design their future workplaces, they redefine their profession. A continuing coexistence of print and electronic cultures requires that librarians act as a bridge between them. Buildings designed to accommodate both worlds seamlessly are the goal toward which librarians and architects are striving. The purpose of this book is to enhance their collaboration.

Notes

1. William Madison Randall, "Constitution of the modern library building," in *Library Buildings for Library Service*, ed. H. H. Fussler (Chicago: American Library Association, 1947), 183.

2. Carol Tenopir and Lisa Ennis, "The digital reference world of academic libraries," *Online* 22 (4): 22–28 (July/August 1998).

3. Suzanne E. Thorin and Virginia D. Sorkin, "The library of the future," in *The Learning Revolution: The Challenge of Information Technology in the Academy*, ed. Diana G. Oblinger and Sean C. Rush (Bolton, Mass.: Anchor Publishing, 1997), 167.

4. Michael Margolis, "Brave new universities," *FirstMonday* 3 (5) (1998) <http://www.firstmonday.org/issues/issue3_5/margolis/index.html>.

5. Geoffrey T. Freeman, "An architect's view: Libraries in the twenty-first century," *Harvard Library Bulletin* 4 (1): 33 (spring 1993).

6. See <http://www.utexas.edu/world/lecture> for up-to-date information.

7. R. Anders Schneiderman, "Why librarians should rule the Net," *E-Node* 1 (4) (September 5, 1996) <http://www.igc.org/e-node/1996/enode0104a.htm>.

8. Sheila D. Creth, "The Information Arcade: Playground for the mind," *Journal of Academic Librarianship* 20 (1): 22–23 (March 1994); Anita Lowry, "The Information Arcade: A library and electronic learning facility for 2000 and beyond," paper presented at the 1993 CAUSE Annual Conference, San Diego, December 1993, CAUSE Information Resources Library Document CNC9346 <http://www.educause.edu/asp/doclib>; and Joanne Fritz, "Playground for the mind," *Iowa Alumni Review* (spring 1993): 22–26.

9. See <http://www.ems.psu.edu/~fraser/Meteo Basic/Foyer/mainFrame.html>.

10. Harold B. Schill, "Bibliographic instruction: Planning for the electronic information environment," *College & Research Libraries* 48 (5): 449 (September 1987).

11. Patricia Battin, "The library: Center of the restructured university," *College & Research Libraries* 5 (3): 176 (May 1984).

12. Richard J. Bazillion and Connie Braun, "Technology and library users: Automation and outreach: Library services to off-campus students," *Journal of Distance Education* 7 (2): 67–75 (fall 1992).

13. Thomas Mann, "Reference service, human nature, and copyright—in a digital age," *Reference Service in a Digital Age: A Library of Congress Institute* (June 29–30, 1998) <http://lcweb.loc.gov/rr/digiref/mann.html>.

14. James F. Corey, "A grant for Z39.50," *Library Hi Tech* 12 (1): 39 (1994); see also William Moen, "The ANSI/NISO Z39.50 protocol: Information retrieval in the information infrastructure" <http://www.cni.org/pub/NISO/docs/Z39.50-brochure>.

15. Maribeth Ward, "Expanding access to information with Z39.50," *American Libraries* 25 (7): 639–641 (July/August 1994).

16. For more information on ISDN, see <http://www.ralphb.net/ISDN>; for more information on ADSL, see <http://www.cs.tamu.edu/people/jhamann/adsl/node3.html>.

17. American Library Association, Presidential Committee on Information Literacy, *Final Report* (Chicago: American Library Association, 1989), 1.

18. CAUSE membership materials, October 1994.

19. Network Wizards Internet Domain Survey at <http://www.nw.com>.

20. Clifford A. Lynch and Cecilia M. Preston, "Internet access to information resources," in *Annual Review of Information Science and Technology (ARIST)* 25, ed. Martha E. Williams (Washington, D.C.: American Society for Information Science 1990), 288.

21. Richard De Gennaro, *Libraries, Technology, and the Information Marketplace: Selected Papers* (Boston: G. K. Hall, 1987), 33.

22. Karl Beiser, "CD-ROM—middle-aged crazy after all these years," *Database* 16 (6): 95 (December 1993); see also Karl Beiser, "Specs for a CD-ROM workstation," *Online* 17 (4): 101–104 (July 1993).

23. *Chronicle of Higher Education* (October 28, 1992): A22.

24. Tenopir and Ennis, "The digital reference world," 28.

25. John M. Nevison, *Computing as a Matter of Course: The Instructional Use of Computers at Dartmouth College* (Hanover, N.H.: Dartmouth College, Kiewit Computation Center, July 1976), ERIC, ED 160061, p. 1.

26. Marc S. Tucker, "The 'Star Wars' universities: Carnegie-Mellon, Brown, and M.I.T.," in *Computers on Campus: Working Papers: Current Issues in Higher Education*, ed. Marc S. Tucker (Washington, D.C.: American Association for Higher Education, 1983), ERIC, ED 240947, p. 6. Seventeen years later, CMU remains committed to incorporating information technology into the teaching and learning process.

27. Quoted in Peggy Brown, ed., *Computer Literacy . . . Would Plato Understand?* (Washington, D.C.: Association of American Colleges, May 1983), ERIC, ED 231263, p. 5.

28. Quoted in Carolyn Marvin and Mark Winther, "Computer-ease: A twentieth-century literacy emergent," *Journal of Communication* 33 (1): 105 (winter 1983).

29. Richard A. Detweiler et al., "Opportunistic planning for information technologies: Upside down or downside up?" Paper presented at CAUSE92, Dallas, Texas, December 1992. CAUSE Information Resources Library Document: CNC9203.

30. Peter Lyman, "What is computer literacy and what is its place in liberal education?" *Liberal Education* 81 (3): 15 (summer 1995).

31. Ibid.

32. Ernest L. Boyer, *College: The Undergraduate Experience in America* (New York: Harper and Row, 1987), 167.

33. See <http://www.vcsu.nodak.edu/offices/itc/notebooks/other.htm> for up-to-date information.

34. Jay David Bolter, quoted in *Chronicle of Higher Education* (September 30, 1992): A17.

35. NREN Overview <http://www.nren.nasa.gov/overview.html>.

36. See <http://www.canarie.ca>; and Jeffrey R. Young, "Superfast Canadian network opens without much to carry," *Chronicle of Higher Education* (July 1, 1999) <http://www.chronicle.com/ search97 cgi/s97_cgi>.

37. *Proceedings of the NREN Workshop*, Monterey, Calif., September 16–18, 1992 (EDUCOM, 1992), A32, A84.

38. See <http://www.internet2.edu> for more information.

39. Andrew Odlyzko, "The slow evolution of electronic publishing," <http://www.research.att.com/~amo/doc/slow.evolution.txt>.

40. Samuel Demas, "Collection development for the electronic library: A conceptual and organizational model," *Library Hi Tech* 12 (3): 71 (1994).

41. Frank Quinn, "Consequences of electronic publication in theoretical physics," in *Scholarly Publication at the Crossroads: A Subversive Proposal for Electronic Publishing*, ed. A. Okerson and J. O'Donnell (Washington, D.C.: Association of Research Libraries, 1995), 170–174.

42. Gregory J. E. Rawlins, "The new publishing: Technology's impact on the publishing industry over the next decade," *Public-Access Computer Systems Review* 3 (8): 34 (1992).

43. George P. Landow, "Twenty minutes into the future, or How are we moving beyond the book?" in *The Future of the Book*, ed. Geoffrey Nunberg (Berkeley: University of California Press, 1996), 216.

44. See Peter R. Young, "Periodical prices, 1988–1990," *Serials Librarian* 18 (3/4): 1–21 (1990), which cites the sources in which increases in periodicals prices since 1975 may be tracked.

45. Michael Les, "How can we get high-quality electronic journals?" *IEEE Intelligent Systems* 13 (1): 12 (January/February 1998).

46. Ethel Auster, *Retrenchment in Canadian Academic Libraries* (Ottawa: Canadian Library Association, 1991), 156.

47. Brian L. Hawkins, "Planning for the national electronic library," *EDUCOM Review* 29 (3): 29 (May/June 1994).

48. Richard P. Hulser, "Prepare today for the digital library of tomorrow," in *The Future Compatible Campus: Planning, Designing, and Implementing Information Technology in the Academy*, ed. Diana G. Oblinger and Sean C. Rush (Bolton, Mass.: Anchor Publishing, 1998), 225.

49. This argument is convincingly made in Bernard Naylor, "The future of the scholarly journal: Clearing the ground," paper delivered to the general meeting LIBER, July 7, 1994: 1. Published in *LIBER Quarterly* 4 (1994): 283ff ; A survey of electronic-publication projects is: Michael Malinconico, "Electronic documents and research libraries," *IFLA Journal* 22 (3): 211–225 (1996).

50. Naylor, "Clearing the ground," 2.

51. The Naylor-Harnad-Odlyzko discussion is archived and can be found at <http://cogsci.soton.ac.uk/~harnad/subvert.html>. See also Jacques Leslie, "Goodbye, Gutenberg," *Wired* 2 (10): 68–71 (October 1994).

52. Andrew Odlyzko, "Tragic loss or good riddance: The impending demise of traditional scholarly journals," *Surfaces* 4 (105) Folio 1: 6, 24 (February 28, 1994) <http://www.research.att.com/~amo/doc/tragic.loss.txt>.

53. Harnad's reply to Naylor, August 14, 1994.

54. Mathew Wills and Gordon Wills, "The ins and outs of electronic publishing" [n.d.] <http://www.mcb.co.uk/literati/articles/insandouts.htm>.

55. Odlyzko, "The slow evolution of scholarly publishing."

56. Andrew Odlyzko, "The economics of electronic journals" (1997) <http://www.press.umich.edu/jep/04-01/odlyzko.html>.

57. Gail McMillan et al., *Report of the Scholarly Communications Task Force*, report presented to the Library Administrative Council, University Libraries, Virginia Polytechnic Institute and State University, May 10, 1994 <http://scholar.lib.vt.edu/reports/task-force.html>.

58. Dru Mogge, "ARL directory tracks growth in e-publishing" <http://www.arl.org/newsltr/196/dej.html>.

59. Stevan Harnad, "Implementing peer review on the Net: Scientific quality control in scholarly electronic journals," *Proceedings of the 1993 International Conference on Refereed Electronic Journals*, Winnipeg, Manitoba, October 1993 (Winnipeg, Manitoba, 1994), pp. 8.1–8.14.

60. Eldred Smith, "A partnership for the future," *Scholarly Publishing* 22 (2): 91 (January 1991).

61. F. W. Lancaster, "Electronic publishing," *Library Trends* 37 (3): 319 (winter 1989).

62. Declan Butler, "Briefing: The writing is on the Web for science journals in print," *Nature* 397 (6176): 1, 2 (21 January 1999).

63. Ibid., 1, 2.

64. Elisabeth Geake, "Network set to put journals in the picture," *New Scientist* (November 21, 1992): 18.

65. Eldred Smith, "The print prison," *Library Journal* 117 (3): 51 (February 1, 1992).

66. Paul Metz and Paul M. Gherman, "Serials pricing and the role of the electronic journal," *College & Research Libraries* 52 (4): 323 (July 1991).

67. Sanford G. Thatcher, "Towards the year 2001," *Scholarly Publishing* 24 (1): 32 (October 1992).

68. Goldie Blumenstyk and Vincent Kiernan, "Idea of online archives of papers sparks debate on future of journals," *Chronicle of Higher Education* (July 9, 1999): A25–A26.

69. Priscilla Caplan, "You can't get there from here: E-prints and the library," *Public Access Computer Systems Review* 5 (1): 21 (1994) <http://info.lib.uh.edu/pr/v5/n1/caplan.5n1>.

70. "Project SCAN: University of California seeks trailblazers for the electronic frontier" <http://www.ucpress.edu/scan>.

71. Brian Kahin, "Scholarly communication in the network environment: Issues of principle, policy, and practice," *Electronic Library* 10 (5): 280 (October 1992).

72. Peter Lyman, "What is a digital library? Technology, intellectual property, and the public interest," *Daedalus* 125 (4): 6 (fall 1996).

73. Lyman, "What is a digital library," 28.

74. Kenneth D. Crews, "Copyright law, libraries, and universities: Overview, recent developments, and future issues," working paper for presentation to the Association of Research Libraries (October 1992) <http://palimpsest.stanford.edu/bytopic/intprop/crews.html>.

75. Scott Bennett, "Copyright and innovation in electronic publishing: A commentary," *Journal of Academic Librarianship* 19 (2): 87–91 (May 1993).

76. "Fair use in the electronic age: Serving the public interest," draft statement prepared by the Coalition for Networked Information, November 8, 1994.

77. Canadian and British readers should know that their copyright law recognizes "fair use" only as a defense against a charge of infringement. There is no legal recognition of a right to fair use. It is consequently easier in Canada for publishers and their agent, CanCopy (the copyright collective), to assert proprietary control over information. See AUCC/Cancopy "Model Licence," March 1994; John R. Garrett and Patrice A. Lyons, "Toward an electronic copyright management system," *Journal of the American Society for Information Science* 44 (8): 468–473 (September 1993); J. Eric Davies, "Intellectual property," in *Security and Crime Prevention in Libraries*, ed. Michael Chaney and Alan F. MacDougall (Brookfield, Vt.: Ashgate, 1992), 152–181; and the Preliminary Draft of the NII's working group in Marjorie Hlava, "A vision for ASIS: 1993 inaugural address," *Bulletin of the American Society for Information Science* 20 (3): 2–4 (August/September 1994).

78. Kahin, "Scholarly communication," 281.

79. Scott Seaman, "Copyright and the electronic library," *DIGIT* (May/June 1994): 1 <http://www.colorado.edu/CNS/Digit/mayjune94/copyright.html>.

80. *Report of the Joint Funding Council's Libraries Review Group* ("Follett Report") December 1993, par. 71 <http://www.niss.ac.uk/education/hefc/follett/report>.

81. Rawlins, "The new publishing," 12.

82. Canadian Association of Research Libraries, "Brief to the national information highway advisory council" (September 1994).

83. Mary Anne Kennan, "The impact of electronic scholarly publishing," *LASIE* 28 (3): 24–33 (September 1997).

84. Paul J. Korshin, "The idea of an academic press at the *fin de siècle*," *Scholarly Publishing* 22 (2): 71–72 (January 1991).

85. A balanced explanation of the slow growth of electronic journal publication is found in Cliff McKnight, "Electronic journals—past, present . . . and future?" *Aslib Proceedings* 45 (1): 7–10 (January 1993).

86. On the current uses libraries make of the Internet, see Sharyn J. Ladner and Hope N. Tillman, "How special librarians really use the Inter-net," *Canadian Library Journal* 49 (3): 211–215 (June 1992).

87. Vartan Gregorian, Brian L. Hawkins, and Merrily Taylor, "Integrating information technologies: A research university perspective," *CAUSE/ EFFECT* 15 (4): 10 (winter 1992).

88. Gordon B. Neavill, "Electronic publishing, libraries, and the survival of information," *Library Resources and Technical Services* (January/March 1984): 81.

89. Norman D. Stevens, "Research libraries: Past, present, and future," *Advances in Librarianship* 17 (1993): 95–96.

90. Clifford Lynch, "Rethinking the integrity of the scholarly record in the networked information age," *EDUCOM Review* 29 (2): 39 (March/ April 1994).

91. Neavill, "Electronic publishing," 80; see also David A. Hockema's remarks in the symposium edited by Paula T. Kaufman and Tamara Miller, "Scholarly communications: New realities, old values," *Library Hi Tech* 10 (3): 70–73 (1992).

92. Lynch, "Rethinking the integrity of the scholarly record," 40.

93. Robert Darnton, "The new age of the book," *New York Review of Books* 46 (5): 7 (March 18, 1999).

94. Bil Stahl, "Networked information resources: Not just a library challenge," CAUSE Information Resources Library Document (CEM9239), 1992.

95. Jacques Barzun and Henry Graff, *The Modern Researcher*, 5th ed. (Boston: Houghton-Mifflin, 1992), 361.

96. Anthony M. Cummings et al., *University Libraries and Scholarly Communication: A Study Prepared for the Andrew W. Mellon Foundation* (New York: Association of Research Libraries, November 1992), 125.

97. Karen Horny, "Digital technology: Implications for library planning," in *Advances in Librarianship* 16, ed. Irene P. Godden (1992), 122.

98. Geoffrey Nunberg, "Will libraries survive," *American Prospect* 41 (November–December 1998): 16–23.

99. A balanced discussion of the issues may be found in Cummings et al., *University Libraries*, chapter 9. On the complex issue of copyright in the electronic environment, see Brian Kahin, "The copyright law: How it works and new issues in electronic settings," *Serials Librarian* 24 (3/4):

163–172 (1994); and Robert L. Oakley, "Copyright issues for the creators and users of information in the electronic environment," *Electronic Networking* 1 (1): 23–30 (fall 1991).

100. Lucy Siefert Wegner, "The research library and emerging information technology," *New Directions for Teaching and Learning* 51 (fall 1992): 88.

101. William Y. Arms, "The institutional implications of electronic information," paper presented at a conference on Technology, Scholarship, and the Humanities: The Implications of Electronic Information (Irvine, Calif., September 30–October 2, 1992), 7 <www.cni.org/docs/tech.schol.human/Arms.html>.

102. Laverna M. Saunders, "The virtual library today," *Library Administration and Management* 6 (2): 66 (spring 1992).

103. Raymond Kurzweil, "Futurecast," *Library Journal* (January, February 15, March 15, 1992).

104. See Project Mercury at <http://www.andrew.cmu.edu:80/user/gm3g/mercweb/ProjMerc.html>.

105. William Y. Arms, vice president for Academic Services, quoted in *Chronicle of Higher Education* (September 2, 1992): A19.

106. Academic Planning Board, The University of California, Berkeley, "Toward electronic scholarly information: The IST five-year vision (1993–1998)" <http://ist.berkeley.edu/IST5>.

107. S. Michael Malinconico, "What librarians need to know to survive in an age of technology," *Journal of Education for Library and Information Science* 33 (3): 233 (summer 1992).

108. Joan Blair, "The library in the information revolution," *Library Administration and Management* 6 (2): 73 (spring 1992).

109. Quoted in Kaufman and Miller, "Scholarly communications: New realities, old values," 66.

110. Susan J. Barnes, "The electronic library and public services," *Library Hi Tech* 12 (3): 51 (1994).

111. De Gennaro, *Libraries, Technology, and the Information Marketplace*, 42.

112. Mark Sandler, "Transforming library staff roles," *Library Issues: Briefings for Faculty and Administrators* 17 (1) (September 1996) <http://www.libraryissues.com/pub/LI9609.html>.

113. Jane E. Klobas, "Information services for new millennium organizations: Librarians and knowledge management," in *Libraries for the New Millennium: Implications for Managers*, ed. David L. Raitt (London: Library Association Publishing, 1997): 39–64.

114. Nicholas von Hoffman, "Checking out electronic libraries: Repackaging information for the next millennium," *Architectural Digest* 53 (10): 130 (October 1996).

115. Stahl, "Networked information resources."

116. Michael Gorman, "The academic library in the year 2001: Dream or nightmare or something in between?" *Journal of Academic Librarianship* 17 (1): 5 (1991).

117. Barnes, "The electronic library," 58.

118. Eldred Smith, *The Librarian, the Scholar, and the Future of the Research Library* (New York: Greenwood Press, 1990), 82.

119. Ibid., 83.

120. Antony E. Simpson, "Information-finding and the education of scholars: Teaching electronic access in disciplinary context," *Behavioral and Social Sciences Librarian* 16 (2): 9 (May/June 1998).

121. Stanley Chodorow and Peter Lyman, "The responsibilities of universities in the new information environment," in *The Mirage of Continuity: Reconfiguring Academic Information Resources for the 21st Century*, ed. Brian L. Hawkins and Patricia Battin (Washington, D.C.: Council on Library and Information Resources and Association of American Universities, 1998), 71.

122. Matthew Allen and Lothar Retzlaff, "Libraries and information technology: Towards the twenty-first century," *Australian Library Journal* 47 (1): 97 (February 1998).

123. Eldred Smith and Peggy Johnson, "How to survive the present while preparing for the future: A research library strategy," *College & Research Libraries* 54 (5): 393 (September 1993).

124. For example, S. Michael Malinconico, "Technology and the academic workplace," *Library Administration and Management* 5 (1): 26 (winter 1991).

125. David W. Lewis, "Inventing the electronic university," *College & Research Libraries* 49 (4): 292 (July 1988).

126. Dell Johnson, *The Future of Electronic Educational Networks: Some Ethical Issues* (Texas: 1991), ERIC, ED 332689, p. 10 (12).

127. Peter Lyman, in Kaufman and Miller, "Scholarly communications," 77.

128. Clifford A. Lynch, "Networked information: A revolution in progress," in *Networks, Open Access, and Virtual Libraries: Implications for the*

Research Library, ed. Brett Sutton and Charles H. Davis (Urbana-Champaign: University of Illinois Graduate School of Library and Information Science, 1991), 23.

129. Richard A. Lanham, *The Electronic Word: Democracy, Technology, and the Arts* (Chicago: University of Chicago Press, 1993), 134.

130. James J. O'Donnell, *Avatars of the Word: From Papyrus to Cyberspace* (Cambridge, Mass.: Harvard University Press, 1998), 90. At the time of writing, O'Donnell was vice provost for information systems and computing at the University of Pennsylvania.

131. Pieter van Brakel, "Education and training for information professionals in the face of the Internet and World Wide Web," in Raitt, *Libraries for the New Millennium,* 247.

132. June Lester, "Library and information studies education," in *Creating the Future: Essays on Librarianship in an Age of Great Change,* ed. Sally Gardner Reed (Jefferson, N.C.: McFarland, 1996), 180.

133. W. Lee Hisle, "Roles for a digital age," in Reed, *Creating the Future,* 36.

134. John M. Budd and Lisa K. Miller, "Teaching for technology: Current practice and future direction," *Information Technology and Libraries* 18 (2): 78 (June 1999).

135. Frode Bakken, "The possible role of libraries in the digital future," *Libri* 48 (2): 82 (1998).

136. Raymond Kurzweil, "The future of libraries, part I: The technology of the book," *Library Journal* 117 (1): 80 (January 1992).

137. Brendan A. Rapple, "A new model of librarian education for the networked environment" <http://www.ala.org/acrl/paperhtm/d37.html>.

138. Lawrence Dowler and Laura Farwell, "The Gateway: A bridge to the library of the future," *RSR: Reference Services Review* 24 (2): 9 (1996).

Designing an "Intelligent" Library

It would appear . . . that all concepts, policies, and standards of librarianship must be challenged if we are to successfully plan buildings that will encourage efficient and effective service in this new environment.[1]

Redefining the Intelligent Building

Almost fifty years ago, Ralph Ellsworth perceived a change in the relationship between architects and their librarian clients. Building planning had passed from the architect's hands to those of people who eventually will operate the library. "The architect's task," wrote Ellsworth, "is to create a building that will perform the functions described in the program." A beautiful library, though a worthy goal, ought not to "waste money or interfere with the desired operations of the building."[2] Several developments, including modular design and the desire to create physically inviting space, converged to produce academic libraries that were intelligently conceived, rather than simply large and ornamental. With the advent of information technology and its application both to research and to environmental controls, came the opportunity to design truly intelligent and functional buildings. After all, "the architect is the only artist who has to consider utility."[3] Elsewhere, Ellsworth observed that architects "tend to think of the beauty of the [building's] shell rather than the beauty of the operation."[4] Some forty years later, this judgment still pertains.

Furnishings, equipment, and shelving are conventional occupants of library space. A less tangible, though pervasive, presence in the building is information technology. The associated equipment occupies three general categories: (1) the library's integrated automated system; (2) networked workstations for staff members and library users; and (3) portable computers, many equipped with Ethernet cards, brought into the library by users. A power and communications grid that reaches every corner of the building enables a simple connection to the campus information network. There are also more traditional devices: photocopiers, microform reader/printers, fax machines, and scanners. All these machines occupy space, generate heat, and therefore affect interior design and layout, air-handling systems, electrical-power requirements, and furniture construction. Existing information technology must be accommodated, along with provisions for future developments. Before the architect can be instructed properly, the electronic terrain has to be scouted and mapped.

Electronic information networks transformed the world of academic libraries after 1994. Already it is clear that scholarly journals and reference sources are migrating toward an electronic format. Specialized monographs may be next. The economics of print publication and distribution push strongly in this direction. Libraries respond by providing cost-effective and seamless access to electronic resources. Collection size matters less than does timely access to needed materials, wherever they reside.[5] Many academic libraries, often working through consortia, now offer direct access to such full-text sources as JStor, Project Muse, and a universe of indexes, abstracts, and bibliographies. One of JStor's aims is "to reduce eventual capital costs for library building," because researchers will have most of their information needs met electronically.[6] This result is the natural culmination of decisions, made over thirty years ago, to embrace library automation. Eli Noam and Caterina Alvarez again raise that troubling question: "Electronics can rescue the storage function of the library. But will they in the process make the library irrelevant"?[7] Our answer, for reasons noted in chapter 1, is no. Libraries as institutions remain strong, although functional change is occurring.

Over a quarter-century ago, librarians realized that many quotidian tasks—mainly cataloging and circulation—lent themselves to computerization. Integrated library systems are now universal. During the first epoch of library automation, which ended about the mid-1980s with the arrival of increasingly powerful microcomputers, online public-access terminals received the same treatment as the card catalog they were about to replace. Banks of these terminals appeared where multidrawered cabinets had once stood and usurped at least as much floor space. To be sure, many buildings constructed after 1970, such as the

McLaughlin Library at the University of Guelph, had power grids and raceway systems to manage miles of wire and computer cable.[8] But in most other ways, library architecture preserved its traditional form. Study tables, carrels, and bookstacks were still arranged to support a pen-and-paper, jotted-note approach to research. Networked information services have evolved to the point that they, along with new ways of teaching and learning, determine the architecture and interior design of today's academic libraries.

As the library's warehousing function declines in relative importance, its involvement in the university's teaching activity will grow.[9] Libraries designed and built from this point onward are teaching and learning centers in which students acquire a mastery of research techniques that will serve them long after their formal education is completed. Design, therefore, should reflect the fact that providing access to the campus information network is one of the library's primary services. Facilities for comprehensive online work must be available in a setting that is both comfortable and conducive to study. Heating, ventilating, and air-conditioning (HVAC) systems should create an environment that is congenial to books, people, and machines. The library's electric power and communications grids, moreover, must deliver service to every study space in the building and to areas in which library staff members work.

With less emphasis on the library-as-warehouse comes more attention to the building's physical amenities. Users may well spend significantly more time in the library, because of the research potential available in the campus information network and because of easy access, through the same network, to Webpage-creation, text editing, and data-analysis software. All work associated with a research project—from generation of a bibliography to production of a finished paper—can be done in the library, perhaps using a notebook computer leased from the university.[10] Study furniture and the ambience in general should be as comfortable as possible, because time spent in the library is likely to increase in the years ahead. Particularly on residential campuses, the library will continue to offer a refuge from raucous dormitories. The soft clicking of keyboards will distract few library users from the task at hand; consequently there will be in fact less "need to provide physical separation between people using traditional printed materials and those using keyboards, printers and other things that click or whir."[11]

Contemporary academic libraries, then, are in transition from repositories for printed materials to participants in the full range of scholarly activity. This new role is a product of several currents that are converging from different directions: (1) rapid acceptance of the Internet and the World Wide Web as essential to academic research and communication by most institutions of higher education in the United States and Canada; (2) inflation of paper-journal prices to a point at which this form of scholarly communication is very likely to disappear; (3) arrival of electronic publishing as an alternative to the print media; (4) affordable broadband transmission that allows multimedia use on local information networks; and (5) availability of portable computing power capable of connecting to local networks or to any information source available on the Internet. Each of these developments, in its own way, affects both the design of library buildings and the library's educational mission.

Building-design implications lie in the evolution of electronic services and the changing role of librarians. Traditional distinctions between technical and public services, for example, are already breaking down with the advent of networked information sources and cataloging data. Some observers predict "flatter" staffing structures and the use of "flexible and project oriented" teams to operate libraries.[12] Others foresee an expanded role for library assistants. When designing a building to last for decades, thought should be given to the way in which personnel are deployed. Roles and activities are being transformed, and the prospect of a new building offers a good opportunity to rethink and revise existing structures. The relationship between library personnel and information technology defines space assignments throughout the building. The basic organizing principle, one that is becoming increasingly clear, is that new academic libraries are central to the teaching and learning process. Librarians in general will "become the guide and counselor through the maze of systems, command languages, and access points, not to mention the instructor in bibliographic control of not only the documents to be obtained, but also of those documents held by the individual researcher and those then created by the researcher."[13]

One of the most significant innovations of recent years is the advent of ubiquitous student access to computers. Sonoma State University requires that all students have twenty-four-hour-a-day access. Wake Forest University, along with several other institutions, has initiated a notebook-computer leasing program. There is an obvious national and international trend toward placing portable computing power in the hands of students and faculty. Teaching is migrating steadily toward a Web-based environment in which students have anytime-anyplace access to course materials of all kinds. The dividing line between classroom instruction and distance learning is blurring swiftly under the influence of new teaching and learning strategies. Electronic media, thanks to high-speed networking, have entered the educational mainstream. What are the consequences for library design and library personnel? Are the predictions of Lewis, Lanham, and others becoming reality?

Ubiquitous computing and campus networking are two of the strongest influences on contemporary library design. Together with the curatorial function inherited from the age of print, they create the hybrid library of today. Few library planners are bold enough to propose a completely electronic environment, even when taking into account the massive growth in digitized information sources. The question, therefore, is one of designing space that accommodates both formats and, at the same time, is flexible enough to be reorganized as needs change. Flexibility applies equally to public services and to the housing of (and access to) library materials.

Considering the scope and intensity of changes affecting library design, it is helpful to recapitulate some examples:

- electronic publishing
- Web-based teaching and learning
- broadband networking
- furniture design and materials
- ubiquitous computer access
- growing need for information literacy
- new models of reference service
- expansion of electronic learning space
- legal public-access mandates: ADA (Americans with Disabilities Act), academic libraries as community resources
- increasingly sophisticated clientele
- multimedia knowledge resources

Each of these items in some way influences design and space decisions in a building project. How many and what sort of computers should be provided for users? What kinds of learning spaces are needed? Will storage needs change significantly during the building's lifetime? What services should the library offer, to whom, and by whom? Some of these questions defy clear answers, especially in an environment defined mainly by the speed of technological change. Consequently, the need for flexible yet functional library space is paramount.

Flexibility and functionality are best achieved by (1) maintaining as much open space as possible, (2) avoiding monumental pieces of millwork, such as imposing reference desks, (3) creating as fine-grained a power and communications grid as can be afforded, and (4) selecting furnishings, equipment, and color schemes that are durable and timeless. Arrangement of furnishings and equipment must observe ADA regulations, which prescribe 36-inch aisles (preferably 42 inches) and 32-inch wheelchair passage between tables and fixed items of furniture. Physical accessibility to all spaces, including hallways, is required in new and renovated buildings.[14] Signage, door handles, signals, plumbing fixtures, doors, elevators, and alarms must also comply. ADA regulations in no way interfere with interior space configurations, and, in fact, encourage greater openness. As custody of physical volumes diminishes, storage areas can easily be converted to other uses. Quality study and research space has to emerge seamlessly from what once were stacks. That can happen only if the power and data grid permeated the building in the first place, with an eventual transformation of space in mind. Atria or stairwells that intrude into the building's interior space militate against flexibility by preventing reconfiguration. That is why they are best limited to the building's entrance, where their impact on assignable space is greatly reduced.

Technology associated with information retrieval and electronic-document construction should be accessible and unobtrusive at the same time. Hundreds of network connections give library users the chance to plug in their portable computers. (As wireless technology matures, library users will be liberated from the physical network connection.) An information gallery situated in prime library real estate, far from compromising the building's integrity, acknowledges the growing importance of digital resources. Provided that equipment and service are functionally related to each other, library users will benefit: "The application of information technology to library-related functions only helps the evolution of libraries into entities that are more relevant to the users they serve."[15] Interior design and environmental control, along with the technology, determine the library's success in meeting user expectations.

An "intelligent building" is one that is comfortable, attractive, and functional. These qualities are neither accidental nor spontaneous, but require careful planning. Sometimes, amid the competing claims of rival technologies and automation strategies, recourse to auguries from ouija boards and the entrails of birds may be tempting. In making sense of a library world turned upside down, librarians are for the most part on their own. There is no point in relying on the wisdom of architects, for most of them know little of how traditional libraries work, let alone the gateway library now emerging. As electronic access supplants print archives, buildings themselves need to be adaptable and amenable to change. That is why flexibility is so important. Librarians not only manage such buildings, but are also their creators and renewers. The challenges inherent in design and renovation can best be met by librarians who understand the implications of information technology. Research, study, site visits, and practical experience are good defenses against architects who insist on substituting their judgment for that of librarians.

Features of an Intelligent Building

An intelligent building is one in which computerized systems control security, lighting, and air-handling functions. Sensors allow the building to monitor its own condition, an especially important feature in earthquake zones.[16] Remote sensing also is needed to maintain a constant relative humidity level in the building. The building envelope, for its part, "reduces heat loss and gain through insulation and thermal mass."[17] Glazing, moistureproofing, vapor barrier, and construction materials all are components of the intelligent building. They help to determine the type of computerized controls that will be linked to the lighting, HVAC, and security systems. The result is a building that offers a healthy, secure environment to its occupants.

Computers, both on- and off-site, monitor lighting systems, motion detectors, and door access. Each program can be tailored to the library's operating schedule, so that lights are turned on shortly before staff arrive in the morning and off after the building closes. (Manual switching is also provided, with ganged circuits to control many fixtures using few switches.) Access cards, carried by all staff (library, maintenance, and security) can be programmed to permit access at designated times, depending on the card's security level. Some libraries use keypad access, which can be tailored to prevent after-hours entry. Entries that occur when the building is closed are recorded in a computer file. Surveillance systems, monitored by security-company personnel, perhaps located in another city, are now common. If an intrusion occurs, the company calls two or more persons on a preestablished list to investigate; the local police also may be summoned. None of these computerized systems is absolutely reliable, but together they provide a high degree of building security. Monitors connected to the HVAC systems ensure that malfunctions are recorded and reported, so that the building does not damage itself. Vandalism and burglary are enough to worry about, especially in modern buildings full of expensive equipment.

When computerized control systems fail to operate as advertised, frustration and disappointment result. Perhaps the design was too complicated: "Seeking to improve control led to loss of control."[18] Often overlooked is the fact that every intelligent building needs smart people who know how the computer programs work. When renovation projects are under way, staff must know how to bypass certain motion detectors. And, as the years pass, someone in the physical plant department has to update the record on the "as builts." If this is not done, succeeding generations of maintenance people will lose touch with the building's systems and be unable to fix them when they break down. Stewart Brand advises that "computers are ideal for keeping dynamic records of this sort." [19] But the data are useless if not regularly updated, studied, evaluated, and used as guides to action.

Lighting

Even today, many years into the computer revolution, lighting remains a neglected or misunderstood aspect of library design. Architects treat it cavalierly; electrical engineers waste little time on its nuances. Libraries consequently are still overlit by "the old-style recessed fluorescent ceiling 'troffers' that have, for many years, been the standard" and that create too much glare for computer use. [20] Yet lighting technology has advanced beyond this style, along with the means to analyze a proposed lighting system.

As is the case with other aspects of library design, lighting configurations may now be created with the aid of a microcomputer. [21] Many manufacturers offer their photometric data on floppy disks, thus allowing architects to simulate actual installations. On the horizon are programs that will permit "an integrated analysis of electric lighting and daylighting." [22] Just because CAD (computer-aided design) software for lighting exists does not mean that architects and their electrical consultants will use it. Because lighting is outside building codes, and because lighting design is not usually included in a project budget, the whole issue is often ignored. It is easier to look up illumination requirements in a handbook than to create a functional design for a particular project. [23] The simple and the slapdash are no longer acceptable approaches to the lighting of libraries, if indeed they ever were. Library lighting is not a trivial matter and therefore deserves more attention than it typically receives from architects and their consultants. Proper illumination is worth fighting to achieve during the design-development phase.

Contemporary lighting fixtures emphasize energy conservation and glare control, two concerns that lend themselves to computer analysis. [24] Fluorescent tubes have almost replaced incandescents, mainly because they are more economical to operate. Electronic ballasts, together with T-8 lamps, help to save up to 35 percent over conventional ballasts; they also appear to reduce eyestrain and headaches in comparison with magnetic ballasts. [25] Two-tube systems can replace older three-tube ones and be just as effective at less cost. Selecting the appropriate fixtures is more difficult now than it once was, because "it is no longer simply a question of cool versus warm white lamps." [26] Other factors must be taken into account, such as color quality of the light produced by a particular fixture, which varies according to the phosphor mix, and, of course, the fixture's cost. Most libraries will combine fluorescent lighting and high-intensity discharge (HID) lamps. Both types of lamps now offer excellent color rendition, especially metal-halide HIDs and phosphor-coated fluorescents. HID bulbs have a life span of some 24,000 hours and are energy efficient. Fluorescents can be equipped with polycarbonate, UV-filtered lenses that are stronger than either glass or acrylic. In summary, modern lighting will not detract from the interior design by altering colors. Lighting, moreover, is a vital component of the library's environment.[27]

This simple fact often escapes architects, who routinely pass responsibility for lighting design to electrical engineers. Less than satisfactory results often ensue. Glare and UV radiation from unshielded fluorescent tubes are two common, yet easily avoidable, problems created by inadequate lighting systems that are "designed independently of all other building systems."[28] PC-based programs, such as RADIANCE, Lawrence Berkeley Lab, and *Lumen Micro* (Lighting Technologies), can model a lighting environment.[29] Something as simple as providing dimmer switches for fluorescent lighting can go far to tailor ambient light to the preference of users. One such system, the Mark 10 ballast produced by Advance Transformer of Rosemont, Illinois, allows "5 to 100 percent dimming."[30] Mylar-film inserts for light fixtures convert cool white light into full-spectrum. The ability to alter illumination levels is essential where computers are used; in a library, this means the entire building.

Libraries require two types of lighting: general and task-specific. In the first case, illumination is provided to stack areas and to any work or study spaces that are located within the stacks. Task lighting is used to give extra illumination where needed, especially at study stations and staff work areas. Fluorescent tubes generally are used for reasons of economy and efficiency. New "triphosphor" fluorescent lights are energy efficient and, at the same time, offer color that is superior to traditional cool white tubes.[31] Glare reflected from light fixtures, work surfaces, and architectural surfaces is "the single most important problem in lighting."[32] Surfaces should not be highly reflective, nor should the library be overilluminated. Users should be able to work comfortably either with a computer or with pen and paper. The *IES Lighting Handbook* has been, until quite recently, the standard guide to desirable levels of illumination, and now is less prone to advise excessive levels.[33]

Over twenty-five years ago, Keyes D. Metcalf criticized the high intensities then being recommended by lighting engineers and "question[ed] the necessity or desirability of going beyond the 30 to 35 maintained foot-candles at table height in most reading areas."[34] Computer simulations subsequently have confirmed Metcalf's ideas, and, indeed, the 1999 edition of his book on academic library design (revised by Leighton and Weber) cites evidence "that intensities greater than 20 foot-candles (215.2 lux) have no practical significance."[35] Opinion nevertheless remains divided on the issue of proper illumination levels, and some authorities still recommend higher intensities than Metcalf proposed.[36] Ellsworth Mason is one consultant who favors a level between 50 and 70 foot-candles (550–770 lux).[37] Another recent study recommends a range of 45 to 55 foot-candles for office work.[38] The Illuminating Engineering Society of North America recommends 30 to 50 foot-candles for offices.[39] Expert opinion therefore suggests that lighting designers try to achieve about 40 to 50 foot-candles in stack areas, so that spine labels may be read easily on the lowest shelves. For work areas, the recommended ambient light level is 30 to 40 foot-candles.[40]

Overillumination, prevalent in the prosperous 1960s and 1970s, is today less a problem than glare in library settings. "Glare," writes Mason, "is most acute at a 45 degree angle to the eye, and it can be controlled by placing the fixtures out of sight."[41] Several methods may be used. Mason points approvingly to the Colorado College solution of placing fluorescent fixtures in 18-inch concrete coffers molded into the open-ceiling design. Another common approach is to use refracting lenses that also act as UV filters. A latticework of acoustic baffles below the lighting grid can also help to remove light sources from line of sight. In the absence of reliable professional advice on illumination questions, the best idea is to specify a general lighting level no greater than 50 foot-candles and to equip fixtures with suitable lenses. Reducing the area composed of glare-producing surfaces, such as tabletops, will also help.

Lighting quality depends heavily on "color temperature," which measures the "warmth" or "coolness" of illuminated space. Color temperature is expressed in degrees Kelvin, according to the following ranges:

Warm	yellow/white	> 3500K
Neutral	white	3500–4000K
Cool	blue/white	< 4000K

Color temperature is unrelated to color rendition. Thus, "the selection of color temperature is an architectural consideration and should be based on 'taste' or 'preference' rather than on a strict metric."[42] Type of bulb, in other words, depends on the application. In the case of a library, neutral-to-warm is better.

No consensus exists on the best configuration for a fluorescent lighting grid. Mason advises that "lighting strips should run at right angles to stack ranges, because it [sic] provides more even lighting within the stack aisles than lighting centered on the aisles."[43] Charles Gosnell, whom Mason cites disapprovingly, prefers aisle-centered fixtures. Writing in 1961, Keyes Metcalf observed that "the fixtures and tubes do not need to be in rows. Different patterns can be used."[44] Agreement exists only on the truism that lighting quality is more important than quantity. This principle appears to mean that coverage and the type of light emitted from particular lamps are the two primary considerations. C. L. Crouch suggests a handy test that library planners might well perform in a lighting environment they would consider normative: "If one sits or stands at the end of a room looking horizontally and shades the eyes with the hand, there will be a shock of brightness if the installation is glaring."[45]

In a library where computers are heavily used, glare is of critical concern. Screens must be legible almost anywhere in the building in order for flexibility to be maintained. Windows therefore have to be at least somewhat reflective. Furniture surfaces, walls, floors, and mechanical equipment should not produce glare. Highly polished or light-colored work surfaces therefore are to be avoided in favor of flat or matte finishes.[46] Carpeted rather than tiled floors also are recommended. Metcalf found that polarized fluorescent lights tend to reduce glare that is reflected from surfaces within the library.[47] Plastic covers designed to filter out UV radiation also can perform a polarizing function.

Library lighting systems are now designed to complement the introduction of natural daylight. In this respect, modern buildings differ from their predecessors, from which natural light was excluded to eliminate glare and to shield library materials from damaging ultraviolet rays. Today's window glass screens out up to 98 percent of UVA and UVB radiation and greatly reduces both glare and heat gain. Yet it is curious that even some recently completed buildings made little use of the new window technology. Reflective surfaces reduce heat gain and glare, thus allowing fairly large windows in staff areas and those parts of the building where materials are not stored.

Windows meet the "need to preserve some relationship with the external world," which, in turn, helps to reduce "sick-building syndrome." This problem may result, in part, from the sensory deprivation that occurs in sealed, windowless buildings in which fluorescent lighting is used extensively.[48] Glazed reading and work areas are now possible, and indeed desirable. Building codes in Japan and Europe, in fact, mandate minimum standards for worker exposure to daylight.[49] Reasonable quantities of natural light help to combat Seasonal Affective Disorder (SAD); daylight also contains the full spectrum and produces less heat than artificial light, as long as reflective window glass is used. Thus, for psychological as well as technical reasons, libraries should admit as much daylight as possible. Care must be taken, however, in the selection of window glass, whose properties must include reflectivity and UV filtering. Regardless of how an appropriate level of ambient light is calculated, "photocatalyzed degradation" threatens library materials. Fluorescent tubes emit UV radiation that generally falls within the acceptable range for libraries and archives (10 mw/lumen). Total elimination of UV can be achieved by using plastic filters. Natural daylight, of course, contains ultraviolet radiation and must not be introduced into stack areas without being filtered.

Librarians who wish to use natural light should know something about window construction in order to make an informed decision. Windows with R-values (insulation effectiveness) higher than 8 are now available. "Other new developments in the industry," according to a 1990 article in *Architecture*, the American Institute of Architects journal, "include windows that block out most solar heat gain yet are perfectly transparent." Low-E reflective coatings improve insulating qualities and protect against UV radiation. Heat gain, even in large, westward-facing windows, is greatly reduced by low-E coating. Argon gas is generally used as an insulator in double-glazed or triple-glazed window systems.[50]

Lighting systems being installed in new library buildings today seek to balance economics and performance. With the advent of high-efficiency fixtures, a consensus is emerging among lighting professionals on reduced levels of luminescence to lower operating costs while improving the quality of ambient light. Quality is enhanced by the light-diffusing capability of the lenses, which in turn lessens reflected glare coming from an overhead light source.[51] Many library staff members prefer light projected upward rather than downward from parabolic fixtures, assuming that both are lensed to reduce glare and UV radiation.[52] If 20 foot-candles is an acceptable illumination level, then glare probably will not be a problem that requires correction by means of expensive polarized lenses.[53] The basic question that must be addressed early in the design process is: How much light is required? Finding the right answer is by no means simple, but the effort is well worth making.

"Architects," wrote Ellsworth Mason some years ago, "are remarkably inept in evaluating lighting."[54] Twenty years later, little has changed. "Very few architects and engineers," observes Frederic H. Jones, "ever give more than lip service to truly designing the lighting environment."[55] They typically leave the matter to their electrical consultants, or else accept advice from lighting-equipment vendors. Neither approach serves the client's interest, which is to receive the highest-quality installation for the money invested. Although librarians are unlikely to be conversant with lighting technology, they nevertheless should resist accepting whatever system is offered. There is no reason why they cannot work closely with the electrical consultant to achieve the best results. This will involve some discussion of engineering principles relating to such vital concerns as glare and ambient illumination. Related issues, such as finishes, wall colors, and carpet type, inevitably will come up. As a result, librarians will have an opportunity to consider all facets of interior design and to reach more informed judgments about the furniture, equipment, and accessories to be placed in the new building.

Glazing, like lighting, often receives short shrift during design development. Aesthetic considerations, pushed by architects wedded to certain design principles, sometimes outweigh functional ones. It is important to make the correct decision when the opportunity presents itself, because alterations are very difficult to make later. At Winona State University, for example, campus facilities officials vetoed reflective windows because no other buildings had them. When the glare problem became obvious, venetian blinds appeared on all windows—a maintenance nightmare for years to come. Postconstruction application of reflective filming may void the manufacturer's warranty, thus complicating replacement of units that lose their seal and fog up. Thorough research and analysis can avoid subsequent distress over the building's fenestration.

Environmental Controls

An essential construction feature is the building envelope, the purpose of which is to form a barrier between the interior and exterior environments. HVAC systems are capable of driving moisture-laden air throughout the envelope of an improperly sealed building, which leads to wall damage caused by the freezing and thawing of condensation on the backside of the building's outer skin. The envelope is intended to exclude water, dampness, and other pollutants that may invade the building through its walls, foundation, and roof. Moisture is responsible for "80 percent of damage in building envelopes," so it is important that the barrier system include under-slab protection. Electronic equipment must be shielded from "moisture moving upward through the concrete slab."[56]

As any librarian can attest, water also flows downward from the roof. Most library roofs are flat and, sooner or later, they all leak. Century-old built-up roof technology cannot maintain the integrity of the membrane used for waterproofing. This membrane is vulnerable to puncture, and it is almost impossible to trace the source of a leak. A pitched roof, sheathed with Teflon-coated steel, will shed water, last longer, and provide cover for mechanical equipment. "Metal roofs," writes Stewart Brand, "have become tremendously popular since architects began getting sued for leaks."[57] Brand has harsh words for modern wall construction: "[B]rick cavity walls now share the vilest attribute of aluminum and vinyl siding: they hide their problems."[58] Today's construction techniques can, and probably will, defeat the librarian's quest for a watertight building.

If well designed and correctly installed, by no means a certainty, the envelope allows a proper internal environment to be maintained. Many factors impinge on envelope design, including cost and the ability of the contractor to install the envelope without compromising its integrity. A great deal of information about weather patterns, construction types, building materials, and architectural design must be collected and analyzed in order to create the best envelope design. Knowledge Craft is an example of a program that can assist in identifying optimum solutions. Code specifications, weather data, the properties of building materials, construction features, costs, and similar kinds of information may be correlated to yield the most appropriate design. Library planners should expect the project architect and his or her consultants to be conversant with computer applications in all phases of the design process, including such potentially vexing challenges as the design of building envelopes and HVAC systems.[59]

Environmental problems have plagued libraries for centuries. Constant changes in temperature and humidity, not to mention assorted leaks in the building's structure, have caused deterioration of collections and uncomfortable working conditions. HVAC systems are expected to do the following: (1) maintain steady, appropriate temperature and humidity levels; (2) remove airborne pollutants, such as pollens, formaldehyde, and other "outgasses"; and (3) operate economically. Variable air volume (VAV) systems regulate air flow to all parts of the building by using a system of dampers to respond to conditions in each room. Fan speeds may be raised or lowered to respond to the thermal demands of various spaces. The overall result is more efficient and economical operation.

Placing the building under slight positive pressure, at a relative-humidity (RH) value of 40 to 45 percent, with seasonal variation of no more than 5 percent, will slow the deterioration of older materials and retard the decay of works printed on acidic paper. Ultraviolet (UVA and UVB) filtering of fluorescent fixtures and daylight is an additional precaution, of benefit to both people and materials. Ambient temperature necessarily has to suit the people who work in the building and can never be as low as ideal preservation conditions demand (about 50°F). Mechanical systems capable of producing a stable environment across the seasons are a costly investment and deserve to be treated with respect by those who inherit responsibility for them. As Kenneth Toombs observes, this is not always the case:

> After forty years of increasing use of air conditioning the institutions are increasingly unhappy about the performance of the systems. My personal feeling is that most of the problems are due to poor maintenance personnel

who do not have the knowledge or the ability to properly maintain the HVAC systems. In the budgets of the institutions of higher education in this country only the maintenance and operation of buildings have a lower priority than the library budget.[60]

A large cumulative investment in paper collections and computer equipment demands that the building's internal climate receive the care and attention it deserves.

Computerized monitoring devices analyze all the variables noted in the preceding paragraphs and control the HVAC systems accordingly. Reports can be printed that allow maintenance staff to evaluate system performance over time and to make needed adjustments. It is technically possible, though more expensive, to create customized local environments within the building. A rare books room, for example, should be maintained at optimal values for preservation of materials, while an adjacent work or reading area could be made comfortable for humans. At the same time, a microcomputer tracks energy consumption and reports on the performance of all system components.

Systems capable of maintaining consistent temperature and humidity levels year round are now common, thanks in large part to computerized controls. Physical plant staff members, however, may prevent a system from offering optimum performance—ostensibly in the pursuit of economy. A generation ago, Ellsworth Mason complained of buildings "run, for economic reasons, on the crude basis of banking the fires at the end of May, and turning off the refrigeration system at the end of September."[61] Nothing much has changed, especially on those campuses where a central steam plant produces heat and cooled water for all or most of the buildings. Maintenance departments prefer to draw outside air, however humid it may be, to "cool" a building, rather than to leave the chiller online to respond as needed. Mason advised that "it is necessary to have both heat and refrigeration available constantly" to sustain a proper indoor environment. His wisdom, even now, is honored more in the breach than in the observance. The answer is to design a system that meets Mason's requirements, yet is economical to operate. New technology is bringing mechanical engineers closer to this goal.

Automated controls are improving constantly, in response to demands for greater operational economies. Some awareness of developments in this area will assist librarians in making their needs clear to the architect's mechanical consultant. Mechanical engineers design HVAC systems to meet the client's specifications, so building designers must know what they need. If computer workstations are omnipresent, then refrigeration capability must be increased to compensate for a greater heat load. Desired humidity levels must balance comfort, preservation, and generation of static electricity (especially in carpeted areas). The librarian ultimately defines the system's parameters and must therefore acquire some knowledge of quite technical matters. Fortunately, the literature is diverse and easily accessible by means of several electronic databases (CARL UnCover and numerous others).

Intelligent buildings provide tailored environments that allow staff members to enjoy temperatures that are comfortable for them. Digital wireless controllers signal the HVAC system directly, without going through the central computer. The trend in building automation is to allow greater individual control over the workplace environment. Libraries should avail themselves of the chance to improve indoor conditions for their users and for staff members.

Psychological comfort demands that the air-handling system produce thirty decibels of "non-directional" "white noise" to mask distracting background sounds.[62] An environment that is silent is as distracting as one in which background noise exceeds a tolerable level. Mechanical engineers pride themselves on designing quiet HVAC systems, despite the librarian's desire for white noise. In this case, it is important that the librarian prevail.

Security Systems

Several types of security systems are available, ranging from human patrols to video cameras and direct links to the local police station. A relatively inexpensive yet effective type, often used by libraries, is the motion detector which, depending on type, sweeps between 1,000 and 2,200 square feet. When staff members close the building at the end of the day, one person keys a security code into a wall-mounted panel to activate the system. The procedure is reversed the next morning. When the system is armed, incursions will be noted by the motion detector and the monitoring service notified automatically. The service then phones the first person on a list provided by the institution. Investigation, at least in the first instance, is the owner's responsibility. Whether to involve the local police at the first alarm is an administrative policy decision.

The motion detectors monitor all doors leading to the outside, including emergency exits. In jurisdictions where permitted by code, the security system may be interconnected with the fire alarms to prevent surreptitious exits and theft of library materials. Magnetic locks (mag-locks) that require considerable force to open may be installed on emergency exits. If the panic bar is pushed, an alarm will sound locally and at the circulation desk. Staff consult the annunciator panel to discover which exit has been breached, and then investigate. Those who attempt to leave by means of emergency stairwells may find themselves trapped between sets of alarmed doors, since typically one cannot reenter the library's security perimeter once the emergency door closes. If the fire alarms should be activated, however, all the maglocks release and the emergency exits are used to evacuate the building. A sad fact of modern life obliges library planners to anticipate the vilest possibilities, such as bomb threats or rampages by crazed gunmen. Any person who, in an extreme emergency, must escape the building is able to do so by pulling a fire-alarm box anywhere in the building. Security considerations produce constant tension between the requirements of human safety and the protection of library materials. Computerized controls do allow conflicting demands to be reconciled to the greatest possible extent.

Heat and smoke detectors give early warning by sounding alarms and locating the source of combustion. Annunciator panels identify the zone where trouble is brewing, thus facilitating a quick response. In the normal course of events, emergency systems and building status sensors will remain silent guardians of the library's premises. If fire is detected, the alarm system overrides all others. Fans are adjusted, smoke dampers closed, and magnetic locks and hold-opens on fire doors released. The interconnection of computerized systems is regulated by fire codes that differ from one jurisdiction to another. When designing security systems, fire codes must be followed rigorously. Furthermore, it is essential that linked systems be thoroughly tested to expose programming errors when the building is being commissioned.[63]

In addition to providing building security, computerized systems contribute to general campus safety. Staff members who enter the building after hours by using their security code are logged in and out. Physical plant administrators therefore are able to track patterns of building use and to know who is on the premises and when. This information helps to determine the level of building access granted to certain staff members. At the outset, all staff receive an access card, which contains a computer chip programmed to open entrance doors between certain predefined hours. Numeric keypads are an alternative that allows personal access codes to be keyed in. The chief librarian and senior staff normally would be accorded twenty-four-hour access, while other staff members might be restricted in their access privileges. In this way, it is possible to limit the number of persons to whom the building is accessible and thus, at least in theory, to improve security. Should need-for-access patterns change, the cards or codes may be reprogrammed. If the entire campus is outfitted with electronic locks, the need for regular patrols by security personnel will be reduced, along with the considerable cost of providing a human presence during the night and on weekends.

The computer that monitors library security need not be located in the library building. In fact, it probably will be set up elsewhere, because it will also track movements in other campus buildings. Members of the university community may carry smart cards that grant them access to various facilities, depending on their status and role in the institution. These cards may also perform other functions, such as debiting for photocopiers and other equipment or identifying the holder as authorized to use university facilities. Campus security as well as the safety of individuals in increasingly violent times demands that computer-controlled surveillance be used in many settings, including the library. This fact of life must be taken into account when budgets are being developed for new building projects.

The security of expensive equipment, such as desktop computers and laser printers, is also of concern. Some libraries connect lighted fiber-optic cable to each device in an area and link these tethers to their building-security system. If the light stream is broken, an alarm signals the source of the problem. Thieves or vandals may be apprehended in the act. This approach is an alternative to cumbersome locks and steel cables. Theft of memory chips from unguarded PCs may be prevented by placing a security strap around each computer case.

Surveillance or security cameras are another safety device, one that may raise hackles among privacy advocates. Library staff cannot be everywhere in a large building, so technological means of protecting library users become necessary. Cameras need not be operating constantly, but periodic visual monitoring of the building needs to be provided. Campus communities are growing used to surveillance cameras mounted on the roofs of buildings, and to emergency call boxes located around the premises. Cameras in libraries, sadly, are a logical response to increasing societal violence. Individual security has to be the primary concern of all university administrators, even in the library's relatively sheltered precincts. The presence of security cameras is simply a matter of "due diligence" in preserving a safe campus environment.

Respecting the Americans with Disabilities Act

The Americans with Disabilities Act of 1990 (ADA) requires higher-education institutions that receive any kind of federal funding to make "reasonable accommodations" for anyone with physical or mental infirmities. Failure to do so is a discriminatory act under the law, unless the institution "can demonstrate that the accommodation would impose an undue hardship on the operation of the business of such covered entity."[64] Accommodation with respect to academic requirements is not our concern here, but rather physical accessibility of the library's premises for disabled individuals. Once inside the building, disabled people must have access to the library's resources, including computers, study spaces, shelved materials, and rest rooms. "Reasonable accommodation" may include work surfaces high enough to allow wheelchair access, low door sills, elevators of an appropriate size, spaces in which to use voice-recognition software, easily accessible catalog terminals, and appropriate aisle widths, as well as rest rooms with large stalls and grab bars.

Library users desiring special accommodation must provide evidence of their disability, and there must be mutual agreement on what is "reasonable." Aside from making the library generally accessible, about all administrators can do is to await special cases and handle each on its own merits. Disagreements over what is reasonable are bound to arise and the library may find recourse in litigation. Library planners can address some obvious ADA-related issues in the design-development phase.

Ramps, elevators, aisles at least 36 inches wide, low sills, and wheelchair-friendly study furniture are a few examples of accommodations that may reasonably be anticipated. Other potential demands are more difficult to foresee or manage. Should an academic library lower shelving height from the typical 88 inches to 42 inches, so that all materials can be reached by a seated person? Considering the catastrophic effect on a building's storage capacity, this sort of accommodation would be considered unreasonable. The ADA's Accessibility Guidelines in fact state that "shelf height in stack areas is unrestricted." Should manually operated mobile shelving be electrified if it uses 88-inch standards? This situation is not as clear-cut, because someone in a wheelchair and without adequate physical strength could not gain access to an aisle. How many private spaces should be available to students who use voice-recognition software? Must hard-surface flooring, such as terrazzo, be treated to reduce a slipping hazard? Each case must be judged and responded to individually, using the elusive concept of "reasonable accommodation."

It may be argued in some cases that an effort to accommodate is itself discriminatory. Setting aside a specific area in which furniture is wheelchair-accessible is one example. Disabled library users should not be restricted to one part of the building when seeking basic accessibility that anyone would reasonably expect to enjoy. They should be able to study in any part of the building, despite their disability. Assuming that physical barriers to movement and location choice are minimal, what must be done to meet other special needs, such as retrieval of library materials or assistance in their use?

Library staff routinely advise patrons on how to find and use resources. A reasonable accommodation is to retrieve materials from high shelves or microform cabinets on request. If a visual or hearing impairment is involved, the student services office typically provides a reader, a note-taker, or an ASL (American Sign Language) signer to help disabled students. The library's legal obligation is to make every reasonable effort to accommodate these special needs. This may mean providing some private space, such as a group study room that contains adjustable work surfaces and required computer equipment.

Work surface height poses a challenge in itself. Libraries on campuses with laptop computer programs have found that 29 inches is a generally acceptable height for work surfaces. People of average height will find this to be reasonably comfortable for several hours. Taller or shorter people may, however, disagree. Those in wheelchairs will require a height of at least 33 inches. Ideally, all work surfaces should be adjustable electrically, but the cost of providing this feature is prohibitive. At least two adjustable carrels must be available in each study area, if ADA is to be respected (figs. 3 and 4). Carrels must be at least 30 inches wide, with a total depth (including space occupied by the wheelchair) of 48 inches. ADA minimally requires a knee height under work surfaces of 27 inches, which is too low to accommodate many types of wheelchairs. Thus it is advisable to have 5 percent of study spaces with adjustable (up to 34 inches above the floor) surfaces. If this accommodation is not made at the outset, it may be required later and at much greater expense. Furniture need not be adjusted until the demand arises.

FIGURE 3
Study carrel at Indiana University–Purdue University at Indianapolis (IUPUI)

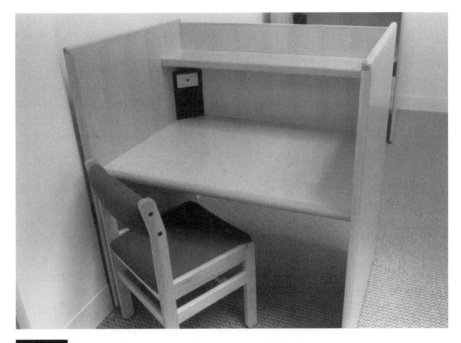

FIGURE 4
Study carrel at Winona State University (WSU)

Aisle widths, in buildings with a 30-foot module, are not a problem. The ADA guidelines stipulate a minimum width of 36 inches and a preference for 42 inches. When ranges are evenly spaced 30 feet on column centers, aisle width works out to about 39 inches, well within the ADA's range of tolerance. Forty-two inches is unreasonable in dense-storage, open-shelf stacks. All doorways must be a minimum of 32 inches when open 90 degrees; typically they are 36 inches. Enough experience with the ADA has now accumulated to impart some precision to such terms as "reasonable accommodation": It is a measure that is "effective" or one that works.[65] If a proposed solution will work, then the burden of proof is on an employer who argues that it imposes undue hardship.[66]

Bringing It All Together: The Planning Process

Complex building projects, like everything else in the contemporary academic world, emerge with the aid of (often in spite of) a planning committee. This group typically represents every sector of the campus community with the slightest interest in a new library. In practice, this means just about everyone, from the president to the maintenance staff.

The committee envisions a library that meets all needs, real and imagined. Initial conceptions may include, in addition to library functions, an art gallery, a snack shop, perhaps a carillon, and enclosed walkways to oblige faculty, who also want their own private studies. A review of the financial implications usually dampens enthusiasm for the more grandiose schemes. It is the job of architects, the library director, and campus facilities people to define a financially realistic project. Handled circumspectly, even the most excitable building committee can be persuaded to see reason.

We assume that the library director is willing to participate fully in a planning and implementation process that may last for the better part of a decade. Especially in publicly funded systems, layers of bureaucracy may pose seemingly insuperable obstacles. Bidding requirements of byzantine complexity, along with glacial approval mechanisms, are daunting but ultimately surmountable. Perseverance and self-confidence are the librarian's strongest assets, particularly when dealing with architects and their technical consultants.

The library director who accepts an active role in the building project will spend many hours on schematic designs, design development, and the preparation of construction documents. Close collaboration with the architectural consultants is assumed, because the client's wishes must be paramount. Incumbent on the librarian is the obligation to be clear and detailed about expectations. Points may need to be reiterated several times before mutual comprehension dawns. No one can read another's mind, but everyone should read each other's memos. Long paper trails produce good buildings by contributing to clarity of design. Both sides must be prepared to realize the building committee's program in a library that is *both* attractive and functional. If the architect rejects this sort of partnership with the librarian, the contract should be terminated. There is no point in trying to work with a willful or opinionated architect. Life is too short.

An architect is obliged to create a building that embodies the program written by those who will use the new library: students, faculty, administrators, staff, and librarians. Yet anyone who has ever been involved in a building project knows that reality is somewhat more complicated. Visions of atria, soaring staircases, and vaulted ceilings dance in the heads of many architects when they hear the word *library*. Library buildings offer a chance to make the architectural "statements" that win awards and, thus, new commissions. Functionality may take a back seat to such artistic values as beauty, symmetry, grace, and splendor. A functional library indeed can have all these qualities, but never at the expense of its primary mission: to be an efficient gateway to the knowledge its users seek. A beautiful building will be a miserable library if its form and layout interfere with its primary mission and if money spent on ostentation is not available for basic library purposes, such as materials or technology.

One way to reduce the chances for conflict between librarian and architect is to add a third person to the team, an experienced construction person called an "owner's representative" or "construction manager." This expert may come from private industry and work under contract for the institution. "As an agent," according to an industry source, "the CM is held to a higher standard of care in his [or her] service to the owner [than is the general contractor], similar to that of a design professional."[67] His or her role is to solve construction-related problems through timely negotiation, and to ensure that the client's interests are protected. Impartial arbitration is another useful role, especially when egos collide on such issues as furniture selection or interior design. The following specific responsibilities are assigned to the owner's representative:

- review drawings and specifications
- oversee budget control
- review all bid packages
- act as liaison with general contractor and subcontractors
- coordinate the commissioning process
- maintain contact with architectural and engineering consultants
- coordinate all warranty claims
- attend all site meetings and inspect work in progress
- administer change orders
- engage in general problem solving
- refer questions to appropriate consultants
- work closely with the librarian on the team

Another strategy, discussed in chapter 5, is to adopt "commissioning" as the best means of achieving a satisfactory building. Commissioning is a process that stretches from the design phase through the end of the building's warranty period. Its aim is to ensure that all parties work together to produce the best possible result. The basic rule is that the owner's will prevails, unless it is obviously perverse. Every owner is entitled to get the building for which it is paying, the *amour propre* of architects notwithstanding.

Conflict can be reduced, though probably not eliminated, by means of a good building program that serves as a kind of charter for the whole project. Time invested in the program repays itself many times over in the clarity of purpose it conveys to the architect. It describes the functional relationship among various library operations and indicates which spaces must be adjacent to each other. All spaces—offices, group studies, communications closets, classrooms, and so on—are dimensioned and assigned. Storage and stack areas are sized to meet future needs. The program also describes the features desired in a new building, including materials and general configuration. If you want to prevent "statements" from compromising functionality, then say so in the program. Although the program is not a blueprint, it must be an unambiguous guide to the library that its owners expect to receive. For their part, the architects deserve to know the constraints being imposed on their creativity.

Once the program is accepted by all campus constituencies, the architects produce a preliminary design that is consistent with the project budget, and suggest layouts and floor plans. These also should have the approval of the building committee. Acceptance of the schematics leads to the project's design development phase, in which a refined and practical building plan emerges. If the financial signals are strong, then the grueling task of creating construction documents begins. During this phase, the library director's involvement is optional. Some people enjoy immersion in such details as concrete mixes, floor-slab cambers, air-handling capacities, and other engineering esoterica. More germane to the building's eventual operation are the electrical specifications. The director's job is to ensure that the power and data grids reach everywhere in the building and provide adequately for every work and study space. No grid, however dense, ends up delivering power or data to every spot that needs it. But there is no excuse for failing to provide it on all four walls of an office, an oversight that even seasoned engineers commit. Avoiding this mistake depends, in large part, on the librarian's willingness to study and understand construction drawings. If something is missing or unclear, say so in writing and be sure to follow up. As so often is the case, the devil is in the details.

The project team, consisting of the library director and such other persons as the owner's representative (or construction manager), campus facilities manager, and physical plant director, must review carefully every set of drawings to make sure that all the program's criteria are met. A strenuous review will reduce the number of change orders that are issued during construction, which significantly benefits the project budget. Change orders are expensive. They cannot be avoided entirely, but should be held to a minimum. Sometimes they are the only way to assure that a building, in the end, lives up to expectations.

A strategy to contain costs and deliver a better building, called *design build*, has recently emerged in the construction industry. This approach ensures that the contractor is involved from the outset, so "there is little excuse for the contractor not to understand the design intent [which] results in fewer change orders."[68] In typical design/bid/build projects, on the other hand, the low bidder may well intend to recoup through the numerous change orders generated in the course of the work. A design team that includes both contractor and owner's representative can help avoid higher costs.

Engaging the services of an experienced owner's representative can spare a project much grief. This person, who will have a construction or engineering background, keeps a close eye on details as site work gets under way and the building develops. The owner's representative is a bridge between the architects and contractor, to ensure that the owner ultimately receives full value for the investment. Many potential problems can be solved in a timely fashion by an alert and capable owner's representative. We venture to suggest that no library director should begin a building project without such an ally at his or her side.[69]

Only a smoothly functioning management team can devise and execute a successful building plan. Mutual respect allows all members to make their decisions in the best interests of the project and the institution. Egos inevitably will clash, especially on esthetic matters, such as colors, textures, and materials. As always, the owner's will must prevail unless it arises from egregious error. Architects who accept this principle will enjoy a better client relationship than those who try to dominate the owner. We have worked with both types of architect and have little tolerance for the second kind. If you encounter such an architect, fire the company and find another that is more congenial. The project will benefit as a result.

Notes

1. Margaret Beckman, "Library buildings in the network environment," *Journal of Academic Librarianship* 9(5): 284 (November 1983).

2. Ralph Ellsworth, "Library architecture and buildings," *Library Quarterly* 25 (1/4): 67 (January/October 1955).

3. Arthur E. Bostwick, "The librarian's idea of library design," *Architectural Forum* 47 (6): 507 (December 1927).

4. Ralph Ellsworth, "The college and university library as a building type," *American Institute of Architects Journal* 43 (5): 70 (May 1965).

5. Gregory C. Farrington, "Higher education in the information age," in *The Learning Revolution: The Challenge of Information Technology in the Acad-*emy, ed. Diana G. Oblinger and Sean C. Rush (Bolton, Mass.: Anchor Publishing, 1997), 63–64.

6. Susan Rosenblatt, "Information technology investments in research libraries," *EDUCOM Review* 34 (4): 31, 44 (July/August 1999).

7. Eli M. Noam and Caterina Alvarez, "The future of the library," *Business and Finance Bulletin*, no. 107 (winter 1998): 30.

8. Stephen Langmead and Margaret Beckman, *New Library Design: Guide Lines to Planning Academic Library Buildings* (Toronto: J. Wiley and Sons Canada, 1970), 38.

9. Ann de Klerk and Joanne R. Euster, "Technology and organizational metamorphoses," *Library Trends* 37 (4): 463 (spring 1989).

10. Raymond Kurzweil, "The future of libraries, part I: The technology of the book," *Library Journal* 117 (1): 80–82 (January 1992).

11. David C. Weber, "The future capital funding of university library buildings," *IFLA Journal* 16 (3): 317 (1990).

12. Colin Steele, "Millennial libraries: Management changes in an electronic environment," *Electronic Library* 11 (6): 397 (December 1993).

13. James H. Sweetland, "Humanists, libraries, electronic publishing, and the future," *Library Trends* 40 (4): 798 (spring 1992).

14. Scott F. Uhler and Philippe R. Weiss, "Library building alterations under the Americans with Disabilities Act," *Illinois Libraries* 78 (1): 5–7 (winter 1996).

15. James Shedlock and Faith Ross, "A library for the twenty-first century: The Galter Health Sciences Library's renovation and expansion project," *Bulletin of the Medical Library Association* 85 (2): 185 (April 1997).

16. Dryver R. Huston and Peter L. Fuhr, "Intelligent materials for intelligent structures," *IEEE Communications Magazine* 31 (10): 40–45 (October 1993). Librarians who wish to acquire some technical knowledge of concrete work may consult William S. Phelan, "Guide for concrete floor and slab construction," *ACI Materials Journal* 86 (3): 252–296 (May/June 1989).

17. Fred S. Dubin, "Intelligent buildings: HVAC, lighting, and other design trends," *Construction Specifier* 43 (2): 51 (February 1990).

18. Stewart Brand, *How Buildings Learn: What Happens After They're Built* (New York: Viking Press, 1994), 170–171.

19. Ibid., 129.

20. Peter Murphy, "Making libraries more people friendly: Lighting for a computerized world," *Journal of Academic Librarianship* 22 (1): 57 (January 1996).

21. David Lord, "Simulation of lighting designs," *Architecture: The AIA Journal* 71 (June 1988): 106–108.

22. David Lord, "Computer aided lighting," *Progressive Architecture* 11 (November 1990): 126. This article identifies currently available analytical software.

23. Howard Brandston, "A design process for lighting," *Interior Design* 60 (7): 126 (May 1989).

24. Joseph Spiers, "Let there be light," *Architectural Record: Lighting* (August 1990): 21.

25. Helen J. Kessler, "In the right light," *Journal of Property Management* 63 (5): 1 (September/October 1998).

26. Alex Wilson, "Achieving energy efficient lighting," *Architecture: The AIA Journal* 71 (June 1988): 110.

27. "Category 9: Lighting," *EC & M: Electrical Construction and Management* 92 (12): 92 (November 15, 1993).

28. Lori Garcia, "Communication is key to efficient lighting controls," *Energy User News* 22 (8): 16 (August 1997).

29. Ian Ashdown, "Visual reality: Computer techniques for lighting design," <http://www.ledalite.com/library-/ldp.htm>.

30. Jane Schogel, "Lighting advances offer new options to designers," *Energy User News* 22 (4): 18 (April 1997).

31. Vernon Mays, "P/A technics: Light for the site," *Progressive Architecture* 69 (November 1988): 108.

32. Ellsworth Mason, "A guide to the librarian's responsibility in achieving quality in . . . lighting and ventilation," *Library Journal* 92 (2): 201 (January 15, 1967).

33. Lester K. Smith, "Lighting and air-conditioning in libraries," in *Planning Library Buildings: From Decision to Design*, ed. Lester K. Smith (Chicago: American Library Association, 1986), 168–169.

34. Keyes D. Metcalf, *Library Lighting* (Washington, D.C.: Association of Research Libraries, 1970), 79.

35. Philip D. Leighton and David C. Weber, *Planning Academic and Research Library Buildings*, 3d ed. (Chicago: American Library Association, 1999), 505.

36. For example, Frederic H. Jones, *Architectural Lighting Design* (Los Altos, Calif.: Crisp Publications, 1989), 63, advises 70 foot-candles in reading rooms and carrels, and 30 foot-candles in stack areas.

37. Ellsworth Mason, "The development of library lighting: The evolution of the lighting problems we are facing today," *Advances in Library Administration and Organization* 10 (1992): 136–137.

38. Richard Katzev, "The impact of energy-efficient office lighting strategies on employee satisfaction and productivity," *Environment and Behavior* 24 (6): 777 (November 1992).

39. "How many footcandles do I really need?" SDGE An Enova Company at <http://espsun3.esp-net.com/sdge/bull8.htm>.

40. Pete Samaras, "Lighting basics for computerized work environments," *Interior Design* 68 (10): 169 (August 1997).

41. Mason, "The development of library lighting," 139.

42. Damon Wood, "The elements of quality lighting," *Lighting Upgrades: A Guide for Facility Managers* (New York: UpWord Publishing, 1996), 14.

43. Ellsworth Mason, *Ellsworth Mason on Library Buildings* (Metuchen, N.J.: Scarecrow Press, 1980), 33.

44. Keyes D. Metcalf, "Library lighting," in *Reader on the Library Building*, ed. Hal B. Schell (Englewood, Colo.: Libraries Unlimited, 1975), 225.

45. C. L. Crouch, "Too much light is poor light," in Schell, *Reader on the Library Building*, 234.

46. Illuminating Engineering Society, "Recommended practice of library lighting, RP-4," reprinted from *Journal of the Illuminating Engineering Society* (April 1974): 10.

47. Metcalf, *Library Lighting*, 53.

48. P. T. Stone, "Fluorescent lighting and health," *Lighting Research and Technology* 24 (2): 59–60 (1992). The author concludes that fluorescent lighting is not in itself a health hazard.

49. Lucie Young, "Natural light at work," *Metropolis* 12 (8): 51–71 (April 1993).

50. Alex Wilson, "Glass: Window developments: An improved outlook," *Architecture: The AIA Journal* (August 1990): 95–98.

51. Ellsworth Mason, "Lighting and mechanical progress in universities," *Library Trends* 18 (2): 247 (October 1969).

52. Alan Hedge et al., "Effects of lensed-indirect and parabolic lighting on the satisfaction, visual health, and productivity of office workers," *Ergonomics* 38 (2): 260–280 (1995).

53. Mason notes that polarized lenses reduce light output by 50 percent; see *Mason on Library Buildings*, 29.

54. Mason, "Lighting," 251.

55. Jones, *Architectural Lighting Design*, 1.

56. Mark Bomberg and William Brown, "Building envelope: Heat, air, and moisture interactions," *Journal of Thermal Insulation and Building Environments* 16 (April 1993): 308; and Bruce A. Suprenant, "Vapor barriers under concrete slabs," *Concrete Construction* 37 (4): 292 (April 1992).

57. Brand, *How Buildings Learn*, 116–117. The foregoing comments are based on chapter 8, which deals with building maintenance.

58. Ibid., 124.

59. P. Fazio, C. Bedard, and K. Gowrie, "Knowledge-based system approach to building envelope design," *Computer Aided Design* 21 (8): 519–527 (October 1989).

60. Kenneth E. Toombs, "The evolution of academic library architecture: A summary," *Journal of Library Administration* 17 (4): 30 (1992).

61. Mason, "A guide to the librarian's responsibility in achieving quality in . . . lighting and ventilation," 203.

62. Philip M. Bennett, "Users come first in design: Physiological, psychological, and sociological factors," *Wisconsin Library Bulletin* 74 (March 1978): 55.

63. David Hine, "Integrating fire-safety systems," *Canadian Architect* 38 (8): 25 (August 1, 1993).

64. 42 U.S.C. ¶ 12131 (2) 1995.

65. *Helping Employers Comply with the ADA: An Assessment of How the United States Equal Employment Opportunity Commission Is Enforcing Title I of the Americans with Disabilities Act*, a report of the United States Commission on Civil Rights (Washington, D.C.: The Commission, September 1998), 108.

66. A good source on the ADA's applicability to libraries is Susan E. Cirillo and Robert E. Danford, *Library Buildings, Equipment, and the ADA: Compliance Issues and Solutions* (Chicago: American Library Association, 1996).

67. "Construction management and the evolution of construction project delivery," *ENR: Engineering News Reports* 236 (23): C-45 (June 10, 1996).

68. Gordon Wright, "A civic success," *Building Design and Construction* 36 (5): 60 (May 1995) and Dennis L. Mulvey, "Project delivery trends: A contractor's assessment," *Journal of Management in Engineering* 14 (6): 51–54 (November–December 1998).

69. Albert R. Russell, "Avoiding building failures: The role of the owner's representative," *Construction Specifier* 47 (11): 143–144 (November 1994).

Building Infrastructure

We need to substitute for the book a device that will make it easy to transmit information without transporting material, and that will not only present information to people but also process it for them, following procedures they specify, apply, monitor, and if necessary, revise and reapply. To provide those services, a meld of library and computer is evidently required.[1]

Architects may come and
Architects may go and
Never change your point of view.[2]

Envisioning a New Building through Computer-Aided Design

Academic libraries derive both their form and function from the institutions to which they belong. Libraries associated with community colleges, liberal arts colleges, or research universities share the common goal of satisfying their users' needs for information and other services, but they do so in different ways and by emphasizing one type of activity over another. Yet all academic libraries belong in the mainstream of the educational process. This is especially true now that research universities are beginning to pay more attention to the quality of teaching. Although a research library's primary mission is to support scholarship, it will need facilities that strengthen the teaching mission: wired study spaces, electronic classrooms, group studies, information commons. The same is true of smaller institutions, every one of which will have to obtain some sort of electronic infrastructure in the years ahead.

Type of library is less important in determining the range of facilities provided than is the balance of services to be offered. Every new academic library needs teaching and learning spaces, as well as storage for print materials. The challenge is to create a functional relationship among these elements within a building that will serve the institution's particular mission effectively. The key is general agreement on basic principles of electronic infrastructure and access to library resources.

Even before a project architect is engaged, there must be a clear conception of the new building's purpose and the best means of realizing it. If planners generally agree that access to information is becoming more important than ownership of specific resources, this principle has certain design implications. So does the idea that both research and writing can be done in the library, provided network access to text-editing utilities and databases is widely available. Taken together, these thoughts imply that library users well may spend more time there than in the past. Interior design, therefore, should create a pleasant environment conducive to study. Carpet, wall, end-panel, and upholstery colors ought to contribute to a cool atmosphere, one that is warmed by the use of wood accents and wall-hung artwork. No color scheme, in other words, should impose itself on the user in such a way as to be a distraction.

Not every architect, and certainly not every interior-design consultant, would agree with the foregoing. Designers of the Leavey Library at the University of Southern California, for example, created a colorful environment intended to be "stimulating" to undergraduates, whose need for extrinsic stimuli is debatable. Librarians who accept this view must prepare to defend themselves against the prevailing opinion among design consultants, who may propose color schemes that reflect current fads. A few years ago, maroon and grey combinations were popular; in the 1970s earth tones combined with splashes of orange and yellow were *de rigueur.* Teal green and pastels characterized interior design in the early 1990s. Some institutions decorate the library in garish school colors. The authors had to decline their architects' suggestion that shelving in the new Winona State University library be "electric green." Regardless of the color scheme chosen, the aesthetic judgment ultimately is the owner's to make. Project architects need to appreciate this point because some of them tend to give their interior-design consultants a free hand. They should understand from the outset that the building's owners will have the final say on interior-design issues.

More will be said later in this chapter on the topic of interior design. We raise the matter here to illustrate a basic point: Good communication between client and architect underlies the success of any building project. Librarians have a duty to explain their vision of the new building and its mission candidly and fully. For their part, "architects [should be] facilitators and chroniclers of the design process" who "guide [building] team members in establishing priorities and projecting a bold vision of the facility's future."[3] An unsympathetic or uncomprehending architect should be replaced by one who is able to understand the intellectual content of library service in a computerized environment. The safest approach is to include a brief statement of principle in the building program itself. Librarians who are unable to articulate their position in a few paragraphs cannot expect an architect to create a functional design. Left to their own devices, architects normally do not display an intuitive grasp of how an automated library should operate. Only librarians can impart that knowledge, and then only to a receptive architect.

Computer-aided design (CAD), which creates three-dimensional models, enables clients to "experience" the space in which they will work (figs. 5 and 6). Shepley, Bullfinch, Richardson and Abbott, a Boston firm that has built many libraries in the United States, uses this technique to help "architects learn about the clients' concerns much earlier."[4] Collaboration ultimately can save money for the owners and time for all concerned, because problems are identified and solved much earlier in the design process. With construction costs running in excess of $170 per square foot, each volume requires $20 to store.[5] Accurate space planning, therefore, is essential. Architects who are unwilling or unable to offer CAD may not be the best choice for a library project in which design must serve functional purposes. Those who do use CAD may charge more for their services, on the theory that clients "should be educated to pay for results, not the tools used to produce them."[6] There is no reason to pay more for architectural services than the customary 7 percent of the construction contract's value.

Once the vision has achieved expression and won acceptance by all concerned, the next step is to capture it within four walls. Building design is a collaborative effort involving those who create, operate, use, and pay for the new structure. Administrators, boards, and politicians demand maximum value in new capital projects, a position that may cause some friction when it collides with the architect's desire to make a "statement" with her or his creation. Librarians usually are inclined to value efficiency over architectural features, such as balconies, atria, monumental staircases, or interior fountains. Flexibility, economy of operation and maintenance, and functionality are the basic principles that planners have to keep in mind as they produce a design. Oblongs best meet these criteria. As Aaron and Elaine Cohen observe: "No matter if the library is large or small, to be built from the ground up or simply rearranged, the

FIGURE 5
Isometric drawing of WSU first floor

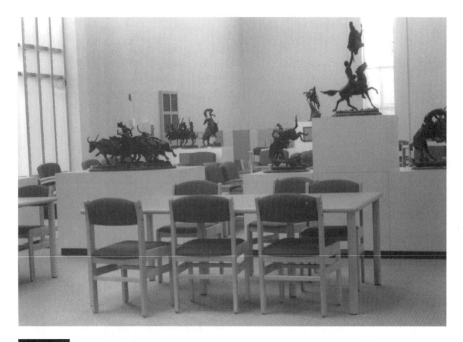

FIGURE 6
Second floor lounge/study area at WSU

square always works."[7] Every library does not have to resemble a crackerbox out of the 1960s, for even the humble square acquires grace from appropriate architectural enhancements. A cruciform design, for example, produces four opportunities to locate stairwells and the main entrance. Its virtue is that a "statement" can be made on the building's edge, where it interferes least with functionality (figs. 7 and 8).

The role of librarians is to analyze the functional relationships among their activities in order to determine how interior space should be organized. This task, as Robert Rohlf advises, ought not to be left to architects.[8] Librarians are the ones who are primarily responsible for creating a functional library by clearly describing how each space relates to adjacent areas throughout the building. These relationships among various parts of the library operation are described in a building program, which guides the architect in designing the physical space. A committee composed of librarians and library users, perhaps advised by a library-building consultant, usually writes the program. Included in it is a philosophical statement concerning the library's role within the university. Planners may decide that the new library should be primarily a book warehouse rather than a "people place." Or they may offer just the opposite conception. In the end, the structure will reflect its designers' underlying philosophy.[9]

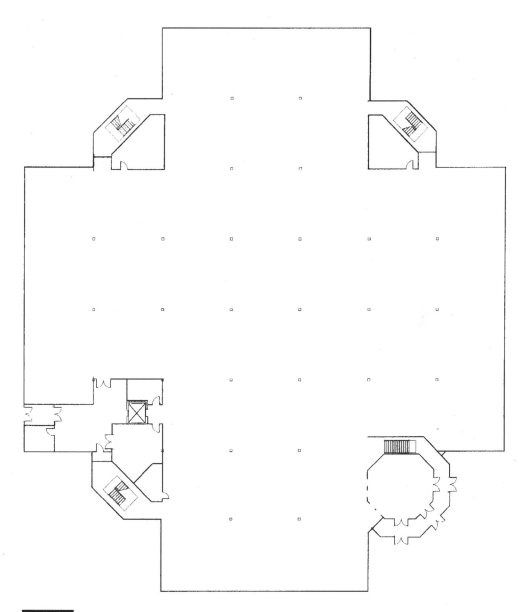

FIGURE 7
Outline of WSU library

Most projects emanate from a building committee made up of people who, for the most part, understand how libraries work and what users expect of them. They are overseen by a small team, which may include a campus facilities person, the library director, and, perhaps, an external consultant or owner's representative. This group collaborates with the architect to achieve a design that suits its owners both aesthetically and

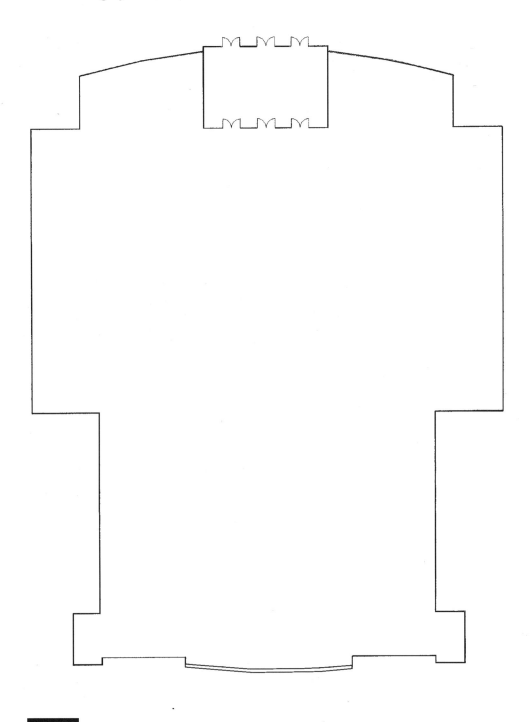

FIGURE 8
Outline of Middle Tennessee State University library (MTSU)

financially. Building-committee members should expect to be involved in a lengthy process of discussion and compromise as they bring into focus the limits of what is possible. The team then assumes responsibility for the building's final design and sees the project through to completion. In an age of financial accountability, everyone involved in the enterprise probably will have to sacrifice something in order to ensure that the result is affordable and workable. This means holding architects and their consultants to a budget that gives the library the greatest possible assignable space for the money available.

An accurate estimate of building size is the essential first step in coming to terms with a finite budget. Many projects today are, in fact, budget-driven. That is to say, a source, such as government, will appropriate funds and planners are expected to work within that amount. If the sum is indeed a realistic one, then a successful accommodation is possible. The place to begin is the size of the building itself. Before this can be determined, existing collection size must be known and certain assumptions must be made about its future growth. As indicated earlier, the second part of this calculation is influenced by several factors, including acquisitions budgets, technological developments in the publishing world, and the library's commitment to information technology. There is no point in overbuilding, provided that future needs have been forecast accurately. As Margaret Beckman advises, "[E]very penny saved in the total square footage, from height or building perimeter, is money that can be applied to internal systems, whether air quality, acoustics or new technology." [10] Keep in mind, though, that "one of the myths, as far as building design is concerned, is that the introduction of information technology will mean that libraries will automatically require less space." [11] Computer technology imposes space demands of its own, and the only collections that may soon require less storage room are bound periodicals. User space easily can consume warehousing space as functions change over time. [12]

There are two ways to calculate space requirements, each of which factors in expansion room. One is to apply national standards, such as those published by the Association of College and Research Libraries (ACRL). These guidelines are rather generous in an age of tight acquisitions budgets and strict accountability. Given the exponential growth in scholarly publishing, not to mention the cost of library materials and construction, space estimates escalate rapidly to the point of financial meltdown. Another option is to make certain assumptions about the effect of information technology on space planning, and to size the building accordingly. Growth in e-journal publication since 1995, for example, is evidence that the paper version's days are numbered; on the other hand, plenty of titles still appear in print and thus demand prime shelf space.

OPAC terminals and scholars' workstations already are familiar objects in libraries; so, of course, are bookstacks. Print and electronic media still compete for library space and financial resources. Cornell University library planners warn that "it would be imprudent to develop a planning strategy for the next two decades with technology as the linchpin."[13] This is a rather conservative position, given the rapid growth of digitized information bases, but it does underscore the hybrid nature of today's academic libraries. Space planning between now and 2010, therefore, has

FIGURE 9
Lobby at the University of Kentucky

FIGURE 10
Lobby at MTSU

to do with creating buildings that maintain print collections alongside evolving information technologies. The library as a structure will be around for at least another generation or two, and it will continue to house books. Print collections, therefore, will expand alongside a lengthening list of electronic titles.

Five functions demand a share of assignable space: (1) materials storage, (2) study stations, (3) work space, (4) public rest rooms, and (5) "architectural" space, which gives the building its scale and proportion. The first three areas have to be calculated before the architect can dimension the building properly. As figures 9 and 10 illustrate, architectural space adds aesthetic interest to the building, ideally without compromising its functionality.

Compact storage is a reasonable alternative to open stacks, provided that the mobile units remain accessible to users. According to Beckman's calculations, this type of shelving can reduce space requirements by about 43 percent. If this strategy is used, compact storage should be incorporated in the design so that rails or channels are provided to accommodate the mobile system. Retrofitting a basement in later years is certainly possible, because manufacturers provide subflooring systems tailored to their particular product.

Provision of study space consumes the next highest proportion of square footage in academic libraries. Carrels and tables must be sized to accommodate users who bring their own notebook computers, which means that each study space will occupy about 25 square feet. The big question, however, is the number of spaces to provide in the library of a residential university. Keyes Metcalf and his successors, Leighton and Weber, recommended that provision be made for 25 to 30 percent of the student body in a typical residential university.[14] Changing economic times have reduced this figure to 20 percent, because of the need to control costs.[15] One consideration that has to be taken into account is the fact that many students may choose to consult the library catalog from a dormitory room or some other location that allows them to connect to the campus network. On the other hand, the library remains a quiet haven from the chaos of residence life and will attract students for that reason alone.

Work space is one of the prime variables in contemporary libraries, because computerization has altered such traditional functions as acquisitions, cataloging, serials control, reference service, and interlibrary loan. Although space devoted to traditional technical services may decline, more may have to go to interlibrary loan (ILL) because of the growing popularity of resource-sharing and distance education. Information (reference) services also are growing in importance, because of the Internet, electronic publishing, and the computer's role in every aspect of scholarly research. The electronic ambience is and will remain in a state of flux, and space allocations, therefore, have to be flexible. An adaptable building is better able to respond to changing circumstances.

Public rest rooms of a certain size are set forth in building codes, based on the intended occupancy. Unless instructed otherwise, architects may provide only minimal accommodation. A high-tech library designed to be a people place, however, requires larger public facilities than the code's minimum. Furthermore, educational institutions (schools and universities) are "public accommodations" under Title III of ADA. Rest rooms, therefore, must be fully accessible to the handicapped. All dimensions and configurations are mandated by law.[16] There is no reason why legal minimums cannot be exceeded in the interest of greater comfort for library users.

A fifth claimant of square footage is "architectural space," in which the building's designer makes an aesthetic or philosophical statement in bricks, mortar, and glass. Monumentality, as Beckman correctly observes, is out, and functionality is in. Modern reading rooms, when they are used, tend to be more intimate than majestic. Maintaining a human scale is the key to successful reading rooms (figs. 11 and 12). The ratio of assignable to nonassignable space, therefore, is higher than it used to be, on the order of 75 to 80 percent. The library at Indiana University–Purdue University at Indianapolis (IUPUI) boasts a ratio of 94 percent. New libraries at Middle Tennessee State University and Winona State University have multistory entranceways of considerable architectural grace, behind which is located library space that is entirely functional. Statements can be made in other ways, perhaps through the use of natural wood finishes on study furniture and service desks or in the use of a particular interior-design theme, such as Native American or contemporary art, or tapestry. The rule stated by Beckman is still valid: Money saved on overall square footage can be spent to greater effect on building amenities and information technology.

Investment should be heaviest in those features that render the building both flexible and livable. An expandable power and communications grid is essential, as is an HVAC (heating, ventilating, air-conditioning) system that assures the comfort and health of those who study and work in the building. Proper zone control of the internal environment is of critical importance. Work areas and storage space have different temperature and RH (relative humidity) requirements, and the HVAC system should allow for independent control. A tightly sealed building envelope will ensure

FIGURE 11
Reading room at the University of Kentucky

FIGURE 12
Reading room at WSU

that HVAC and humidity-regulating systems function efficiently, and that no damage occurs to the exterior façade as a result of humidified air being forced out through fissures in the envelope.

Very early in the design phase, and certainly before space requirements have been codified, library planners should address organizational issues. Wherever separate activities can be combined, space savings will result. For example, monographic government publications might be cataloged and integrated into the general collection, thus reducing the need for special collection space. Faculty opposition, of course, may rule out such an approach in an academic library. Arguments that government publications demand a separate area staffed by specialists often carry the day. More easily accomplished is the elimination of a variety of special-purpose rooms, the existence of which impedes building flexibility. All circulation functions—including general and reserve—can be carried out at the main desk in order to reduce duplication of effort (fig. 13).

Technical services presents another example of computerization's effect on acquisition and cataloging functions. Allen B. Veaner advises "that technology be employed to dismantle massive technical services operations in order to redeploy resources." [17] Online bibliographic utilities, such as OCLC, together with easy access to cataloging-in-publication data, have radically trimmed large in-house cataloging departments. The leading book jobbers, moreover, offer online ordering as part of their

FIGURE 13
Circulation desk at WSU

regular service. By computerizing what traditionally have been labor-intensive housekeeping activities, libraries are able to devote staff resources to public-service duties of direct assistance to users.

Each of the issues raised here needs to be brought to the architects' attention before they begin conceptual drawings. A great deal of time can be saved if the building program describes clearly the way in which the new building will be operated. All functional relationships—notably between public and technical services—must be made explicit so that the architect can provide for an efficient work flow within the building. Distribution of materials and supplies from the receiving room, for instance, should require staff to traverse the least possible distance. Lighting controls should be centrally located and provided with a master switch. Building security also must be designed-in and not treated as an afterthought. If it seems advisable to install surveillance cameras in certain parts of the building, electric power must be provided. Architects and, especially, fire marshals often have little sympathy for the security requirements of libraries. In the best of all worlds, the library will have but a single entrance/exit point controlled by a security system to detect pilfered materials. Multiple emergency exits are, however, mandated by code, and they represent the greatest threat to library security.

Each of the matters noted in this section undoubtedly will receive thorough examination in the building committee, which provides advice to the architect during the design-development phase of the project. The group's librarian member(s) must be prepared to explain and defend the design features that enhance flexibility, security, and efficiency. These concerns may seem unreasonable at first, especially if architects create features that militate against building functionality. The preference of most librarians for a plain, rectangular building may be resisted by architects to whom a simple square is unappealing. Yet there is no more efficient shape for a library building in which every square foot of assignable space has to justify itself. Several recent buildings illustrate the possibility of having it both ways: an efficient library that also is aesthetically pleasing in an architectural sense.

In Praise of Flexibility

Libraries, to reiterate our central theme, will continue to house print materials for some time to come. Electronic publication nevertheless will comprise a growing proportion of scholarly communication from now on. This transformation has implications for library design, especially for the ratio between study space and collection-storage areas. As electronic publication acquires respectability within the academic community, it will make its influence felt in library space planning. Storage requirements may diminish, while demand rises for the computer workstations that provide access to networked information sources. Space devoted for a time to one function therefore must be convertible to others over the building's life span. Hence the need to design for flexibility in order to keep all options open.

New library buildings, from this point on, will not house comprehensive research collections. It is no longer financially or physically possible to collect a reasonably complete record of scholarly publication. Both the volume and the price of printed material preclude thorough coverage. Accordingly, the idea that libraries should be capable of significant expansion as collections develop can be abandoned. Some growth naturally is to be expected, but less than in the past. Local collections well may reach a steady state circumscribed by acquisitions budgets, capital funds, and available land on the central campus. Instead of maximizing the holdings under their direct control, librarians will concentrate on providing access to materials owned by other institutions or to a central warehouse facility that houses rarely used titles. An example is the new Minnesota Library Access Center, from which member libraries can quickly retrieve items they have deposited there. (The exception is continued growth where there is "an established need in a given area of research."[18]) Libraries will also make use of electronic databases, especially those that offer full-text documents. In other words, librarians will help to organize the transition from traditional research in printed sources to reliance on many types of electronic media, for example, bibliographic databases, citation indexes, text editors, publication software, and electronic journals. Furthermore, librarians will work in settings quite different from those of the past.

No one is suggesting, we hasten to add, that the library as a building is in danger of becoming obsolete. New structures are still needed to house print materials already owned; book publishing is a healthy industry and is likely to remain so. Buildings will change mainly in their appearance, as they gradually lose their role as warehouses and become what might be called "knowledge centers." There must always be a special place where those in search of knowledge can come to pursue their quest. Some material will be found in the library's own collections of print or electronic media; some will be accessible online; rare volumes from the past will be acquired physically or in facsimile (digital image) from distant repositories. Each study space in the "electronic library" is wired for power and computer communications. Tables and carrels are equipped with wire-management systems that provide unimpeded work space. All online utilities (databases, word processors, Web browsers) are accessible from each seat.

Libraries, therefore, ought to be designed as "people places" that offer congenial surroundings. Natural daylight introduced into reading areas through ultraviolet-filtered windows is an important part of the ambience (fig. 14). So is a muted, but not absolutely still, auditory environment. Colors that contribute to an atmosphere of contemplation are important, because the library remains a place to think with minimal distractions. Most of the furniture should be constructed of wood, because natural materials are aesthetically preferable to artificial ones. (Work surfaces necessarily have to be plastic laminates to reduce the ravages of wear and tear; chairs may be of welded-steel or reinforced-wood construction to withstand the abuse they are expected to endure.) Seating needs to be comfortable, in consideration of the increasing time that many users will spend in the library.

These amenities, intended to make the library an inviting place to be, conceal a sophisticated infrastructure. Computers and their paraphernalia—wires, printers, and so on—should not be obtrusive. "The most profound technologies," observes Mark Weiser, "are those that disappear. They weave themselves into the fabric of everyday life until they are indistinguishable from it."[19] Therefore, a building designed to facilitate online work should provide a smooth interface between human and machine. For this reason, every effort is made to accommodate the use of portable computers, which users are encouraged to bring with them to the library.

FIGURE 14
South atrium/reading room at WSU

Each study space receives network access through extensive power and communications grids in walls and floors. Once the furniture plan is ready, power and data can be brought to each table or carrel through an exactly placed floor box or wall outlet. In addition to these specific provisions, there also should be a grid that covers floor areas and runs beneath shelving that may be removed some years ahead to create additional study space. Within a 30-foot building module, covered floor boxes can be located every 15 feet. When midfloor power and data are needed later, they are easily accessible. An overlaid wireless network, of course, offers ubiquitous data linkage and, therefore, deserves serious consideration.

Power plugs and RJ45 network jacks are built into carrels and tables (figs. 15 and 16). Study spaces thus become self-contained work areas in which research and writing may be done with relative ease: the "scholar's workstation." Libraries should plan to provide networked printing capacity for all study spaces and workstations. Networking technology and an extensive communications grid allow these printers to be located in convenient spots throughout the building or elsewhere on campus. Debit card devices may be used for printer control: When the user's card is inserted, the print job may be retrieved from a queue. Or, as in the Leavey Library, a print room is located adjacent to the Information Commons, and students collect and pay for their copies at a service counter. Winona State adopted a model similar to Leavey's, and situated its print room on the main floor close to the Information Gallery. Very quickly it became clear that printers would have to be located closer to point-of-use, an adaptation made easier by the fact that all printing is covered by the students' technology fee.

It is unnecessary to install many smart terminals for public use, unless they are in an information arcade or commons where help is readily available. Most online catalogs are now Web-based, thus requiring the use either of microcomputers or of network computers (NCs) as OPAC terminals (fig. 17). Larger libraries may wish to scatter OPACs throughout the

FIGURE 15
Top of wired study table at WSU

FIGURE 16
Top of wired study table at the University of Kentucky

FIGURE 17
OPACs at WSU

stacks, while smaller ones can provide a bank of terminals on each floor or in the vicinity of each separate collection. There is no need, however, to devote large amounts of floor space to blocks of terminals that appear to emulate the old card catalog. OPACs can easily be wall- or column-mounted to save space. Inexpensive printers—one per OPAC—are adequate for the job of recording short citations and call numbers. Users who access the catalog from their own PCs, of course, may download citations to disk.

Because computers are omnipresent in modern libraries, special attention needs to be paid to the power and communications grids within the building. Ideally, no point on any floor should be farther than 3 feet from a potential connection. Budget considerations usually mandate a less-flexible grid, one that perhaps is five times more dispersed. If the building module is 30 feet, there are power and data in the centers and 15 feet from each column in all directions (fig. 18). The point is to have as much in-floor connectivity as can be afforded. Technology changes too quickly for one-time installations intended only to meet current needs. The safest approach is to provide a far more extensive grid than seems to be necessary at the moment. Four-plex outlets are advisable, because library users may wish to plug in several pieces of equipment.[20] A grid may be constructed by embedding conduit in each floor, so that tapping-in can occur as the need arises. Wire trays also may be used to create a gridwork. Ceiling design, therefore, should be kept simple so that easy access is possible above the light fixtures. Dropped ceilings present problems, because of the difficulties involved in working above the ceiling-tile channels. Conduit housing fiber optic cable and electric wires must be expandable, and this means making ample use of junction boxes from which additional conduit can be run in the future.

Within the overall power and data grid, a conduit system feeds specific pieces of study furniture. It is essential to design the furniture to fit the architectural space *before* laying out the conduit runs. If furniture is not appropriately sized, and wiring is provided without reference to carrels and tables, furniture cannot be installed in optimal proximity to power and data outlets. A chaotic layout can easily result. Our firm advice is *not* to leave the critical issue of matching furniture and outlets solely to architects and engineers. They may have no idea what the issue is, let alone how to ensure that the contractor follows instructions *precisely.* One way to get satisfactory results is to relate furniture dimensions to shelving lengths, which relate in turn to the building module. Figure 19 illustrates the connection among building module, shelving, and furniture.

Figure 19 depicts the shelving and furniture configurations that can occupy a 30-foot bay, provided that all dimensions relate to each other as described earlier. This diagram also shows a 15-foot power and data grid

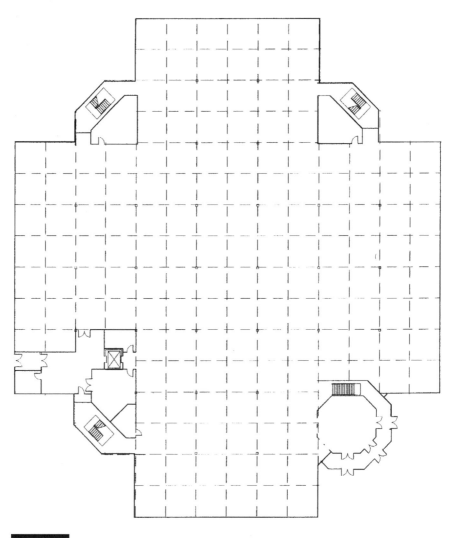

FIGURE 18
Network grid on first floor at WSU

quartering each 30-foot bay. Although this grid does not feed directly into furniture, provisions for it to do so can be made during construction. Conduit channels can be built into the concrete deck, running from each junction box (already installed) to each table or carrel. This arrangement will handle furniture programmed for various bays. If, at some time in the future, furniture replaces shelving, channels will have to be cut as part of a building retrofit. Relating all power and data channels, whether installed at the outset or added later, to the 15-foot grid reduces the chances of an awkward furniture arrangement.

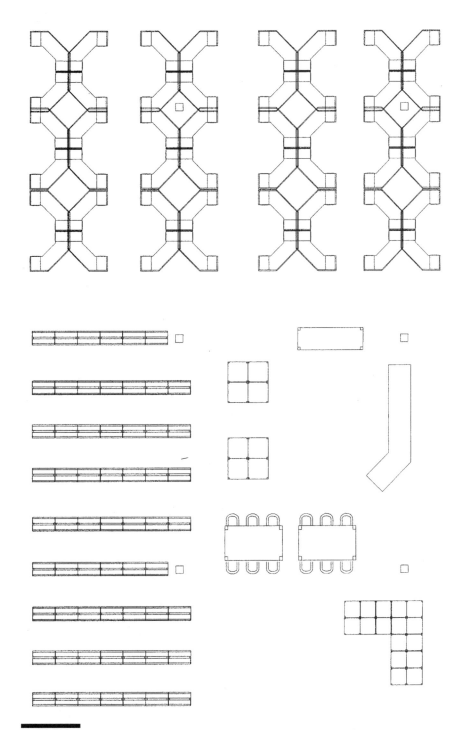

FIGURE 19
Relationship among building module, shelving, and furniture

Success in achieving the proper alignment of wired furniture depends on following this sequence:

1. Design the furniture to conform with the idea of the 30-foot bay.
2. Lay out the 15-foot power and data grid on the architectural drawings.
3. Superimpose the furniture layout on this grid to locate the power and data connections.
4. Check the installation of all junction boxes before concrete is poured, after which you must take what you get.

Building flexibility requires the construction of as few permanent internal walls as possible, but flexibility has other dimensions as well. A diagonal lighting design, for instance, contributes to flexibility by offering good illumination no matter how the stacks are configured. It is a mistake to assume that they will always remain as originally situated and, accordingly, to run the lighting along the aisles. Over the building's life span, stacks may be shifted from time to time in response to changing space demands. The rate at which high-acid-content paper is deteriorating suggests that much of the existing book stock may well disintegrate within several decades. Photocopiers and laser printers are accelerating the process by emitting damaging quantities of ozone, an oxidizing agent that destroys paper by breaking down carbon molecules.[21] Republication of a significant proportion of that scholarship probably will occur in electronic rather than print format. Consequently, the square footage that has to be devoted solely to book storage may well decline for reasons beyond the control of librarians, whose conservation efforts cannot prevent the inevitable destruction of printed material currently in existence.

. . . and Modularity

Modular construction has distinguished library buildings for some sixty years, ever since Angus Snead Macdonald first proposed the idea in 1933 and the University of Georgia followed his advice a year later.[22] Briefly out of fashion in the 1960s, when atria were much in vogue, modular design is now generally respected. Kenneth Toombs calls it "the greatest innovative development in library architecture since electric lighting," while David Kaser credits it with "allowing the development of utilitarian library structures appropriate to their present-day egalitarian societal role."[23] Modularity, in this context, does not refer to pre-fab construction techniques, but rather to the dimensioning of interior space. Module size is based on a predictable, recurring measure, such as the length of a section of shelving or the footprint of a study carrel. The building is then designed so that its structural columns are integrated into the configuration of furnishings and equipment and thus do not impede traffic flows. If carefully calculated, the module can accommodate either storage or study space and allows functions to be interchanged.

Flexibility of space is the virtue of modularity. If structural columns divide the total space into rectangles of the same dimensions, then areas intended for book stacks may be used for other purposes should circumstances change (fig. 20). Shelving configurations may be altered, and the mix between storage, study, and work space modified as appropriate. This philosophy of building design is even more cogent in the new century, when the influence of technology on library design is growing. No matter what form of construction is selected, modular design is the sine qua non of a successful library building. Its full potential is realized, however, only if the power and communications grid reaches every part of the building in which it one day may be needed. If load-bearing walls are completely absent, then any part of the building theoretically may be used for any other purpose at some point in the future. Too great a fascination with the idea of flexibility, on the other hand, can upset space planning in the present. It is important to sort out functional relationships early in the design process.

For more than a generation, library planners, such as Metcalf, Mason, Ellsworth, and Beckman, have recommended the modular approach as a means of achieving building flexibility. If, for example, a book stack measures 36 inches from the center of one upright to the center of the next, then a range of nine sections will fit between columns spaced at 30 feet (center to center). Because the module is square, seven ranges with six aisles will fit within the module (fig. 21). Aisle width will be 39 inches (assuming that double-face shelving is 21 inches wide), which exceeds the minimum width mandated by the Americans with Disabilities Act. Aisles between fixed ranges of book stacks now must be wider than the traditional 34 inches in order to accommodate wheelchairs: 42-inch aisles (36 inches is the ADA minimum) will permit wheelchairs to turn. Should planners wish to create 42-inch aisles and thus achieve the ADA optimum, the module would have to expand to 31 feet 6 inches in order to accommodate the same number of ranges. Or the module could shrink to 26 feet 4 inches (precisely) and allow only four ranges between columns. In both cases, assuming that shelving sections are 21 inches wide (9-inch shelves), all ranges are centered on columns. Regardless of module dimension, it is then a matter of sizing the building to meet storage and study-space needs. Keep in mind, however, that the smaller module will complicate conversion from one purpose to the other, because furniture designed for computer use fits best in the larger module. Carrels, for example, could be only 36–38 inches wide with a downsized module in order to accommodate the same number in the equivalent space.

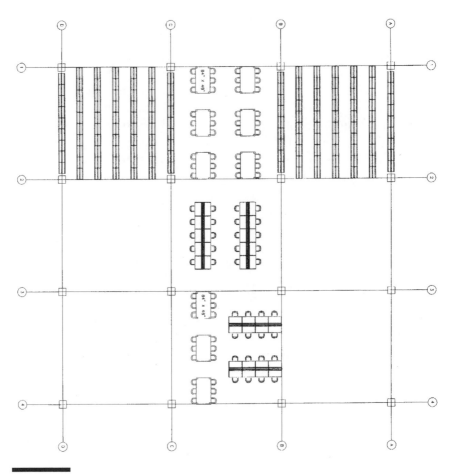

FIGURE 20
Relationships on first floor at WSU

Furniture designed to fit the 30-foot module can be located between columns in a similar way, and space may be reassigned in the future with greater convenience. Another advantage to modular construction is that the columns may be integrated into the shelving layout so that they do not obstruct traffic flows through the stacks. At the same time, the columns can carry power and communications needed by building cleaners or notebook computer users who may wish to work in leisure-reading areas where columns are also present.

Rather than rely entirely on the architect to articulate the module, librarians can experiment on their own by using a CAD program. A good example of design software is DataCAD, which is both inexpensive (approximately US $500) and relatively easy to learn. Two- and three-dimensional drawings, complete with scaled furnishings and equipment, can be produced. Various design hypotheses may be tested informally

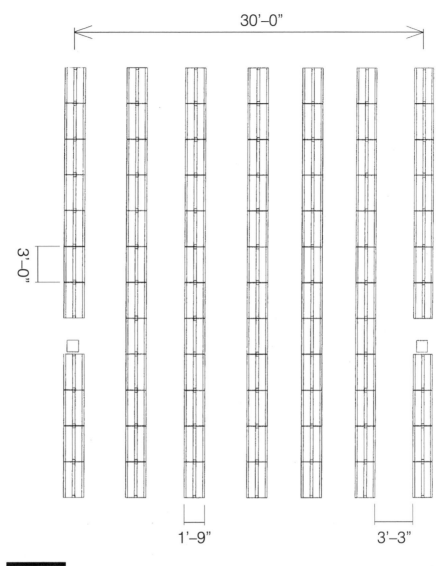

FIGURE 21
Shelving and aisles

before the building program is completed. Librarians may wish to experiment with various furniture placements and locations to create a proper relationship between study and leisure-reading areas. Like a well-designed page layout, a good library requires architectural "white space" for the psychological comfort of its users. Crowded accommodations produce the same sort of unease as an acoustical environment that is unrelieved by white noise. Sound and space can be used to give each person surroundings that are conducive to study. In addition, such drawings enable the client to communicate more cogently with the architect. Misunderstandings and misinterpretations are minimized if both parties begin with a clear perception of the client's wishes. Librarians certainly should not attempt to be architects, but there is no reason to avoid the technicalities of space planning, now that the right tools are available.

Organizing the Interior Space

Several traditional functions continue to occupy library space:

- book stacks
- study stations
- shared staff work space, for example, technical services, circulation, the information desk, interlibrary loan
- offices for professional librarians
- administrative offices

Although some rooms and offices are created by building walls, none of these need be load bearing. Each space conforms to the building module and theoretically may be converted to other uses. Demountable partitions and modular offices may be used to create work space for staff. Again, electricity and communications are provided by tapping into conduit below or in the floor slab. Modular offices are engineering marvels with internal wire-management systems, soundproofing, and convenient work areas. Modular work spaces also can be created in larger rooms in which several professional staff members regularly work, as has been done in the Leavey Library and the University of Kentucky library. The idea is to create private spaces that, at the same time, do not isolate staff members from each other or from library users who may require assistance.

Study areas, at least in relatively small libraries, should occupy the margins of the stack areas on each floor (fig. 22). Power and computer connections are most easily provided along the walls, although it certainly is possible to bring wiring up through the floor to service tables situated in interior space. Floor plugs also can be installed wherever needed. Larger libraries can group carrels and tap into conduits or wire trays fixed to the ceiling of the floor below. The point, in every case, is to conceal, as much as possible, evidence of the connections themselves.

Permanent office space ideally should be built along the building's periphery, so that occupants have natural daylight in the rooms where they work. When staff members are consulted during the initial design phases, they predictably ask for two things: windows and windows that open. The second of these requests often is denied, because environmentally controlled buildings tend to be sealed. But there is no reason at

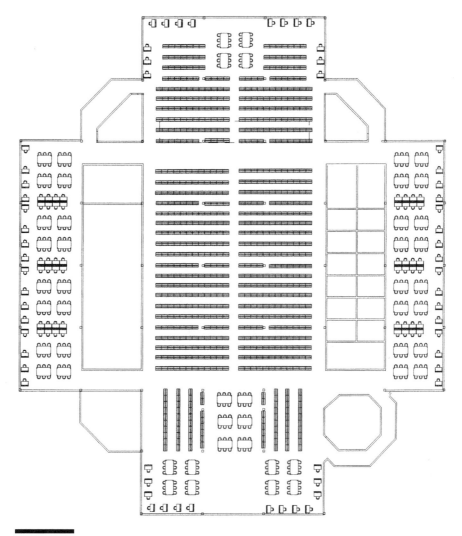

FIGURE 22
Second floor layout at WSU

all to begrudge staff windowed work spaces. Visual contact with the outside gives a psychological lift that is well worth providing.

Professional librarians, especially those who are department heads, require offices close to the areas they supervise. These offices should be accessible, but not to the extent that constant interruptions are likely to occur. Glass sidelights convey a sense of accessibility, but preserve a necessary degree of privacy. The same general comments apply to administrative offices, which should be neither isolated nor too prominent. The library director has to be close enough to the action to remain aware of what is happening on a daily basis. But he or she is not required to be at the disposal of every library user in search of assistance.

Offices, study areas, and the book stacks occupy most, but by no means all, of the library's interior space. Other functions that have to be accommodated are: (1) microform reading areas with their associated cabinets and machinery; (2) photocopiers situated conveniently close to point of use, and not in separate, isolated rooms; and (3) leisure-reading space for contemplation or relaxation (but not excessive socializing), equipped with soft seating and low tables. (Each of these areas inevitably requires staff supervision.) Staff members require a lounge in which to take breaks and eat lunch.

The circulation area is a multipurpose workstation that may also administer the reserve-reading collection and other collections (such as videotapes or computer programs) that require special handling. Enough terminals should be provided to accommodate peak demand for service. Easy access to the security system is necessary for those occasions when the alarm sounds and the situation has to be investigated. Behind the circulation desk should be a walled or partitioned office in which staff can pursue essential tasks that require concentration, when they are not actually performing desk duty (fig. 23). It is a good idea to locate the interlibrary-loan office in the vicinity of the circulation desk, because ILL should be easily accessible to faculty and students. This is especially true now that resource-sharing among academic libraries is growing in importance.

FIGURE 23
Circulation workroom at WSU

Finally, within the library itself are several spaces that must be situated correctly if the building as a whole is to function properly. The receiving room is a place where mail, packages, and other deliveries are handled on their way into and out of the library. Convenient elevator access to all floors should be adjacent to this area, which is separated from the loading dock by a weather vestibule (fig. 24). Elevator access to all levels is an ADA requirement; elevators should be large enough to accommodate both passengers and freight. Skimping on size to save a few dollars is false economy. Not to be overlooked are the rest rooms, which, sadly, seem to

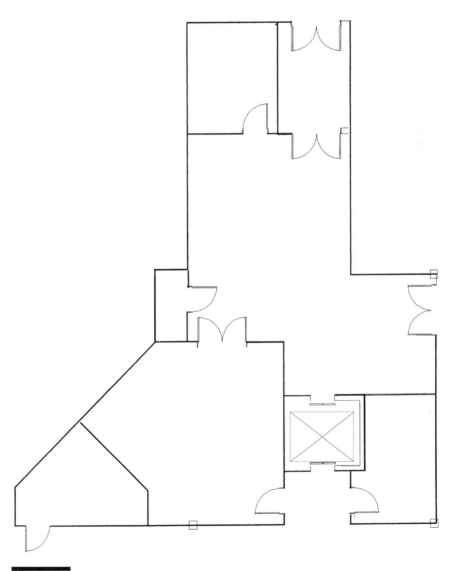

FIGURE 24
Loading dock relationships at WSU

attract vandals. High-quality fixtures resist depredations somewhat more successfully than cheaper alternatives. For this reason, the additional investment is recommended. These facilities naturally must be fully accessible to the handicapped.

Experience confirms that computerized workplaces are not necessarily danger free. Radiation emissions from CRTs are still being studied for potential health hazards. (The issue will disappear as LCD flat-panel monitors come into general use.) Repetitive strain injuries are frequently reported by staff members who keyboard at uncomfortable angles.[24] As automation progresses, such complaints as carpal tunnel syndrome appear to increase.[25] Circulation and information desks, along with other workstations, ideally ought to be designed according to ergonomic principles to reduce the possibility of harm to library employees. Left to their own devices, some architects will happily specify kitchen cupboards and call them circulation desks. Now that circulation functions are fully automated, desks should be built to accommodate terminals and keyboards in positions comfortable for staff use (fig. 25). It is advisable to consult a physiotherapist skilled in workplace ergonomics when designing millwork and selecting furniture. Precautions at this stage can help to avoid complications later.

FIGURE 25
Circulation desk at Leavey Library, University of Southern California

Calculating Shelving Requirements

The first step toward producing an accurate estimate of shelving requirements is to determine how many volumes the library currently possesses. A good automated cataloging system can provide this count with relative ease, but that is about all that the computer can do to simplify the task ahead (fig. 26). Every shelf in the existing inventory must now be counted and note made of how full each one is. When this information is combined with a projection of annual rates of acquisition, it is possible to extrapolate shelving requirements and to provide adequate room for collection growth. Net assignable space in the new building is established on the basis of storage needs projected at least twenty years ahead by combining current standards and formulas with an estimate of the impact

Classification	Main	Education	Documents	Periodicals	Storage	Total
A	183	84	49	10	41	367
B	12,187	879	22	3	626	13,717
C	698	266	33	0	97	1,094
D	9,829	586	70	0	891	11,376
E	4,369	515	572	1	113	5,570
F	4,665	721	369	5	93	5,853
G	2,996	1,452	247	4	194	4,893
H	18,637	1,241	2,853	1	255	22,986
J	4,063	74	552	0	257	4,946
K	1,121	448	469	0	11	2,049
L	65	12,422	236	0	659	13,382
N	131	1,971	92	0	71	2,265
P	22,164	3,921	137	3	2,520	28,745
Q	11,962	2,280	1,216	1	1,252	16,711
R	2,375	441	392	0	96	3,304
S	1,213	109	1,122	0	71	2,515
T	1,742	1,237	1,065	0	113	4,157
U	342	17	87	0	46	492
V	45	15	33	0	4	97
Z	2,756	466	241	25	209	3,697
TOTAL	101,543	29,145	9,857	52	7,619	148,216

FIGURE 26
Collection breakdown according to location and LC classification

of information technology on warehousing space. The second factor, technology, adds an element of suspense to the calculations.

If financial constraints prevent planners from designing a building of appropriate size, then serious thought must be given to how the library will cope with overcrowding during a period in which the print medium remains dominant. Electronic publishing indeed may come to the rescue, but planners should not rely too heavily on this possibility within the next fifteen years. A better fallback position is to plan for the eventual installation of compact shelving, or even to use this option at the outset to get the most value from limited space. The precast or poured floor slabs of modern library buildings can be reinforced to bear the weight of this storage system (250 pounds per square foot of live load). Assuming, however, that fixed stacks will be provided throughout the new building, the next task is to determine how much shelving is needed.

Shelving requirements cannot simply be estimated, but must be precisely measured in order to obtain just the quantity needed. Until recently, the only way to do this was to draw shelving ranges to scale on a set of architectural drawings. With the advent of affordable CAD programs, librarians themselves can produce scaled drawings of the stack areas and easily position the ranges. Once this is done, quantities may be established very quickly. These drawings also serve as the basis for the stack and collection maps required to move a book collection to its new quarters.

The *stack map* (fig. 27) is a two-dimensional placement of the shelving on the architectural drawing. The *collection map* depicts where each LC classification fits on the shelves (fig. 28). Empty bays and shelves can be included for expansion, based on such factors as the size of the acquisitions budget, rates of book donations, and so on.

Shelves are considered full when there is less than 8 inches of vacant space on each. The average capacity of a shelf is eighteen volumes. Expansion room must be provided between Library of Congress classifications, and it is advisable to keep bottom shelves free throughout the collection to reduce the need periodically to shift large portions. Top shelves also may be left vacant, if shelving capacity substantially exceeds current collection size. The standard double-face bay contains fourteen shelves on an 84-to-90-inch upright. Assuming that two shelves per bay remain free, then a double-face bay can hold approximately 216 volumes. Knowing these estimates helps planners to provide all the stack space they can afford.

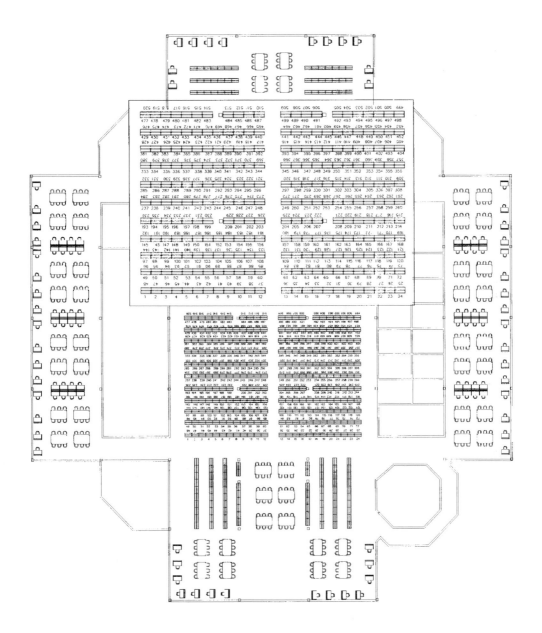

FIGURE 27
Stack map with inset

1	2	3	4	5	6	7	8	9	10
AC	AE	B	VACANT	B	B	B	B	B	B
AC	AG-AP	B	VACANT	B	B	B	B	B	B
AC	AS	B	VACANT	B	B	B	B	B	B
AC	AS	B	VACANT	B	B	B	B	B	B
AC	AY-AZ	B	VACANT	B	B	B	B	B	B
AE	B	B	VACANT	B	B	B	B	B	B
VACANT	VACANT	VACANT	VACANT	VACANT	VACANT	VACANT	VACANT	VACANT	VACANT

11	12	13	14	15	16	17	18	19	20
B	B	B	B	B	B	B	B	B	B
B	B	B	B	B	B	B	B	B	B
B	B	B	B	B	B	B	B	B	B
B	B	B	B	B	B	B	B	B	B
B	B	B	B	B	B	B	B	B	B
B	B	B	B	B	B	B	B	B	B
VACANT	VACANT	VACANT	VACANT	VACANT	VACANT	VACANT	VACANT	VACANT	VACANT

21	22	23	24	25	26	27	28	29	30
B	B	B	B	B	B	B	B	BC	BC
B	B	B	B	B	B	B	BC	BC	BC
B	B	B	B	B	B	B	BC	BC	BC
B	B	B	B	B	B	B	BC	BC	BD
B	B	B	B	B	B	B	BC	BC	BD
B	B	B	B	B	B	B	BC	BC	BD
VACANT	VACANT	VACANT	VACANT	VACANT	VACANT	VACANT	VACANT	VACANT	VACANT

FIGURE 28
Collection map

Calculating Study Space

Building size is calculated on the basis of the space needed to accommodate materials, staff, users, and services. The number of potential library users defines space requirements: student enrollment and faculty complement. General guidelines are found in ACRL's "Standards for College Libraries, 1995 Edition, Draft." [26] "When less than 50% of the FTE [full-time equivalent] enrollment resides on campus," seating for 20 percent is to be provided; when more than half of FTEs live on campus, the recommended proportion is 25 percent. Once the allocation is known, the space needed may be calculated.

Another factor that impinges on the calculation of study space is the personal computer. If planners assume that notebook-computer use will be widespread on campus, then study spaces must be sized accordingly. Carrels, for example, should be 42 inches wide and about 30 inches deep, to allow room for the machine, research materials, and perhaps a portable printer (figs. 29 and 30). Table space should offer enough room to work comfortably with a computer and source materials: 84 inches by 48 inches. Tables will seat six people; in practice, they will never do so except perhaps at the height of the exam period. Some research suggests that library users avoid table seating because proximity to others threatens their personal space.[27]

Individual study carrels, suitably dimensioned for computer use, have a footprint of 10.5 square feet. If carrels are spaced 42 inches apart, to allow plenty of room for the chair, then the footprint of the entire study station is about 23 square feet. Carrels designated for use by those in wheelchairs need more space between them. The ACRL standard of 25 to 35 square feet per study station is rather generous, even taking computer usage into account.

Once the amount of space for study purposes is known, thought must be given to its type. Some library users prefer carrels to tables; others feel the opposite. Depending on the shape of the architectural space,

FIGURE 29
Study carrel at Leavey Library

FIGURE 30
Ganged study carrels at Leavey Library

it probably is best to install as many carrels as possible, and to situate tables either in glazed reading areas (areas with windows) or throughout the stacks. A safe assumption is that most people, especially those with a portable computer, will gravitate toward a carrel.

Calculating Work Space

Each professional librarian, including the director and associate directors, requires private office space. Sizing guidelines may be found in Philip D. Leighton and David C. Weber, *Planning Academic and Research Library Buildings* (1999), chapter 8. Desktop computer use is assumed in each case, and rooms are laid out accordingly.

Staff work space is calculated on the basis of several factors: (1) progressive decline in the size and scope of technical-services operations; (2) concomitant expansion of public-services and interlibrary-loan activities; and (3) self-check-out units, such as the 3M SelfCheck system. Libraries must plan to accommodate staff already on the payroll, but should build flexibly so that workstations can be converted to other uses when positions become vacant.

Each staff member at a computerized workstation requires 100 square feet. Technical-services areas need ample room for shelving. Most libraries have automated serials control, using either in-house or vendor-supplied systems, and thus can dispense with cabinets for paper records. Generous circulation space, in which book carts can maneuver, therefore can be provided within budgetary constraints.

One new claimant for a portion of the total work space is the wire closet. The power and communications grids converge on the wire closets from their network of conduit and wire trays. From there, cabling is routed to specific rooms and workstations throughout the building. Wire closets should provide easy access to connector panels, relays, and so on. They must be accessible to technical staff at all times.

Interlibrary-loan (ILL) activities deserve special mention at this point. Electronic access to bibliographic data and the growing popularity of regional consortia are creating an upsurge in resource-sharing. Rationalization of collection-development strategies among groups of academic libraries means that access to information now outweighs ownership of specific titles. "Just-in-time" delivery of documents is becoming the norm. All this has raised the profile of interlibrary-loan departments everywhere. Until interactive ILL is generally accepted, more space will have to be devoted to this department of the library, at least 200 square feet (Leighton and Weber, appendix B). The ILL area should not, however, be encompassed by load-bearing walls, because it may contract again as library users become direct borrowers from remote sites, with requested items delivered by e-mail.

Growth in distance-education programs will mean that more space and staff resources must be devoted to off-campus library services. Some activities associated with scanning and mailing physical items can be amalgamated with ILL. As staff involvement in ILL declines, emphasis can shift to distance-learning support within the same space. With electronic communications as the main engine of change in library operations, all staff work space must be easily convertible from one kind of activity to another.

Another work area whose size and design is influenced strongly by information technology is the information/reference desk. Some librarians are suspicious of any structure that physically separates library users from public-services staff. This need not be the case if the desk is designed to attract those in need of assistance. A desk built in the form of a bifurcated doughnut, clearly visible from the entrance, works well. High enough on one side to enable seated staff to meet library users at eye level, the doughnut's other half is regular desk height. This configuration allows staff to invite users to sit down for a consultation. Networked computers are, of course, located on this part of the desk. Assistance can be offered to persons in wheelchairs with such an arrangement. Several staff members can work with questioners at the same time, on either or both sides of the lower half.

Another type of information desk is found in the Leavey Library at USC, where librarians and computer experts work side by side to assist users of the Information Commons. The service counter is located close to the workstation carousels. Staff routinely leave the desk to assist users as required. Iowa's Information Arcade employs graduate assistants to explain the technology and to supply subject-matter expertise. In both cases, a dynamic relationship exists between staff members and library users, and in neither of them is a large, imposing desk required. Here, then, are two good examples of how work-space design emerges from a service philosophy.

When planning the location of staff work spaces, functional relationships are important. Off-campus library operations, for example, should be adjacent to ILL because of the frequent contact between them. The receiving room should offer easy, behind-the-scenes horizontal or vertical access to the technical-services area, so that materials can be moved out of the public eye. Administrative offices need to be accessible, but not necessarily on the building's main traffic artery. Strategically located internal phones allow library users in need of assistance to contact the information/reference desk. Appropriate separation between work and study areas will preserve a quiet environment in the library.

In the end, the quality of library space and not its quantity will determine a building's success or failure. If efficient design is combined with attractive surroundings, the library will justify its substantial cost. The affordability of good CAD programs makes possible an even more active role for librarians in the design process than is usual. Computer-assisted design (CAD) has been available for some years and is now an indispensable design tool.[28] Architects require elaborate and expensive CAD software in their design work. Prices for such software range from $50 to $10,000. More-sophisticated products will allow the interior space to be modeled by including a variety of elements: light and shadows; color and texture of carpet, upholstery, and fabrics; perspectives based on several camera angles; and furniture "built" to exact proportional dimensions. An example is DataCAD, which the authors used to create the architectural drawings in this book (fig. 31). Still greater elaboration can be achieved using computer animation, which allows an "observer" to walk around the room and to examine it from all points of view. All components may be shifted and rearranged in order to discover an optimum pattern.

CAD programs are available that allow actual fabric samples and product images to be scanned in and manipulated. Computer simulation is unnecessary, and there is no "need for color boards, tiny fabric swatches, color renderings, floor plans and elevations."[29] Disks containing images of furniture and equipment are available from manufacturers. Designers thus are

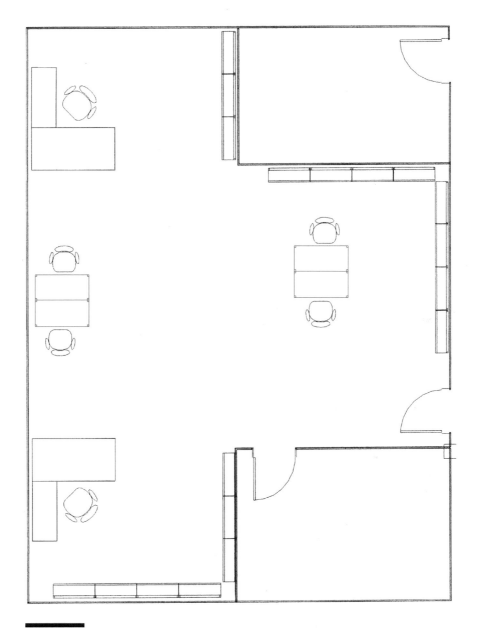

FIGURE 31
Technical-services work area at WSU

able to include real products, colors, and textures in their CAD-generated layouts. Librarians, at the same time, have an accurate picture of their new space as well as an opportunity to make appropriate changes during the design phase.

Networking

Every library-design consultant advises building planners to provide ample electric power (more than one could imagine will ever be required) to meet present and future needs, and to make outlets easily accessible. Though determined to follow this counsel, librarians often fail in the attempt. Power connections can turn out to be awkwardly located after furniture is installed, or staff must resort to extension cords in order to bring power to their work areas located midfloor. One way to avoid this kind of embarrassment is to use a computer program to model the interior space by placing all furnishings and equipment, represented to scale, in their proper setting (fig. 32). Computer modeling depicts perspective, the spatial relationship of objects, the texture of materials, and the effects of lighting.[30] Architects and clients obtain a good idea of how the interior will look. Power and communications outlets may then be situated exactly where they should be, including those in the floor.

Building flexibility derives mainly from an accessible grid, perhaps a conduit network poured into the concrete floors or a system of cable raceways. Power and communications grids are designed to fit the particular construction technique used by the architect. Precast floor slabs, for example, contain cells through which wires may run across the building; deck-hung raceways are used to carry wires in a direction perpendicular to the in-slab channels. In the case of poured concrete floors, a conduit grid or duct system may be laid down between the two layers of reinforcing rods and thus become part of the floor slab. This technique is usually applied to the main-floor deck, especially if it is slab-on-grade. Both types of building make use of structural columns to transport wire vertically. A third strategy, which offers easier access to the home runs, is a system of cable trays within the plenum space (fig. 33). Connecting to cable in trays is easier than locating conduit buried in the slab and offers greater flexibility in placing power and data boxes.

In jurisdictions where permitted by code, flat cabling may be used to enhance flexibility, because it can be run virtually anywhere on a floor and can also be retrofitted. Flat cabling has a few drawbacks: It can only be used with carpet tiles (which are expensive) and may leave lumpy ridges in the carpet; data cable can run only 50 feet; and flat wire is generally more expensive than other options.[31] Wiring run through cells in precast floor slabs, through conduit in poured slabs, or through a system of raceways is preferable.

Early in the design phases, planners have to decide on the type of internal cabling to be used: twisted-pair, coaxial, or fiber-optic. Among these alternatives, fiber-optic provides maximum bandwidth needed by streaming multimedia. Electrical signals are transformed into light,

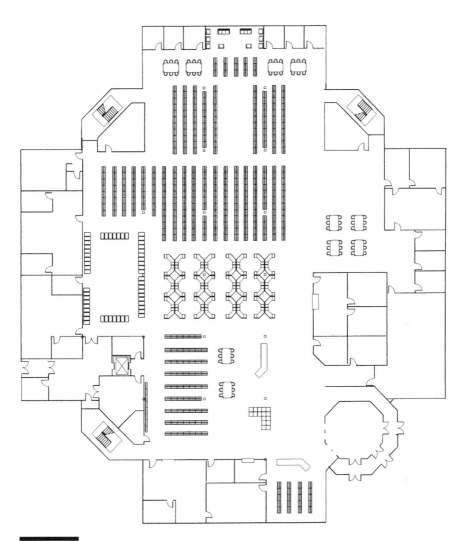

FIGURE 32
Layout of furnishings and equipment

which is then transmitted by light-emitting diodes (LEDs). An adapter at the other end converts the light signal back to an electrical one. Because glass fiber is rather fragile, in comparison with copper wire, it cannot be pulled through tight bends in a conduit system. A conduit grid designed for twisted-pair only may not accommodate fiber-optic cable, should the library wish to make a change in the future. Copper might have to be pulled out before fiber could be installed. The grid, therefore, should be constructed as if for fiber-optic at the outset so as to remain functional. A system of wire trays is best for fiber-optic cable. As campus information networks begin to deliver multimedia, broadband transmission

FIGURE 33
Cable trays in plenum space

capability becomes essential. Category 5 UTP and the new Category 7 can accommodate multimedia data flows on an ATM (asynchronous transfer mode) network. The campus information network, of course, demands a fiber backbone to handle massive data flows headed for other buildings and the Internet. These buildings also must have an adequate power supply to support a sophisticated communications grid.

All outlets into which computing equipment is likely to be plugged must be grounded and connected to an uninterruptible power source (UPS), in the event of a general power failure. Now that paper systems, such as the card catalog and manual circulation procedures, are extinct, there is no recourse when the power fails or the system goes down. Heavy demands for electric power mean that building service should be greater than 600 amps. Less amperage will create the potential for overload and power failure, which can bring the operations of a modern library to a standstill. "A rough rule of thumb," advises Elaine Cohen, "is that each piece of electric/electronic equipment requires five amps."[32] Provision of adequate electrical power, though essential, is a relatively simple matter when compared with computer communications. A library building intended to serve for several decades requires cabling that can accommodate succeeding generations of information networks, not simply the 10/100 BASE-T Ethernets common today.

The requirements and configuration of a proper campus information network are by now well understood:

a fiber-optic backbone operating at a minimum of 56 Kb, but possibly at ATM speeds of 25 Mb to the desktop

category 5 or 7 copper twisted-pair to the desktop

a network menu that offers easy access to the library's online catalog, CD-ROM towers, word-processing and spreadsheet software, other library catalogs, and the Internet

bandwidth sufficient to accommodate streaming multimedia: text, graphics, video, and sound

multiple connections for users' portable computers in the library, residence halls, offices, and other points on campus

e-mail support, with system accounts available to all faculty and staff

network access to management information systems

Library designers need to be conversant with network architecture, because the library is one of the main consumers of network resources. The following examples illustrate the bandwidth demands that are likely to occur:

Faculty who offer Web-enhanced courses provide links to multimedia resources, such as video clips, sound files, graphic representations, and other massive data collections. These resources have to load at a reasonable speed in order to be useful, whether they originate from a local server or from elsewhere on the Internet.

Music students receive listening assignments that traditionally have required them to use tape decks or CD players. Streaming audio over an ATM network, on the other hand, is accessible through any computer that has an ATM card installed. (At present, this does not include the laptop computers that some one hundred U.S. institutions require students to use.) Listening can be done anywhere on the network where the appropriate equipment is located.

As these examples show, bandwidth is one of the most important educational advantages that a university can offer its students. Full network access from all library study spaces therefore must be available.

If the campus network is 10/100 switched Ethernet, a constant bitrate of 4 Mbps reaches the user's computer. Quality of video transmission is not full-motion. ATM offers more than five times this data flow, which results in high-resolution video and CD-quality audio. As demand for bandwidth increases, network speed can be scaled up to 622 Mbps. Prices for hubs, switches, and routers are dropping, as is the cost of interface cards ($250 in 1999). Each ATM port currently costs about $750, which means that universal access is not yet affordable. Yet it is realistic to plan for ATM at each machine in an information arcade or an electronic classroom in the library. The important thing, from the standpoint of infrastructure design, is that ATM will run over Category 5 UTP; it does not require fiber to the desktop. (For detailed information on networking issues, see appendix A.)

Wireless networking can be used to reach parts of the building not serviced by the cabling grid. Wireless is not yet a substitute for conventional infrastructure, because it lacks the carrying capacity. The maximum speed for radio-frequency transmission was increased to about 10 megabits per second, which is still a bit slow for optimal Internet use. Infrared, effective only over short distances, handles 10 megabits per second. It may be some time before broadband wireless networking becomes economically feasible for libraries. Potentially, it will solve the perennial problem of too few data connections caused by the high cost of a fine-grained wiring grid. Although fully functional wireless is not yet available, building planners may anticipate a solution to the challenge of networking an entire library. Extrapolating to the campus at large, wireless LANs (local area networks) may eliminate the need to retro-wire older buildings at considerable expense. Thus, "the fastest connections will probably always be wired."[33] Wireless connections nevertheless can be convenient both for library users and for librarians who require catalog access without having to visit an OPAC terminal. Now that laptop computers have an extra slot for a wireless-network card, students who wish to use their machines outside the building also may appreciate the convenience.[34]

Not only are networks becoming wireless, but also their architecture is changing from a client-server model based on PCs to the so-called thin client–fat server model. "An organization," write Charlie Tuller and Diana Oblinger, "would invest its resources in ensuring that the network is up to date and that its users have information appliances. Changes would be made to the network, not to individual client machines."[35] Word processors, Internet browser plug-ins, or the library catalog would reside on the server, with the "thin client" performing required tasks. At the moment, this architecture works well for an online catalog, thin clients serving as OPAC terminals. As network speeds increase, along with those of central servers, the PC may disappear as the primary means of access to networked resources.

Server capacity is the key to a library's effective use of the bandwidth offered by an ATM network. Planners in fact may decide to locate course and media servers in the library, along with technical staff to operate them. Technically competent librarians could manage servers, thus bringing their traditional service orientation to a task that involves considerable interaction with the teaching faculty. Mediation between information technology and its users is certain to become an important role for librarians as electronic resources grow in number and sophistication.

With this probability in mind, Winona State University created an academic technologies center (ATC) in its new library (completed in 1999). The ATC supports faculty who are making educational uses of technology and who require powerful computing resources, such as media servers and ATM connectivity. A qualified librarian with considerable technical expertise created the ATC, where all Web-course servers are located. Hardware reliability is paramount, and the ATC ensures that servers are always operating. Library support, teaching, and computer services converge in the ATC, which epitomizes the integration of technology into the educational process. The library's data network culminates in the ATC and, from there, connects to the network router in another building.

Today's academic libraries are information hubs on their campus networks. It makes sense to locate course and media servers in a central place, where the required staff expertise is available. An evolutionary process is bringing the library into the teaching and learning activities of its campus. Two developments are driving progress in this direction: (1) broadband networking and (2) faculty interest in Web-enhanced or Web-based instruction. Library resources published in electronic format, then networked, are accessible via hyperlink from course syllabi. Thus, the library becomes a gateway to information resources directly applicable to specific courses.

Special Facilities

Ten years ago, two leading authorities on library design wrote that "over the next decade, the computer will not be an instrument that is carried around more than was the portable typewriter in the 1950s." [36] David C. Weber refers elsewhere to "clusters of microcomputers" that "represent a new and supplemental space requirement in terms of the traditional library." [37] Rather than bringing along their own computer, users would carry disks to use in machines supplied by the library. This prediction failed to materialize. In 1999, a number of colleges and universities have in place programs that facilitate student access to laptop computers. Winona State's Laptop Universal Access (LUNIAC), Wake Forest University's "Project for the Class of 2000," and the University of Minnesota–Crookston's pioneering effort are but three examples of a growing trend. As David Leroy Michaels, a library-design consultant, predicted several years ago, "[l]ibrary users will routinely bring lap-top computers to libraries to combine word processing with research."[38] This prophecy came true. Librarians now "expect many patrons to arrive with computers in hand, looking for a jack to connect them to the network," and new buildings are being designed accordingly.[39] "It is time," writes Robert C. Heterick, former president of EDUCOM, "that our institutions give up the industrial age model of personal computers in laboratories and move aggressively to the expectation that every student will come to school prepared with at least a minimally configured personal computer."[40]

Laptop computer use among students and faculty is increasingly popular at the turn of the millennium. Additional leasing costs, tacked onto tuition and fees, do not deter students who realize that information technology belongs in their educational and professional lives. No campus with a mandatory leasing program suffered enrollment declines; increases of 15 to 20 percent, in fact, are not uncommon. Power and portability continue to improve, along with campus information networks and the range of electronic information services to which they provide access. Library planners, therefore, have to provide network connections at each study space and in leisure-reading areas throughout the building. Laptops will be equipped with PCMCIA network cards, preconfigured by computer services technicians. UL-listed furniture will have surface-mounted power and data modules that plug into floor or wall outlets. Designing the power and data grids, therefore, is critically important, and requires the assistance of a qualified consultant who works with the architects' electrical engineer.

Assuming general use of portable computers, there is no need to provide machines at study spaces. (The information gallery or arcade is an exception.) Electronic information products, such as databases of full-text articles and video materials, are generally available on campus information networks. Course assignments are migrating to electronic format. Faculty are transferring their course materials to the Web and are using such products as Web CT or CourseInfo to organize them. Electronic media are now common in higher education. Their widespread use will influence library design from now on.

Depending on the scale of a building project, the following areas may be programmed into a new library:

an information commons or arcade

one or more electronic classrooms

an auditorium with computerized controls

a support center for faculty who are developing electronic course delivery

a network server area to house course and media servers

Each of these facilities belongs in an academic library that aspires to be a teaching and learning instrument. Their presence enables the library to be an active participant in the educational process. An emphasis on networking, moreover, prepares the library to serve a growing clientele of distance learners, as Web-based education expands. Accommodating and staffing such "nontraditional" components challenge architects and librarians to redefine the nature of library service. The implications deserve further consideration.

At issue here is the need to support technology use by both faculty and students. The emphasis on access to information sources remains, but the prevailing medium is electronic rather than print. No longer is it sufficient merely to acquaint students with information technology, in preparation for the workplace. Since 1995, technology has become integral to higher education itself. Long a bulwark of tradition—the print culture of lecture-based teaching—the university has been engulfed by information technology. Libraries that must serve farther into the future than any planner can see therefore have to incorporate technology into their fabric, and they have to do so while respecting their own heritage as repositories of human knowledge.

Because today's academic library is a hybrid of print repository and electronic gateway, its design features are a blend of the old and the new. Furniture, for example, easily can be traditional wood construction, though with concealed wire management. There is nothing wrong with reading rooms that retain some of the grandeur of former times, although the monumentality of a Widener Library is passé. High windows, with modern filtering technology, remind all who enter of the library's noble past. Yet it is the special-function areas that hold the key to a future in which the library still occupies a central place on its campus.

Let us begin with the Information Gallery, as Winona State calls it (fig. 34), or the Information Arcade, according to the University of Iowa (fig. 35). This is a student-centered facility where expert help is available to create electronic documents from a variety of electronic sources. Although the concept is a popular one among academic librarians, there is no consensus on where to locate an information commons. Iowa has placed it in a corner of the main library, walled off from the rest of the building. The Leavey Library at USC gives it part of a lower floor. Winona State situates its gallery in the middle of the main floor, between the reference area and periodicals stacks. Wherever the arcade is located, librarian and technical support need to be close by, because this is a high-maintenance area. Students will be using sophisticated computers, loaded with a standard software suite and some specialized programs, and attached to such peripherals as laser printers, scanners, and so on. In most cases, the computers' capabilities will exceed the knowledge of their users. Questions and problems will arise in profusion. With multiple workstations

FIGURE 34
Information Gallery at WSU

FIGURE 35
Information Arcade at the University of Iowa

available, staff will be heavily engaged in individual instruction. This labor-intensive effort is teaching of a very high order and is unusual in a library setting. The payoff is an information-literate student who is at home with knowledge sources of all kinds and one, moreover, who is comfortable with the technology. Universities that require students to maintain electronic portfolios throughout their academic careers may find the gallery to be a natural focus for this activity. Gallery furniture should be configured in such a way that consultation can occur without disturbing others. Chairs should be quite spartan, with only a gas lift to accommodate users of different heights.

The gallery's counterpart for faculty is an area that Winona State calls the Academic Technologies Center, or ATC (fig. 36). Occupying 2,700 square feet originally scheduled for audiovisual services, the ATC contains computers for course-development work, a studio classroom used for facilitating discussion of educational rationale and integrating technology into the curriculum, teaching-software applications, staff offices, and a large server room from which streaming multimedia are made available across the campus on the ATM network. Course servers also are located here, so that they are easily serviced by ATC staff. This facility is directed by a librarian who possesses the technical and pedagogical expertise to help

FIGURE 36
Academic Technologies Center at WSU

subject specialists use technology effectively in the classroom. Interested faculty have participated in eight-day "Web Camps" offered several times during the year, after which the ATC provides continuing support and advice. Having this facility in the library means that faculty enjoy a congenial atmosphere in which to apply technology to their teaching.

Electronic products developed in the ATC find their application in the electronic classroom. Such classrooms are now routinely included in new library buildings, primarily for the use of librarians who teach electronic research skills. Each student has a networked computer, which the instructor may control from a lectern. LCD projectors and electronic whiteboards (e.g., SmartBoard or SoftBoard) are essential. With the growing interest in distance education, digital ITV (interactive television) and videoconferencing may be included. Two students share a television monitor recessed into the desk so as not to interfere with the cameras' sight lines. The room should be acoustically isolated and equipped with ambient-light controls. If each computer has an ATM card, the instructor may import multimedia, including full-motion video, from servers located in the ATC. Such classrooms should have the simplest possible controls, so that faculty can teach without interference from the technology. This goal is difficult to achieve, but is worth the effort required to place technology at the service of the academic enterprise.

An auditorium equipped for digital presentations of all kinds is useful when student bodies exceed 5,000 or so. Some demonstrations simply require a theater-like ambience. Not every project can afford to build and equip a large auditorium, and the other facilities mentioned earlier probably would take precedence. The basic principle is that modern academic libraries need plenty of instructional space if they are to fulfill their mission as high-tech gateways.

Building Fabric and Interior Design

The building's fabric comprises all nonstructural elements that complete the overall design and allow the library to function as intended. Included here are floor coverings, windows, display cabinets, and artwork that is permanently installed. None of these items can be taken for granted or left solely to the discretion of architectural consultants. Librarian involvement in the selection process is appropriate and, if the overall result is to be satisfactory, required. Although architects are responsible for designing the building to the program's specifications, they have less authority over the interior. How space is configured and equipped is, and must remain, primarily the concern of those who will operate and live in the building. Their interest consequently extends to all aspects of the building's fabric that affect library functions. They need a good understanding of interior design as it applies to libraries.

While the building itself is taking shape in the CAD program, there should be ongoing discussion of the interior design. The architect should provide sample boards with which the planners can live for a while before offering suggestions for changes. Members of the university's planning team should not hesitate to reject suggestions that contradict their basic notions of functionality and appearance. Under no circumstances should the university accept a "diktat" from the architect or his or her design consultant. "Some designers . . . ," writes Eric Rockwell, "may try to patronize you. However sympathetic you may feel, if your designer is condescending, fire him, too. Remember: *you're* the boss!"[41] To paraphrase an old chestnut, interior design is too important to leave to interior designers.

As Elaine Cohen notes: "Design professionals (architects and interior designers among others) seem to have been taught that designs are best when they are created intuitively."[42] What this approach often ignores is the functionality and atmosphere of the library environment that will emerge from the design process. "Ornament," as Charles C. Soule wrote many years ago, "is the last thing to think of about a library."[43] When "mere librarians" presume to offer their own conception of how things should be, they risk colliding with the *amour propre* of the "professionals," whom architects themselves may regard simply as "merchandisers."[44] Yet, many architects are content to leave interior design to their consultants, who may or may not bother to discuss their ideas with the client. "Most designers," notes William Seale, "have something to sell, and they charge a percentage of it, and of course may take kickbacks besides that."[45] Because the design consultant usually works for the architect, university personnel must ensure that their architect understands their desires and that she or he points the interior designer in the right direction. The goal, according to one architect, is to create an "interior environment . . . so designed by the architect that the average library user will be satisfied."[46] Frequent consultation is essential so as to satisfy the owner while avoiding egregious lapses of taste, such as the orange plastic study chairs one designer once recommended to the authors, or the electric-green shelving proposed by an architect on another project.

Aspects of interior design that are part of the contract—carpet, built-ins, quarry tile, paint, laminates, and other finishes—should be settled before the contractor is hired. Changes made later are either expensive or, if a price is solicited by change order for less-expensive materials, the credit offered is distressingly low. Design features, therefore, should be discussed and decided early in the process, rather than being left until architectural questions are resolved. If this is not done, the result can be disappointing to those who will live in the new building. By the time that the librarian discovers what is afoot, it may be too late to influence the outcome. The architect must understand that no materials are to be ordered without authorization from the building-project committee.

The building program itself should make explicit the basic design features that library planners wish to see realized. These elements then are written into the specifications that become part of the general contract. If matters are handled in this way, certain constraints are placed on the interior designer's artistic license. Designers left to their own devices may become ego involved to an extent not easily controlled or reversed. It is best, therefore, that the client's voice be heard clearly at the outset. Even those who are justifiably modest about their color sense should resist the designer's efforts to incorporate the obvious, and therefore datable, design trends (e.g., teal greens and pinks from the early 1990s) into the building's fabric. "[S]ome of the most colorful buildings in the United States," write Aaron and Elaine Cohen, "are all glass and white walls. The color comes from the furnishings, for which the interior architectural form provides a backdrop."[47] A library intended to last for several generations does not need to advertise its birth date from within. Think how easy it is to spot interiors designed in the 1970s, with their garish primary colors combined with muddy earth tones. Exemplary interior design aspires, on the contrary, to be ageless.

Relationships among proposed colors can be evaluated in low-tech fashion, by arranging various materials on a sample board. If finishes are shown "in proportions similar to those in the actual space," experiments with different kinds of lighting will give an idea of how the total environment will look.[48] A cool atmosphere may be warmed by using incandescent (a prohibitively expensive option) or warm fluorescent lighting. Artwork and accent colors produce a similar effect. Wall-hung art is the best way to enhance a building's interior environment. Our own preference is for an unobtrusive color scheme that does not distract library users from the task at hand.

Interior design is an elusive topic, mainly because it involves aesthetic judgments. One way to avoid a clash with the architect's consultant is to include a few guiding principles in the building program. If there is a consensus among the library planners on, say, the use of wood or wood accents, or the color of shelving and end-panels, this information should be given to the designer. Because end-panels constitute the predominant block of color in the building, everything else must harmonize. Bright, contrasting colors characterized the 1960s; designers discovered earth tones in the following decade; maroon and grey combinations proved to be popular in the 1980s. Blues and greys gained favor in the early 1990s. Nothing will date a building as quickly as its color scheme. When planners are trying to look fifteen years or more into the future, they probably are wise to avoid extreme color statements that identify their building with a particular trend in interior design. "By allowing a building to be striking," warn Aaron and Elaine Cohen, "embellished with all sorts of architectural insignia that cannot be removed without harming the structure, the possibilities of interior change become limited."[49] That is why accents should not be built in or painted on, but rather provided by wall-hung paintings, weavings, and so on. In the words of the distinguished historian of architecture, Vincent Scully, "[T]he traditional architectural aphorism that one should decorate construction, never build decoration is a sound one. . . ."[50]

The color scheme eventually adopted should reflect certain philosophical assumptions about the type of library service to be provided—book warehouse or "people place"? This is a basic choice, the resolution of which determines all matters relating to interior design. If the building is construed primarily as a book warehouse, spartan furnishings and natural colors (e.g., concrete, brick, wood) are appropriate. On the other hand, as information-access sources proliferate and electronic publication develops, library users probably will visit more frequently and stay longer. Planners, therefore, ought to pay attention to the comfort level offered by their new buildings. According to Philip M. Bennett, an architect,

> two types of color surroundings should be developed in the library: the immediate task surroundings and the overall library surroundings. Immediately around the task, colors should be slightly warm or in the middle of the spectrum. In the general surroundings, colors should be slightly cool. The immediate task area thus draws attention and stimulates thought processes, while the surroundings are minimally distractive.[51]

The general ambience should be unobtrusive and calming, with bright colors provided by accents, such as wall-hung artwork. Extensive use of wood in study and lounge furniture contributes to the warmth and comfort of the surroundings and meets Bennett's criteria. Chairs with ergonomic design features are essential if users are expected to remain seated for some time. Carrels and tables should be designed for easy use of personal computers.

As the foregoing comments imply, there is an important psychological element in interior design. Library planners have to take account of the way in which their building is likely to be used as information technology becomes pervasive in society at large. A building constructed now will accommodate users, both faculty and students, who are comfortable with the technology and adept at using it. They comprise a library clientele that requires proper accommodation in the years ahead.

The design and furnishing of libraries, with their long life span, require the gift of clairvoyance. No one can know with certainty how the future will unfold, as new technologies emerge and old ones decline. Yet, decisions have to be made in the present, and in such a way as to place as few constraints as possible on users of the building a generation hence. Durability, utility, and timelessness are criteria that apply to all aspects of the building, from its finishes to its furnishings and equipment. These criteria should be kept in mind during discussions with the architect and his or her consultants, and during preparation of the bid documents for shelving, furniture, carpeting, and equipment. As a corollary to this advice, cheap solutions to any related questions are very likely the wrong ones. To obtain the best value for any investment, extensive research is absolutely essential.

Nothing should be chosen until the marketplace has been canvassed in order to discover the range and quality of available products. Advice from consultants is helpful, but must never substitute for research by library planners themselves. Dealing with a variety of vendors, all of whom vigorously promote their own wares, is time-consuming and sometimes aggravating. But there is no better way to "kick the tires and slam the doors" of many competing products. The ultimate purpose, of course, is to identify items that can serve as "industry standards" when bid documents are written. "Cheap materials," warns Robert Rohlf, "are not the way to bring a building in on budget." [52] How to distinguish good quality from poor is a skill that comes only from experience, and acquiring that knowledge can be an experience in itself.

Local suppliers can help to establish direct contact with manufacturers, who generally welcome potential customers wishing to tour their facilities. The best evidence of product quality comes from observing the manufacturing process. When the time comes to decide, say, between particle-board and plywood cores, it helps to have discussed the issue with an independent expert. The same applies to the evaluation of seating, where the advice of a physiotherapist or occupational therapist is very useful. Achieving the proper color and finish on steel shelving involves negotiation and experimentation that no sales representative can offer. The choice in all these matters is the owner's to make, and those acting on her or his behalf are obligated to become knowledgeable. It is they, after all, who will be held responsible for the outcome.

Once the research is well advanced, bid documents can be prepared with some confidence that the right products are being sought. These documents are best written by librarians, in consultation with the building committee and outside advisors. There is nothing wrong in collaborating with the vendor of a product that may then be cited confidently as an industry standard because of a favorable ratio of price to quality. Vendors who cannot match the standard are thereby excluded, which somewhat simplifies the process; those who propose alternates know the level of quality they are expected to match. The point of the whole process, in the end, is to strike a balance between price and quality in line with budget realities.

Carpet

Most libraries that aspire to be people places elect to install carpeting. A high-grade commercial carpet constructed of solution-dyed nylon with a low, narrow loop may be expected to last at least fifteen years with regular cleaning. Carpet must be antistatic to avoid problems with computer terminals. Low maintenance is another important consideration in an age of budget restrictions, so a multitoned tweed is preferable to solid colors. Loop construction will resist wear in high-traffic areas, such as aisles and around study stations. To prevent the carpet from being overly obtrusive, it should contain subdued accenting colors that reflect primarily the color and material of the end panels.

Until quite recently, nylon was the only suitable carpet material. Its colorfastness and wearing qualities were superior to those of competing products. Antistatic backing, made of a charcoal substance, reduced the risk to computers. Today, polypropylene (or olefin) carpets match the characteristics of nylon but cost less. Some of these products are specifically designed for use in computerized environments and use woven-in metal filaments to dissipate static charges. They come in 32-ounce weight and feature antizippering, which prevents long strands from being pulled loose if a loop is torn away from the backing. An investment in high-quality carpet is economical in the long run, because it is a costly proposition to move ranges of shelving in order to replace the floor covering.

Carpet tiles are an expensive alternative to broadloom, and are sometimes selected when building codes permit flat wiring to be used. If the cost is acceptable, this is a bona fide reason to select carpet tiles. Future replacement of worn patches with new tiles is not a persuasive argument in favor of carpet tiles, because the colors will not match after the passage of time. If broadloom is chosen, we recommend against underlay for two reasons: (1) rolling book carts will eventually cause "delamination" and buckling of the carpet, and (2) shelving ranges are more stable if their glides rest close to the concrete slab.[53]

Areas of highest traffic—the entryway and around the circulation desk—probably should be floored with quarry tile. If the entire area is carpeted, then a sufficient quantity should be purchased initially to allow replacement of worn areas at least once before complete re-carpeting is scheduled. Glazed tile with a matte finish is preferable to the unglazed type, because it is easier to maintain; 8-inch-by-8-inch squares are recommended for coverage of larger areas. Because tile is among the last components to be selected, it is relatively easy to choose a color that harmonizes with the carpeting and the end panels. Terrazzo is an alternative to tile, but must be treated with an antiskid coating because it is a slipping hazard when wet.

Artwork and Display Areas

Publicly funded projects may require that a small percentage of the construction budget be set aside for external or internal artwork. A committee generally makes recommendations, selects appropriate art, or commissions its creation. Assistance from a state agency may be forthcoming and is certainly appreciated. Some projects may include an art gallery within the library building, but even those that do not have a special facility can use the library's ample wall space to hang artworks in various media, such as architectural textiles or large paintings.

An important rule when considering interior decoration is to avoid any permanent embellishments to the building's fabric. Paintings usually are locked in place to discourage theft, but can be removed by using the correct tool. Anything that can be hung also can be removed later and replaced with something else. As with any other design element, art cannot be allowed to interfere with building function. This will not happen if, for example, there is a decision to provide a decorative floor in the lobby. The entranceway is a stable element, even if, in the distant future, the library building should acquire a different function (fig. 37). External works of art, such as statuary, fall into the same category of "permanent installation," though not every artistic sensibility may appreciate their form.

Provision of lockable display space within the library's precincts is advisable, because there will always be requests for it. Libraries are evolving toward community facilities whose role is broader than support for study and research. Visitors expect the library to assume a cultural role that may go beyond traditional functions. To some extent, the library is custodian and curator of its campus's history. This function alone demands that some provision be made for the public display of relevant artifacts. Study areas should be programmed with this expectation in mind.

Creature Comforts and Access

Study and learning are no longer construed as solitary activities devoid of social contact. The new emphasis on collaborative learning is reflected in the number of group studies programmed for academic libraries. Demand

FIGURE 37
Entrance at WSU

is growing for twenty-four-hour access to the library's facilities, not just its study areas (which, in any case, are fully integrated and not isolatable spaces). Quite apart from the staffing implications, how accommodating can the library reasonably be to nocturnal or hungry users, or to those accompanied by infants?

Demands are rising to relax the prohibition on eating and drinking in the library, and even to include snack bars and coffee shops within the building proper. Jacques Barzun attributes the following words to a dean "at a college in the Northeast (1998)": "This library will surprise you. . . . The coffee bar is as far from the image of the old [library] as you can get. We're thinking of the library as a social space as well as a study space."[54] However inhospitable it may seem, we contend that an academic library is not to be compared to national-chain bookstores that offer food for both mind and body. Libraries are custodians of easily damaged materials and equipment that do not need external threats from spilled coffee and ketchup-laden burgers. A library cannot be cleaned as easily as the local fast-food outlet. Debris will accumulate and contribute to preservation problems already complicated by acid-content paper, UV radiation, insects, and other direct threats to longevity. Food, drink, tobacco products, and libraries have been, and remain, a lethal brew.

Although libraries cannot (or should not) feed the hungry and slake the thirst of caffeine addicts, they may consider offering services to their nontraditional clientele. The new library at Middle Tennessee State University, for example, serves a student body that includes a significant number of parents with small children. Several changing rooms are available for students accompanied by infants. Depending on the institution's particular circumstances, this may be an accommodation worth making.

Academic libraries are becoming social venues as they add such electronic services as information arcades and offer greater support to collaborative learning. They need to be designed to fulfill an enhanced public function, but within reason. Libraries remain places dedicated primarily to study and research, activities that depend increasingly on a communications infrastructure tied to network access. Technology is now assumed to be part of a new building's fabric, where it is ubiquitous but unobtrusive. Furnishings and equipment, together with interior design and lighting, should promote a seamless interface between the library user and information technology. That is the essence of the library's role as a high-tech gateway.

Notes

1. J. C. R. Licklider, *Libraries of the Future* (Cambridge, Mass.: MIT Press, 1965).

2. From "So Long, Frank Lloyd Wright" by Paul Simon, Columbia Records, 1970.

3. John W. Focke, FAIA, "The new American library: Technological, educational, and social changes are redefining traditional roles," *Texas Library Journal* 73 (3): 116–117 (fall 1997).

4. B. J. Novitski, "Architect-client design collaboration," *Architecture* 83 (6): 132 (June 1994).

5. Brian L. Hawkins, "The unsustainability of the traditional library and the threat to higher education," in *The Mirage of Continuity: Reconfiguring Academic Information Resources for the 21st Century*, ed. Brian L. Hawkins and Patricia Battin (Washington, D.C.: Council on Library and Information Resources and Association of American Universities, 1998), 139.

6. Jerry Laiserin, "Meeting client expectations," *Architecture* 86 (5): 190 (May 1997).

7. Aaron Cohen and Elaine Cohen, *Designing and Space Planning for Libraries: A Behavioral Guide* (New York: R. R. Bowker, 1979), 67.

8. Robert H. Rohlf, "Library design: What *not* to do," *American Libraries* 17 (2): 100–104 (February 1986).

9. The indispensable guide to all aspects of library-building planning is Philip D. Leighton and David C. Weber, *Planning Academic and Research Library Buildings*, 3d ed. (Chicago: American Library Association, 1999).

10. Margaret Beckman, "Cost 'avoidance' in library building planning: What, where, when, why, who?" *Canadian Library Journal* 47 (6): 405 (December 1990).

11. David J. Jones, "Staying smart: Challenges of library design in the 1990s," *Australian Library Journal* 42 (3): 220 (August 1993). All library planners should read this significant article.

12. Ibid., 221.

13. Michael W. Matier and C. Clinton Sidle, "What size libraries for 2010?" *Planning for Higher Education* 21 (4): 14 (summer 1993). The foregoing paragraph is based on this article.

14. Metcalf, *Planning Academic and Research Library Buildings*, 724.

15. Beckman, "Cost 'avoidance,'" 407.

16. Sam Robb, "Pass to compliance," *American School and University* 70 (11): 36ff (July 1998).

17. Allan B. Veaner, "1985 to 1995: The next decade in academic librarianship, part I," *College & Research Libraries* 46 (3): 222 (May 1985).

18. Richard D. Hacken, "Tomorrow's research library: Vigor or rigor mortis?" *College & Research Libraries* 49 (6): 489 (November 1988).

19. Mark Weiser, "The computer for the 21st century," *Scientific American* 265 (3): 94 (September 1991).

20. This and other useful advice is found in Andrea and David Michaels, "Designing for technology in today's libraries," *Computers in Libraries* 12 (10): 8–15 (November 1992).

21. Michael Trinkley, *Preservation Concerns in Construction and Remodeling of Libraries: Planning for Preservation* (September 1992), ERIC, ED 355959, p. 38.

22. Angus Snead Macdonald, "A library of the future, part I," *Library Journal* 58 (21): 971–975 (December 1, 1933).

23. Kenneth E. Toombs, "The evolution of academic library architecture: A summary," *Journal of Library Administration* 17 (4): 29 (1992); and David Kaser, "Twenty-five years of academic library building planning," *College & Research Libraries* 45 (4): 274 (July 1984).

24. In 1989, 52 percent of reported job-related injuries were caused by this activity. Mark Randel, "PC accessories can ease the PC blues," *Office* 113 (5): 12 (May 1991).

25. Elizabeth B. Winstead, "Staff reactions to automation," *Computers in Libraries* 14 (4): 18–21 (April 1994); and Ganga Dakshinamurti, "Automation's effect on library personnel," *Canadian Library Journal* 42 (6): 343–351 (December 1985).

26. "Standards for College Libraries, 1995 Edition, Draft," *College & Research Libraries News* 55 (5): 261 (May 1994).

27. Cynthia A. Gal et al., "Territoriality and the use of library study tables," *Perceptual and Motor Skills* 63 (2): 567–574 (1986).

28. One such program is AutoCAD, which is IBM-compatible and has been used successfully in several U.S. locations. See "Action exchange," *American Libraries* 20 (5): 412 (May 1989).

29. Paul Eshelman and Kesia Tatchell, "How beneficial a tool is computer-aided design?" *Human Ecology Forum* 20 (1): 18 (winter 1992).

30. A clear description of the modeling process is found in Donald P. Greenberg, "Computers and architecture," *Scientific American* 264 (2): 104–109 (February 1991).

31. Thomas Fisher, "Electrifying floors," *Progressive Architecture* 67 (2): 120 (February 1986).

32. Elaine Cohen, "The architectural and interior design process," *Library Trends* 42 (3): 552 (winter 1994).

33. Alex Hills, "Terrestrial wireless networks," *Scientific American* 278 (4): 76 (April 1998).

34. Clifton Dale Foster, "A wireless future: College and university libraries unplugged," *Broadening Our Horizons: Information, Services, Technology—Proceedings of the 1996 CAUSE Annual Conference* <http://www.educause.edu/asp/doclib>.

35. Charlie Tuller and Diana Oblinger, "Information technology as a transformation agent," *CAUSE/EFFECT* 20 (4): 39 (winter 1997–1998).

36. Philip D. Leighton and David C. Weber, "The influence of computer technology on academic library buildings: A slice of recent history," in *Academic Librarianship Past, Present, and Future: A Festschrift in Honor of David Kaser*, ed. John Richardson Jr. and Jinnie Y. Davis (Englewood, Colo.: Libraries Unlimited, 1989), 25.

37. David C. Weber, "The future capital funding of university library buildings," *IFLA Journal* 16 (3): 315 (1990).

38. David Leroy Michaels, "Technology's impact on library interior planning," *Library Hi Tech* 5 (4): 60 (winter 1987).

39. Charlene S. Hurt, "A vision of the library of the 21st century," *Journal of Library Administration* 15 (3/4): 9 (1991); Richard J. Bazillion, "Personal computing and academic library design in the 1990s," *Computers in Libraries* 12 (3): 10–12 (March 1992); and Richard J. Bazillion and Connie Braun, "Academic library design: Building a 'teaching instrument,'" *Computers in Libraries* 14 (2): 12–16 (February 1994).

40. Robert C. Heterick, "The shoemaker's children," *EDUCOM Review* (May/June 1994): 60.

41. Eric Rockwell, "The seven deadly sins of architects," *American Libraries* 20 (4): 307 (April 1989). This article is essential reading.

42. Elaine Cohen, "Analyzing architectural and interior design plans," *Library Administration and Management* 1 (3): 91 (June 1987).

43. Charles C. Soule, *How to Plan a Library Building for Library Work* (Boston: Boston Book Company, 1912), 114.

44. Stewart Brand, *How Buildings Learn: What Happens After They're Built* (New York: Viking Press, 1994), 166.

45. Quoted in Brand, *How Buildings Learn*, 166.

46. J. Russell Bailey, "Mr. Architect, listen," *Library Journal* 90 (21): 50 (December 1, 1965).

47. Cohen and Cohen, *Designing and Space Planning for Libraries*, 191.

48. Peter Barna, "The light of color," *Interiors* 89 (September 1989): 62, 66.

49. Cohen and Cohen, *Designing and Space Planning*, 189–191.

50. Vincent Scully, *Architecture: The Natural and the Manmade* (New York: St. Martin's Press, 1991), 202–203.

51. Philip M. Bennett, "Users come first in design: Physiological, psychological, and sociological factors," *Wisconsin Library Bulletin* 74 (March 1978): 54.

52. Rohlf, "Library design: What *not* to do," 104.

53. Evelyn Minick et al., "Carpeting your library," *College & Research Libraries News* 55 (7): 410–412 (July/August 1994).

54. Jacques Barzun, *From Dawn to Decadence: 500 Years of Western Cultural Life—1500 to the Present* (New York: HarperCollins, 2000), 784.

CHAPTER 4

Furnishing, Equipping, and Staffing the Building

In light of all the combined wisdom and good intentions, what conspires to thwart the quest for a smart library? Apart from the universal challenge of funding, two major inhibitions are ignorance and inflexibility.[1]

Establishing a Budget

To arrive at a budget for furnishings, fittings, and equipment (FFE) and technology, begin with 30 percent of the estimated construction cost. This amount, in addition to FFE, includes all fees, tests, and inspections that the project is expected to incur. The actual budget assigned to FFE depends on the type of building being designed. A library, for example, will require less office furniture than a building that houses faculty, but considerably more shelving. Steel shelving represents less cost per square foot of construction than does office furniture. Consequently, the budget for furnishings and equipment may be somewhat less for a library, depending on the amount of technology that is programmed. Vendors are generally willing to supply ballpark estimates to help planners build their FFE budget. Actual costs, of course, are discovered during the bidding process.

One important consideration that has budgetary implications is the level of quality desired. A building intended to serve for many years requires durable furnishings. An investment in the highest quality permitted by the budget will repay itself many times over. Study furniture, subjected to the depredations of undergraduates, should last upwards of thirty years, and products are on the market that can meet this standard. Before compiling a list of "equals" for bidding purposes, it is wise to visit factories and observe manufacturing processes. This is the best way to get a feel for quality differences and the real distinctions between competing brands. Also, be aware of the results of furniture stress-tests, such as those sponsored by the American Library Association. Always accept offers to send sample items, such as chairs, tables, and carrels. It is especially important to subject task and study chairs to rigorous, day-to-day on-site evaluation. Only then can a proper decision be made.

Furniture comes in two varieties: custom-built and manufacturer's stock. Large companies offer standard lines in various price ranges through their catalog and may also do custom work according to a client's requirements. The big decision is whether standard designs will fit the ambience of a new building, or whether something unique is a better choice. All manufacturers offer wire-management systems, though it is important to ascertain whether these are UL-listed. Any new academic library will demand that virtually all study spaces be connected to the network. Furniture that accommodates technology unobtrusively is the best. The goal is to have very few, if any, trailing wires once the furniture is in place. Power and data cables must connect with floor plugs in such a way that they cannot be kicked loose.

Durable work surfaces are essential. Plastic laminate is the most common material used on carrels and study tables. Because libraries almost always are overilluminated, colors and textures that are less reflective work best. This is especially true in libraries that admit a fair quantity of natural light. Those using portable computers will appreciate reduced glare. Very high use surfaces, such as circulation desks, may need tougher materials, for example, finished hardwood or Corian. Everywhere in the library—walls, floors, rest rooms, furnishings—the emphasis has to be on durable materials and finishes. Money spent this way will be repaid in lower maintenance and replacement costs in the years ahead. Consequently, an adequate FFE budget has to be provided at the project's outset.

All project-management teams include someone, often the architect or owner's representative, who monitors budgets. Weighing price against quality, while staying within budget, is part of the process of selecting the best products that can be afforded. Compromise is part of this picture, but never at the expense of the project's integrity. Affordability is certainly one criterion in judging competing products. Balanced against it are long-term requirements of serviceability directly related to how well the furniture is made. *Quality* is a relative term, but one that lends itself to empirical testing. The American Library Association, for example, supports a testing program for library furniture, and its publications compare the performance of various manufacturers' products. There is no substitute, however, for personal inspection by the potential customer. The project architect or interior designer can provide valuable assistance in establishing quality standards and in writing specifications that ensure customer satisfaction.

Project budgets build on the estimated cost-per-square-foot for construction of the required space. Thus, a library of 100,000 square feet at $125 per square foot will cost $12.5 million. Added to that will be the architect's fee of about 7 percent of all expenditures directly related to the contract, which also may include certain items of equipment, such as an exit security system. At least 15 percent of the construction budget should be allotted for fittings (e.g., signage, shelving, detection system), furnishings, and equipment (FFE). Information technology will drive FFE toward the 30 percent mark depending on how extensive the power and data grid is and how much computer equipment is to be installed. Budgeting too conservatively for FFE may result in a strain on the contingency (typically 10–11 percent of the construction budget), which by then may have been depleted by the inevitable change orders. Quality furnishings and equipment in sufficient quantity can be acquired only if the budget accommodates them from the outset.

Buildings envisioned by committees often exceed available funding, because initial programs typically try to satisfy everyone. Depending on the construction marketplace at the time of bidding, a building of desired size, and with all the requested amenities, may prove to be out of reach. Under such circumstances, it is better to sacrifice some square footage so as to afford quality furnishings. Design development is a process of compromise, but one that should never produce a library that is equipped with inferior furnishings. More than most public buildings, libraries suffer the ravages of heavy use and often abuse. Replacement of furniture inside twenty years is unlikely, so false economies should be avoided.

We recommend identifying a portion of the overall contingency for FFE demands that are certain to arise during the building's first year of service. There are always items that have been overlooked and must be purchased later. Coatracks, small utility tables, and additional computers are a few examples of afterthoughts with costs attached. Anticipate them because they are virtually inevitable in a complex project, such as a library. Be sure that there is a budget line for FFE contingencies, separate from the overall project contingency.

Developing and monitoring the FFE budget is a process that extends through the entire construction process. Publicly funded projects require that all FFE packages be bid competitively. Sometimes bidding produces happy surprises, such as lower prices for computers. The reverse can also happen, especially when the low bidder fails to offer quality and service. It is important, therefore, to have all quality standards spelled out in the bid documents. If a particular vendor is well known for supplying quality, it is possible to "sole-source" certain items, even on public projects. Private institutions, of course, may sidestep the bidding process altogether if they choose to do so.

Responsibility for budget monitoring falls to the institution's business office, the architect, or the owner's representative (whose role is discussed in chapter 2). Close attention to detail will prevent both unnecessary expenditures and premature depletion of budget lines. Several pairs of eyes on the balance sheet can avoid financial shocks as the project nears completion. The aim is always to obtain the highest quality for an affordable price.

Quality, Affordability, and the Bidding Process

There is a paradox inherent in all building projects: Although libraries are being transformed by information technology, the structures that house them are expected to last for many decades. Functions must be able to change and evolve within a set of walls that surround a library. If space is flexibly designed and the network is ubiquitous, realignment of services will be easier. Furnishings, though they can be moved around and reconfigured, are also part of the building's fabric, because they are expected to serve generations of students. Quality counts when longevity is demanded.

Because power and data to the work surface are essential in all new academic libraries, thought must be given to the construction of all items of furniture. Wood study tables with plastic laminate tops and quality core materials (lumber, plywood, particleboard, timberflake) may be purchased from several well-known manufacturers or built to specification by an independent factory. Standard designs offer the best combination of durability and affordability. They need to be fitted with power and data modules capable of withstanding heavy usage; these, unlike the tables themselves, are easily replaced as necessary. Tables and carrels have to be built for the long haul. Economy is not a virtue in furniture selection. It is better to buy fewer items of quality and to add to the inventory over time than to purchase a full supply of poor-quality furniture.

Adequate power and data modules for tabletop installation are difficult to find. Some are simply awkward to use; others promise to be maintenance headaches. Several months of searching finally turned up a suitable item for the Winona State project, apparently durable and easy to install. The furniture manufacturer placed an order, only to discover some weeks later that his electrical supplier had changed the specifications. Meanwhile, tables had been shipped to the new library. We found ourselves having to solve this problem in the field, with no help at all from the vendor who caused it. The lesson for all of us is to obtain written guarantees from suppliers whose product specifications well may be subject to change without notice. It is the architect's job to make sure that furniture adequately accommodates the power and data modules, a task that sometimes turns out to be more complicated than expected.

Chairs, which are subject to the highest level of abuse, require special scrutiny. Librarians should expect to evaluate dozens of task and study chairs before attempting to balance price and quality. Time devoted to this process is a worthwhile investment, especially if an argument for good seating needs to be made on economic grounds. Manufacturers of high-quality chairs should be willing to extend a multi-year warranty at no extra cost. There is no reason to accept less than twenty years of service from a wood study chair. One-and-one-half-inch tubular steel will do as well, if you like that look.

Campuses often engage their architectural firm to oversee and organize the process of acquiring furnishings. Working closely with the client, the architect will establish specifications and prepare bid packages. All concerned typically agree that certain products by a particular manufacturer will be the standard against which competing items are judged. Standard-setting is not a theoretical exercise. Furniture has to be evaluated on-site and factories visited to assess how well it is made. References need to be checked and test results analyzed. Once this is done, a list of equals can be created before bidding occurs. This process, which usually takes longer than anticipated, protects the library from falling victim to a low bidder presenting itself as an equal. It is the owner's prerogative, in the end, to decide what is equal and what is not. "Alternatives" should be permitted only when the library wishes to have the ability to choose a preferred, more-expensive item if it can do so and still remain within the budget.

Shopping can happen spontaneously. When a library construction project is awarded, eager furniture vendors descend on both the architect and the home institution. There is usually no lack of competitors for the status of "standard" and "equal." Almost all vendors are willing to supply product samples for evaluation. There may be a veritable flood of items when the project is a large one. Visits to representatives' showrooms and furniture factories occur at the companies' expense, and their hospitality should not be declined if quality is a primary consideration.

Only one or two librarians can travel consistently: The same people, insofar as possible, should make the visits and initial selections. All library staff, however, deserve a voice in the evaluation process, because they are the ones who must live with the chosen products. If offices and work spaces are to be furnished with modular units, then staff should choose the modules they desire. Furniture shopping, in fact, is a good way to involve staff members in the project and to share ownership of it with them. It also helps to overcome the inevitable fears and misgivings that arise as moving day nears. Staff who may have responded eagerly to the announcement of a new library building may find their enthusiasm cooling as reality sets in. Nostalgia and commitment to old, familiar ways become more evident as time passes. Because a new building presents the opportunity to do things differently, all means of reinforcing team spirit need to be used. Shopping can help to do this.

In planning the bidding process, it is useful to keep in mind that most furniture manufacturers have a lead time of at least ninety days between receipt of a firm order and delivery of the merchandise. If you expect timely and superior installation, it is best not to back your supplier into a corner. At least as much time is needed to select and obtain furnishings as to work out the building's physical design. In both contexts, it is largely the librarian's responsibility to assert the primacy of function over form. Architects normally do not do so on their own.

Once a furniture contract is awarded, the buyer is in the vendor's hands. A performance bond offers some protection against the supplier's bankruptcy or unavoidable nonperformance. It can do nothing, however, in the face of "reasonable delay" and other annoyances. Reputation is the best guide to potential performance, and ought to figure next to value-for-money in the establishment of the standard. Keep in mind from the outset that the library (probably) has only one loading dock. Staging of deliveries is critical to a successful installation; vendors, having been given the opportunity to perform well, had better be prepared to do so. Otherwise, chaos may reign at the loading dock when shipments that should have arrived in sequence turn up simultaneously.

In public institutions, the bidding process is mandated by law or regulation. Sole-sourcing of items may be difficult. Sometimes there are state contracts with particular companies that simplify things and enable the purchase of products of proven quality. Private institutions may be able to spare themselves some of the aggravations of bidding, but they should not necessarily avoid the bidding process altogether. Competition, provided it occurs among established equals, can yield better prices. Whether operating in the public or private domain, however, librarians should take the proper steps to ensure they eventually receive the quality they expect. The key to success is research.

Shelving and Furniture

Several well-known companies specialize in library furniture, either of a standard design or custom-made. A variety of materials and finishes capable of supporting virtually any interior-design conception is available. The same is true of library shelving, produced by vendors in both the United States and Canada. Cross-border shopping benefits from the North American Free Trade Agreement (NAFTA), which eliminated tariffs on most manufactured products. Large quantities of library furnishings made in Canada find a ready market in the United States, thanks in no small part to the weak Canadian dollar. Librarians thus have a wide choice and can focus on obtaining the highest quality in products and service.

The first step is to define quality standards, then to write specifications so tightly that unacceptable alternates cannot insinuate themselves during the bidding process. Because the architect presides over specification-writing and the call for bids, close collaboration is a necessity. The owner's representative (discussed in chapter 2) can help to ensure that all the safeguards are in place before the bid documents are released. Coordination at all stages of bidding, ordering, manufacture, and delivery must occur, if the building is to open on schedule and with its major components in place.

Shelving

The industry standard is steel-cantilever shelving, slotted to accommodate dividers, and no narrower than 9 inches if intended for use in an academic library (fig. 38). Wood shelving, however attractive it may be, does not stand up well both to normal wear and tear and to the constant shifting of shelves that accompanies library collection growth. If the library's current inventory does not meet this standard, arrangements should be made to replace it as part of the building project. A number of companies manufacture steel shelving. Generally speaking, all brands are sturdy enough to give years of satisfactory service. They differ from each other in such respects as gauge of metal, assembly, finish, and color options. Desirable features are:

> 16-gauge uprights and 18-gauge shelves (minimum standard)
>
> unitary construction of legs and uprights so that bolting together is unnecessary
>
> minimal use of bolting in the installation of end panels and top plates
>
> epoxy-powder-coat finish, which is superior to enamel paints
>
> range of colors, both standard offerings and special orders
>
> welded-frame construction as required by law in earthquake zones
>
> slotted shelves for dividers, to assist in controlling "slumping" of shelved materials

FIGURE 38
Library shelving

Existing shelving that is serviceable in other respects may be equipped with new end panels in a more acceptable color, or perhaps with panels made of wood or plastic laminate. Many choices of color and finish facilitate the creation of whatever atmosphere library designers wish.

Steel shelving comes in several standard colors, with custom colors available at a substantial premium. Manufacturers offer many patterns of plastic laminate for end panels. If wood is preferred, the options typically are oak, maple, or birch, sawn and finished according to taste and budget. The point is that the choices of carpet, upholstery fabric, work surfaces, and wall paint follow from the color selected for the shelving and end panels. Once the dominant color is in place, subsequent decisions have a focus. Shelving color may become an issue, especially if an inexperienced architect tries to use it as a design feature. Vincent Scully's comment warning against built-in accent colors is relevant here: Once miles of shelving are in place, they constitute a permanent addition to the interior landscape. The color should blend with the interior design and not call attention to itself. Standard colors are best, because it will cost far less to order additional components later on. The finish should be epoxy-powder coat, not enamel, which is prone to chipping.

Whether or not shelving is dressed up with kick plates, top plates, and custom end panels is a local decision. Painted-metal or wood end panels do offer the opportunity to create a finished and aesthetically pleasing environment in the stack areas. If the budget will accommodate them, use them. Take care to harmonize the carpet and any other areas of color with end panel colors to avoid a clash of shades. This is especially true if colored plastic laminates are used on tables, carrels, and service-point desks.

When bid documents are prepared, the following points ought to be included:

minimum gauges of metal that are acceptable

dimensions of all component parts

type of construction

color and finish of shelving, uprights, and end panels

type of bracing required by code, e.g., floor bolts, cross-ties

responsibility of the vendor for checking of shipments, installation, and so on

trade-in arrangements for existing inventory that will not be used in the new building

expected delivery date

length of time that quoted prices are to remain valid

Before selecting the winning bid, evaluate a sample of the product and, if possible, visit the plant that produced it. Because the investment in shelving may involve hundreds of thousands of dollars, making the proper choice is crucial. Factors to be considered are sturdiness, appearance, ease of assembly, and, where relevant, ability to withstand seismic shocks.

Shelving installation typically is carried out under the supervision of a manufacturer's representative, using local labor. Because the building module is based on the linear dimensions of shelving ranges, library staff already know how many sections will fit between columns and how wide the aisles will be. One way to ensure that placement is uniform and square is to lay out the footprint of each range with masking tape. Installers then follow these footprints, leveling each range as they go. The taping process is tedious, but speeds up installation and thus reduces labor costs.

Shelving ranges must be level and stable before being loaded. It is important to choose shelving with sturdy leveling glides that have enough extension to cope with imperfections in the concrete slab. Residual cambering, intended to settle out over a period of years, may complicate the job of leveling. If the raw slab has no finishing coat, the glides have to compensate for dips and ridges in the floor. High-quality steel shelving is quite forgiving in this respect.

Many libraries install mobile or compact shelving to gain greater storage capacity within a much smaller footprint. There is a choice between manual and motorized compact shelving, with selection dependent mainly on financial considerations. Quality is more difficult to judge than in the case of open-stack shelving, because important mechanical features are hidden from view. Mobile shelving runs on rails that are set either in the floor slab or in raised flooring. All brands have safety features that prevent browsers from being injured by moving carriages. In deciding which brand to specify, it is important to visit installations and talk with owners. Research and testing are the best guarantors of a sound purchasing decision.

Furniture

Because so many types and quality levels of furniture are available, the bidding process demands careful preparation. Low bids cannot be allowed to determine the outcome. It is perfectly acceptable, indeed advisable, to ask for samples to be evaluated on-site for a period of time. This is especially important in the case of seating, which ought to be thoroughly use-tested before being ordered. Manufacturers whose products are of special interest should be willing to supply samples and to assist in preparing preliminary budget estimates. Once the design and construction features are noted, exact specifications for manufacture can be written. Serious bidders will be prepared to cooperate with a potential customer to ensure that the results are satisfactory.

Planners may wish to make office furniture the subject of a third bidding process. The reason for separating the shelving, study furniture, and office furniture is to allow for better control over the furnishings and equipment budget. Librarians probably will have a priority listing of these items, and will be prepared to defer purchase of some of them if the budget is tight. Manufacturers of different types of equipment require varying lead times between order and delivery. It is therefore convenient to wrap up one category before focusing attention on the next. Assuming that the library is doing its own bidding, rather than using the services of a consultant, this procedure is likely to prove more manageable. If the architect is engaged to provide this service, vigilance is still necessary. It is easy for the librarians to lose control over their own project by allowing architects too much latitude in furniture selection.

Pressures associated with designing, bidding, and laying out a new building may force specific issues, such as furniture selection, into the background, at least temporarily. Sometimes other authorities are responsible for purchasing furniture, and may do so without a librarian's involvement. Furniture that is expected to last as long as twenty or thirty years should not be chosen by someone—perhaps an interior designer or a purchasing agent—who is not as well "attuned to the needs of staff and users as the library manager is."[2] Furniture has to be both functional and durable if it is to perform satisfactorily for a long time. Cheap, poorly designed furniture can compromise any project, regardless of the beauty or functionality of the building itself. Considering the anticipated life span of library furniture, it is best to treat it as part of the building's fabric and to buy for maximum durability. Furniture selection requires patience and the willingness to do comparison shopping. Whenever possible, visit the factory of potential suppliers. Observation of the manufacturing process is the best way to understand how good furniture is designed, built, and finished. If study carrels and tables are to contain wire-management systems, it is instructive to see how these are made. This inspection may suggest improvements in the design. Functionality and durability may both be judged on the basis of firsthand knowledge of how the furniture is produced and assembled. Comparison also may be made between wood veneer and plastic laminates, or among particleboard, plywood, and lumber as alternative core materials. In no case should a salesperson's pitch be accepted as gospel. There is no substitute for personal scrutiny.

If there is to be widespread use of wood—in millwork, study furniture, and accents—type of wood and finish are important considerations. Maple, birch, and oak are light woods that complement an interior into which plenty of natural light is to be introduced. Various manufacturers offer wood study carrels designed to provide privacy, a generous work surface, and wire-management systems essential in an electronic environment. Carrels with wood-paneled sides fit well into an academic-library setting, because they are substantial in appearance and are easily wired. Study tables constructed in a complementary style provide a different kind of study space. In both cases, librarians will find that a high-quality plastic laminate work surface reduces maintenance problems. These laminates also can be found in many colors and textures, including wood grains, so they can be used to tie together the library's overall color scheme. Never choose a solid-color laminate, especially white and its variants. Students treat such surfaces as a *tabula rasa* on which to scribble. A patterned laminate offers a somewhat weaker temptation to graffiti artists. We have tussled with architects on exactly this issue, and are pleased with our decision to reject their proposal of a white laminate.

Study Furniture

Specially equipped study stations are required for reasons nicely described by Heather Edwards in her book on library design:

> The fully electronic library . . . will provide reader stations able to accommodate a wide variety of hardware, and storage systems for a diverse collection of software. It will be conceived as a learning and information center rather than a collection of bookshelves and study spaces.[3]

In this type of library, the study carrel is both a work space and a node on the campus information network.

The carrel is today more than a piece of furniture intended for private study; it is in fact a scholar's workstation. "[L]ibraries," according to Philip Young, "will provide many of these . . . cubicles instead of vast banks of public terminals or work tables, and the building will take on a more individualized atmosphere."[4] Libraries are obliged to provide network access, but not necessarily computers themselves. There is no need, contrary to Richard Boss's advice in the 1980s, to provide study carrels large enough to accommodate desktop PCs and CD-ROM drives.[5] If the library boasts an information gallery, like that at Winona State University, special carousels indeed will be needed for larger computers and their peripherals (fig. 39), but carrels somewhat larger than traditional models will accommodate notebook-computer users.

We recommend, as noted in chapter 3, study carrels with work surfaces 42 inches wide and about 30 inches deep.[6] Proper height is a matter of debate among designers. If chairs are adjustable, then 28¼ inches is the optimum for keyboard use. If not, and it is unlikely that ergonomically designed study chairs can be afforded for student use, we advise a height of

FIGURE 39
Information Gallery at WSU

29 inches for carrels and tables.[7] This is a compromise solution that is reasonably friendly to computer users and that minimally satisfies ADA requirements. Special accommodation may have to be made for wheelchairs, but that cannot have the effect of restricting handicapped users to certain parts of the library where compliant furniture is located. A number of height-adjustable carrel work surfaces should be located throughout the building. Power and communications outlets should be located conveniently, so that personal computers can be connected easily. Power and data modules fit nicely into the corners of carrels (fig. 40). Tables offer several possibilities: half-sphere modules on the tabletop or connections in the table's skirt or legs. "Pop-up" modules are not advisable, because of their fragility (fig. 41). Multiple power outlets will allow computer users to plug in their own portable printers. Those who prefer to use remote printers can send their jobs over the network to the location of choice, which may be the library's print room or other local printers.

Wiring of tables, in particular, poses a few challenges. If multiple data ports are provided, each table requires a hub and power bar. One data and one power cable run down a hollow leg to floor boxes. Ideally, the junction is structural so that there is no danger of dislodging plugs by kicking them (fig. 42). Outlets should be below floor level, so that the connections cannot be accidentally kicked apart. A great deal of thought and investigation is needed to identify suitable equipment and to coordinate the floor boxes

FIGURE 40
Carrel-mounted power and data module

FIGURE 41
Pop-up power and data module

FIGURE 42
Study table with power and data connection in floor

with the furniture plans. Failure to invest the necessary time is sure to produce unsatisfactory results. To avoid subsequent problems, the architects should address these wiring issues early in design development.

Perfectly acceptable production-line furniture is available from several reputable manufacturers. A bit of research will identify leads that are worth pursuing. Some companies may be willing to modify their standard designs, especially because most of them already offer wire-management systems to facilitate computer use. Libraries planning to integrate information technology into their fabric, however, well may find themselves involved in designing furniture to suit specific needs. In such cases, customization is the route to follow. Only those wire management systems that are UL-listed should be chosen, so as to make installation easier and to meet local electrical codes.

Aligning study furniture with power and data receptacles in walls and floors requires meticulous planning. Four 42-inch-by-30-inch carrels will fit between the columns that define a 30-foot bay, with adequate room for chairs to be moved back. Receptacles are covered by the furniture, which should have grommet holes in the proper location to provide direct access to outlets. The aim is to keep wires completely out of sight. Wiring tables is more difficult, because receptacles must be accurately located when concrete is poured. If this job is done carelessly, it will destroy the furniture plan. Ensure that the furniture icons in the architect's CAD program are indeed properly dimensioned. If they are even slightly off, the furniture plan will not work. Do your own measuring to confirm that all dimensions are correct. The whole point is that computer use must be designed into a building, not simply added on.

While on the subject of study furniture, chairs deserve additional mention (fig. 43). No piece of furniture will receive more abuse. Large persons will rear backward, thus placing great stress on two legs. In northern climates, where salt, grit, and mud accompany the seasons, there may be good reason to avoid chairs with upholstered seats. Students inevitably will use chairs as footstools, especially when working on portable computers. Salt runoff will soon degrade any fabric and will break down ordinary varnishes. It therefore may be advisable to select a wood chair, with metal-to-metal fastenings, that has a catalyzed urethane finish. Such a product should be impervious to ordinary wear and tear and abusive treatment. Compromise between comfort and durability may be necessary, but that is a local decision. The investment in quality chairs, however, will be repaid more quickly than almost any other in the library's furnishings.

The best way to identify a suitable chair and to compare various brands is to check test results published by the American Library Association in *Library Technology Reports* (latest results are in the March/April 1995 issue). The rigorous testing program subjects production-line chairs to the stresses they will endure over time in an academic library, the majority of whose clientele consists of young adults. Selecting several hundred chairs, most of which must last upwards of twenty years, represents

FIGURE 43
Various study chairs

an important purchasing decision. Choosing the right chair, in fact, is one of the most time-consuming parts of a building project. Design, comfort, and durability have to be carefully weighed. If a bidding process is required, it is essential to know which chairs are truly equivalent in quality. Structurally sound chairs, because of their number and cost, are the most critical pieces of furniture in the library. Try to obtain an extended warranty, because the passage of time may reveal design or construction defects that the manufacturer must rectify.

Leisure-Reading Areas

Another space that deserves mention before leaving the subject of furnishings and equipment is the library's leisure-reading area. If the architect has been able to provide a suitable space, it is a good idea to accommodate those who wish to browse through newspapers, current journals, or escapist literature. Seating should be comfortable, to be sure, but not to the extent that readers are encouraged to slumber. Access to electric power and communications will assist those who wish to commune with their notebook computer under somewhat more relaxed circumstances (fig. 44). Lounge furniture also must be very durable, because students will consistently abuse it in their quest for the most

FIGURE 44
Lounge area at WSU

comfortable position. As with everything else covered by the FFE budget, you get what you pay for—sometimes. Before selecting leisure seating, become familiar with its construction. In the furniture business, only the strong survives the abuse it will endure.

Staff Work Space

Similar reasoning applies to the design of staff offices and work spaces, which should be comfortably furnished and harmoniously decorated. The idea that carpet belongs only in the executive offices is passé, so whatever is installed in the library proper should be extended into offices, staff rooms, seminar rooms, and other areas in which staff spend their hours on the job. A smaller technical-services staff in the twenty-first-century library can be provided with modular work spaces, using fabric-covered panels equipped with internal wire-management systems. The idea is to combine efficient work flow with an atmosphere that encourages a positive attitude toward the job. Modular furniture arrangements in wood, laminates, or other materials may be used in librarians' offices and elsewhere. Look for panels that can easily be removed to provide access to wall sockets and data connections.

Work surface height is of great concern in computerized areas, such as staff offices. Furniture designers recommend lowering the height from the old standard of 30 inches to either 28 or 28¼ inches. Adjustable chairs enable staff members to reach and use their keyboards comfortably, especially if there are keyboard shelves that pull out from beneath the work surface. Modular panel systems, with internal wiring, offer many alternative ways of configuring an open area into discrete work spaces. These systems can be complex and thus difficult to reorganize in the future. For this reason, the simplest layout is best. Computer-aided design (CAD) is very useful in determining workstation layouts; depending on the size of the project budget, modeling can either be simple or elaborate. In the second case, as explained in chapter 2, CAD also is able to simulate actual lighting conditions, material colors and textures, and, by means of video graphics, work-flow patterns throughout the area.

The rapid deployment of information technology has brought computers to every staff desktop in the library. Ergonomic work-space design, therefore, is a requirement, if compensation claims are to be controlled. Flat-screen technology has reduced the footprint of computer equipment on the desktop. Some libraries prefer a laptop machine that can also serve as a portable presentation device in electronic classrooms across the campus. Every computer quickly becomes obsolete, which is why machines should be leased rather than purchased. A three-year lease is an affordable alternative to the problem of obsolescence. Technology is such an important part of the work and learning environments on all campuses that up-to-date equipment is absolutely essential. This is especially true in universities that require students to lease laptop computers and that are committed to using technology as an educational tool.

Computer-Related Equipment and Staffing

Ideally, all computers and peripherals should be leased, so that the library is not encumbered with a large inventory of obsolete equipment within two years. That said, what types and quantities of computer-related machinery are needed? The answer depends on how the library earlier defined its mission in the building program. A library that considers itself a "teaching instrument" and a "gateway" will have specific technical requirements, based on certain assumptions about such matters as:

>　ubiquitous student access to computers
>
>　extent of Web-enhanced courses
>
>　faculty/student demand for high-end computing facilities
>
>　degree of interest in distance learning
>
>　depth of access to digital information resources
>
>　faculty demand for support in delivering courses electronically

Planners may safely assume that the educational applications of technology will expand, and that libraries will be part of this process. Consequently, the library's teaching and gateway roles will grow. Technology-infrastructure issues, therefore, will require close attention. These include:

>　the building's internal network and its link to the campus backbone
>
>　number of facilities, such as information commons and electronic classrooms
>
>　need for faculty-support space: e.g., development lab, studio classroom
>
>　need to support two platforms (Mac and PC)
>
>　printing needs
>
>　quantity and type of computer peripherals

All these matters receive attention during the design-development phase, but actual purchasing decisions should be deferred as long as possible so that the latest equipment is procured. If the campus is, or is intending to become, "laptop," then there is no need to equip study stations with computers. All they need is a convenient power and data connection. Classrooms, information commons, work areas, and support centers need to have appropriate equipment installed.

Every library- and information-related activity now relies heavily on computers. Librarians and staff should receive computers configured to do the job. This often does not mean the latest high-performance chip. Campus computer services can provide a recommendation and perform the installation work. Printing and fax needs are assessed early in the planning process, then adjusted in light of changing reality.

Computers installed in an information commons or development lab should have a standard software suite that can be supported locally. In addition, there may be specific programs that faculty have identified for their students, but which are of interest to several departments, for example, SPSS, Quark XPress, Adobe Illustrator, and so on. Although librarians should be able to assist with the standard suite, they may lack experience with specialized software. Peer tutoring or direct faculty intervention may have to occur. As far as technical problems are concerned, librarians (as we point out elsewhere) have to improve their hardware expertise, so as to be able to solve common problems, such as device conflicts, reinstallation of device drivers, computer-to-device communication failures, and so on.

No new academic library can prosper, however, unless it has its own technical staff. Qualified computer and network technicians must be housed in the library to ensure that problems receive prompt attention. Information technology demands mediation at all levels, including that of hardware. If the library is going to provide electronic access and research assistance, it is obliged to help users with computer equipment. This is perhaps the most significant way in which library service is changing in response to information technology. Both in expertise and mode of organization, librarians' roles are being transformed by technology's influence on teaching, learning, and research. There are profound implications for building design and for the activities carried out within that building.

A "wired" library is a very busy place, where people need lots of help with the technology. Demand far exceeds the ability of regular staff to respond. Student workers, therefore, are being recruited to provide assistance with both hardware and software. These students require training and space, two matters that building planners need to take into account. The success of such programs as STARS (Student Technology Advisors) at Wake Forest University demonstrates the vital role that student assistants now play in a campus information-technology infrastructure.[8]

Reorganizing Library Operations

An imminent move to new quarters offers a chance to reorganize library operations and thus to achieve efficiencies in space utilization and staff deployment. A year in advance of the move is not too early to begin planning, because there is time enough to involve all concerned in the process. The internal geography of buildings imposes its own logic on the activities that occur there. A new library is an opportunity to do things differently.

No matter how high the level of anticipation that precedes a move, the prospect of change can disrupt any organization. This is especially true of libraries, where long-standing routines breed an attachment to the status quo. Older staff members may resent the loss of familiar territory. Fear of the unknown can dampen enthusiasm quickly. In the interests of a smooth transition, involvement of all staff members in the planning process is essential.

Each higher-education institution has its own culture, within which planning must take place. At Winona State University, for example, librarians belong to the faculty union and are members of the library "department." In this environment, any plan is suspect that comes from the top down. A more effective approach was to make planning a collective effort, involving everyone who chose to participate. The result, with some nudging by the library administration, was a plan that fits the new building and covers the services to be offered there.

Many of those services involve the application of information technology to teaching and learning. Computer and networking facilities pervade the building and, by their very presence, create a new set of demands on library staff. Older staff members, who may have succeeded in evading technology in their former premises, now face the prospect of professional obsolescence. A few individuals may seek early retirement; others may confront new challenges with grace and determination. Yet there is no escaping the fact that modern academic libraries require staff who possess qualifications suited to an electronic information environment. When there is a full complement of tenured, senior librarians present, how are new, computer-based services to be offered?

One answer is to house information-technology staff (IT workers) in the library, thus ensuring that technical expertise is nearby. They can be based in an academic technologies center or network center within the library. Academic technologies, in fact, is one area in which the librarian's role is blending with that of the IT worker, as faculty demand more support in the process of adopting technology. The librarian's service ethic and familiarity with research techniques are especially germane to this situation. An obvious convergence of professional competencies is occurring, spurred on by the creation of sophisticated library facilities. Librarianship is undergoing a transformation, although one that is in its early stages at this point. In the meantime, libraries need the services of IT workers who are not, by education and inclination, librarians themselves. Building designers, in recognition of this fact, have to provide suitable accommodations.

A couple of examples, based on recent experience, will illustrate the point. Two years into the design process, Winona State decided to create an academic technologies center (ATC) and to locate it in space previously assigned to the media center (A/V department). University administration concluded that this vital faculty support service should be in the library, the campus information center. This decision led to another, namely to place all course and media servers in the ATC and make it the campus network center. The ATC now houses two types of IT workers: technicians and faculty whose specialty is applying technology to the teaching/learning process. Classroom faculty thus have two kinds of expertise available to them, as well as facilities in which to do their course-development work. There is, in addition, an electronic classroom in which faculty can experiment with Web-based teaching and the use of interactive television (ITV). ATC personnel, the instruction librarian, and the director of ITV all work with faculty in this setting.

As these examples show, several types of IT workers, including librarians, are members of the library staff. This is just the beginning of an evolutionary process through which academic libraries acquire a broader focus on the world of information resources. Buildings themselves both define and enable this new purpose; through their technological infrastructure, they also reveal the nature of their staffing requirements. If suitably qualified staff members are not on board when the new building opens, then every opportunity must be seized to hire them. One way to force the issue is simply to amalgamate library and computer services, as some institutions have done. Another, less-radical solution is to ensure that all new hires possess the skills to function, as librarians, in an IT environment. In this way, the service ethic long associated with librarians can be preserved, to the ultimate benefit of all library users.

As electronic information sources proliferate, the library's public-service function grows. Reorganization thus involves shifting human resources away from custodial functions, such as maintaining paper-journal collections, and toward "customer assistance." Technical-services departments continue to shrink as salary lines are moved elsewhere in the library. So extensive have online resources become that public service is the library's primary role. To be a knowledge gateway means to enable library users to find, evaluate, and use information stored in a variety of formats. Realignment of staff resources will help a library to meet this challenge, but organizational change is only half the battle. The rest is a matter of ongoing professional development, an obligation imposed on all librarians by the technological environment in which they now work. Clearly, a new building can itself be a change agent.

Notes

1. David J. Jones, "Staying smart: Challenges of library design in the 1990s," *Australian Library Journal* (August 1993): 224.

2. Carol R. Brown, *Selecting Library Furniture: A Guide for Librarians, Designers, and Architects* (Phoenix: Oryx Press, 1989), 1. This book is recommended as a comprehensive guide to furniture selection.

3. Heather M. Edwards, *University Library Building Planning* (Metuchen, N.J.: Scarecrow Press, 1990), 130.

4. Philip H. Young, "Visions of academic libraries in a brave new future," in *Libraries and the Future: Essays on the Library in the Twenty-first Century*, ed. F. W. Lancaster (New York: Haworth Press, 1993), 57.

5. Richard W. Boss, *Information Technologies and Space Planning for Libraries and Information Centers* (Boston: G. K. Hall, 1987), 68–69.

6. Study carrels in an academic library should be sized generously in order to accommodate "the transfer of information between paper and screen." Denis Heathcote and Peter Stubley, "Building services and environmental needs of information technology in academic libraries," *Program* 20 (3): 33 (January 1986). The dimensions recommended by these authors are, in our view, too cramped: 5.15 square feet of work surface.

7. David Leroy Michaels, "Technology's impact on library interior planning," *Library Hi Tech* 5 (4): 61 (winter 1987).

8. For more information, see <http://www.wfu.edu/Computer-information/STARS/index.html>.

CHAPTER 5

Occupying and Commissioning the New Building

The building occupancy and initial period of use can be a sore trial of the staff and a matter of grave disappointment to faculty and students if those final steps of occupying and operating a building are not as carefully managed as were the earlier stages in the planning process.[1]

Planning for Opening Day

Every new library building faces the pragmatic test of day-to-day usage. If its planners aspired to create more than just a storage facility, they will be curious about people's reactions to the environment and services now being unveiled. Planning for occupying and commissioning the new building begins early in the construction phase because of the need to keep university administrators, library staff members, and other interested parties up-to-date on project status and how the building will function once it is open to the public. Attention paid to these matters from the beginning of the project means that staff reorganization efforts, collection moving plans, inauguration of the building's internal networks, and so on will proceed smoothly.

Numerous questions will be asked and answered through observation of the building and the people working in it or using it throughout the first year. Are staff members satisfied with their new working conditions? Does the interior design achieve its goal of encouraging library users to linger? Is the building's internal network design as functional and robust as planned or needed? Do the electrical and mechanical systems work as advertised? What adjustments can and should be made in order to solve obvious problems? Are there construction deficiencies that need to be remedied while the building is still under warranty? How these questions came to be raised in the first place are the result of having spent many hours planning for and anticipating how the building will perform on opening day. The first step toward the goal of a completed library is shelving installation, closely followed by furniture deliveries and the move itself.

Organizing and Moving

A move involves more than the shifting of library materials, particularly when it is to a new building. Interior space will be organized so that all components are installed where they are intended to go: shelving, study tables and carrels, office assignments, and so on. Planning for the receipt of new furnishings that may be supplied by several different vendors will require some scheduling expertise. Deciding who will arrive when, with what, and where it should ultimately go is a complex task. Then, of course, there is the preparation of the library's collections for their transfer to their new home. All these things take plenty of time, and those who get involved in such assignments should be advised to begin almost as soon as the construction gets underway.

Appointment of a move coordinator is crucial to the success of this phase of the library building project. This individual will help to lay out the interior space, decide about the placement of furniture, participate in the installation of shelving and furniture, prepare the collections for moving, and oversee the move itself. Only one person can be charged with this responsibility. Having more than one will result in chaos and confusion, especially when vendors bring in teams from the outside to install shelving and furniture. A single contact person is even more important as the moving company begins the process of transferring the library's collections and other resources.

The library staff, for its part, will focus on getting ready to move to the new building. Staff will be asked to undertake a thorough house-cleaning so that only what is absolutely necessary will be moved. Each individual will be given responsibility for packing up his or her desk, as well as filing and supply cabinets, in boxes supplied by the moving company. Closing each box and applying labels that include name and office assignment in the new facility will complete staff efforts until unpacking can begin. For library staff members who have been employed by the institution for several decades, this task can be intimidating, so it is important to provide adequate time to complete a difficult chore.

Once staff members begin to pack up their offices and the contents of their desks, the imminence of a move strikes home. Until then, the reality of impending change easily can be denied, ignored, or relegated to the background. A library move, as noted earlier, can prove traumatic, both organizationally and psychologically. Apprehension tends to replace anticipation as moving day draws closer. To ease the stress of a move, staff members should be encouraged to visit their new workplace regularly as the building takes shape and is equipped and furnished. Unless everyone feels a part of the process, resistance and recrimination may upset the transition to a new workplace.

Moving the Collections

What are the expectations of library staff in connection with the move? Although most staff members will not be directly involved in its organization, they will have specific tasks to perform as preparations unfold. Labeling or relabeling of bound periodicals and a review of microform titles for chronological order will ease move stresses. Completion of such tasks will ensure that materials are in their proper places when the new building opens. Neither stimulating nor interesting in themselves, these jobs still need to be done well, because collections will be in excellent order when the building opens. Professional movers transfer materials as they find them, so it is best to have collections properly shelved ahead of time.

Different moving strategies are possible, depending on the circumstances. If the library collection is a modest one, say twenty thousand or fewer volumes, the library staff might be encouraged to plan and execute the move. Because few library collections are that small, full staff participation probably is an unrealistic expectation. Packing or loading books, transferring them to their new home, and unpacking and reshelving books, after all, are strenuous tasks. An alternative would be to mobilize a contingent of students. This approach may be less expensive than employing professional movers, but carries with it the potential for confusion and delay. A student workforce is unreliable by nature and, for this reason, may disrupt the most well planned moving schedule. The best solution, for larger moves, is to hire a professional moving company to do the physical work. This is the most expensive alternative, to be sure, but it places the responsibility for the move in the hands of those best equipped to carry it out.

Consultation will occur with the mover, who may or may not be familiar with conducting a library move. The personal involvement of the move coordinator will increase or decrease depending upon the experience level of the mover. Moving company professionals usually are willing to participate in discussions and consultation because it is in their best interest to execute as flawless a move as possible. Taking note of narrow stairwells and other obstacles, as well as location of elevators and the loading dock or staging space all will ease the stress of the move. Analyzing potential problems means that as many traps as possible can be eliminated before the move begins. Despite a moving company's experience in transferring library collections, not all its employees will be familiar with library classification schemes. For this reason, planning early and well is critical to a good move. Procrastination in this matter, as usual, is the enemy of success. The time to start planning for a move is the moment that the building project becomes a reality—that is, when the contracts are signed and construction gets under way.

Among the first steps in the planning process is to produce a plan that specifies the distribution of the library's collection in the new building. The next job—perhaps the most tedious and time-consuming of all—is to produce a collection map that will indicate exactly how the collection is to be arranged in its new home. Mapping entails a walk through the collection in order to record how much space is occupied by each classification area. One shelf is assigned, no matter how few volumes it contains. A generous estimate of space currently occupied builds in additional expansion room that will be appreciated in the future.

Information gathered during this process is then transferred onto scale drawings of the stacks produced by librarians using their own CAD software. The stack map numbers each bay so that the exact number of available shelves is known. Each bay will be labeled with its number, so that movers and shelvers will know precisely where they are in the stacks and so that different LC or Dewey classifications can be moved simultaneously. The next step is to distribute the existing collection on the shelving that is now available to accommodate it, leaving either all top or all bottom shelves (or both) free. The documentation that accompanies the stack map consists of two parts:

1. *Shelf assignment schedule.* Each shelf is numbered within each numbered bay, so that it may be assigned to hold a specific part of the collection. Shelf 1.1 is where the collection begins, and the location of each subclassification can be ascertained (see fig. 45).
2. *Face-on view* depicts the placement of each subclassification on the shelves as it would appear if one looked at the shelves straight on. This adds a second dimension to the stack map, which is essentially an aerial view of the stacks (see fig. 27).

Using the face-on view for reference, the shelves are labeled to show where each subclassification is to go and where vacant space is to be left.

1.1	AC	7.1	B	13.1	B	19.1	B
1.2	AC	7.2	B	13.2	B	19.2	B
1.3	AC	7.3	B	13.3	B	19.3	B
1.4	AC	7.4	B	13.4	B	19.4	B
1.5	AC	7.5	B	13.5	B	19.5	B
1.6	AE	7.6	B	13.6	B	19.6	B
1.7	VACANT	7.7	VACANT	13.7	VACANT	19.7	VACANT
2.1	AE	8.1	B	14.1	B	20.1	B
2.2	AG-AP	8.2	B	14.2	B	20.2	B
2.3	AS	8.3	B	14.3	B	20.3	B
2.4	AS	8.4	B	14.4	B	20.4	B
2.5	AY-AZ	8.5	B	14.5	B	20.5	B
2.6	B	8.6	B	14.6	B	20.6	B
2.7	VACANT	8.7	VACANT	14.7	VACANT	20.7	VACANT
3.1	B	9.1	B	15.1	B	21.1	B
3.2	B	9.2	B	15.2	B	21.2	B
3.3	B	9.3	B	15.3	B	21.3	B
3.4	B	9.4	B	15.4	B	21.4	B
3.5	B	9.5	B	15.5	B	21.5	B
3.6	B	9.6	B	15.6	B	21.6	B
3.7	VACANT	9.7	VACANT	15.7	VACANT	21.7	VACANT
4.1	VACANT	10.1	B	16.1	B	22.1	B
4.2	VACANT	10.2	B	16.2	B	22.2	B
4.3	VACANT	10.3	B	16.3	B	22.3	B
4.4	VACANT	10.4	B	16.4	B	22.4	B
4.5	VACANT	10.5	B	16.5	B	22.5	B
4.6	VACANT	10.6	B	16.6	B	22.6	B
4.7	VACANT	10.7	VACANT	16.7	VACANT	22.7	VACANT
5.1	B	11.1	B	17.1	B	23.1	B
5.2	B	11.2	B	17.2	B	23.2	B
5.3	B	11.3	B	17.3	B	23.3	B
5.4	B	11.4	B	17.4	B	23.4	B
5.5	B	11.5	B	17.5	B	23.5	B
5.6	B	11.6	B	17.6	B	23.6	B
5.7	VACANT	11.7	VACANT	17.7	VACANT	23.7	VACANT
6.1	B	12.1	B	18.1	B	24.1	B
6.2	B	12.2	B	18.2	B	24.2	B
6.3	B	12.3	B	18.3	B	24.3	B
6.4	B	12.4	B	18.4	B	24.4	B
6.5	B	12.5	B	18.5	B	24.5	B
6.6	B	12.6	B	18.6	B	24.6	B
6.7	VACANT	12.7	VACANT	18.7	VACANT	24.7	VACANT

FIGURE 45
Shelf assignment schedule

This can be done by color coding the shelves to correspond with the face-on view, using self-adhesive colored dots. It is essential to show exactly what goes where, so that workers who are unfamiliar with library classification systems can move along briskly during the move. Library staff ensure that books are reshelved in proper order.

If the collection map is well prepared, holdings will be spread evenly throughout the stacks, in which vacant bays and shelves are left to accommodate expansion in the fastest-growing classification areas. Librarians will know with fair accuracy—assuming the absence of unexpected budgetary windfalls or cuts—how long the new premises will serve. It is to be hoped that projections match the space that the institution has been able to build. Libraries do not need to plan for the kind of exponential growth in staff and collection size that occurred over the past generation. All the signs—technological, economic, and financial—point toward a steady-state library in the years ahead. Unless the institution is projecting significant expansion within the coming twenty years, there is no reason to overbuild or to provide excessive room to grow. This is a departure from the conventional wisdom of only a short time ago, but it is justified by current realities.

Moving is not an exact science and demands that flexibility be built into the planning. Because space needs usually are addressed long after problems become obvious, it may be necessary to integrate material that is stored in various locations. Collection mapping, as described here, will reveal how the collections ought to be arranged throughout the stacks. Moving the collection in shelf-list order from the old facility to the new building is vital. If perfectly shelved before the move, the collection will be transplanted in good order and will be immediately useful to patrons wishing to browse and borrow as soon as possible. It is worth the effort to take every possible precaution in advance, including prominent labeling of shelving in the new facility to indicate the location of expansion space.

Collection-management aspects of planning and executing a move can benefit from computer analysis. An accurate machine count of holdings provides the space-planning database. This phase involves laying out the collection in such a way that existing volumes are accommodated and expansion room is appropriately distributed throughout the stacks. Although computers are used for final computation of space needs, there is no substitute for physically counting the shelves occupied by the collection in the existing space. Being aware of donations that are about to appear on the shelves is helpful, too, because large, discipline-specific collections throw off all space calculations. The task of producing an accurate collection map is tedious, but must be done in order to avoid having to shift large portions of the collection in the future, as expansion occurs.

Before the collection map comes the stack map, which is itself an aspect of building design. A building's storage capacity, even in the age of electronic information, is still its defining feature. Except in the case of budget-driven projects, where square footage is decreed by the funds available, library planners build their space estimates around the following elements:

linear measurements of existing collections

size and quantity of space not devoted to materials storage in the new facility (i.e., offices, meeting rooms, locked storage)

estimated annual growth in collection size based on anticipated acquisitions budgets

Leighton and Weber explain how to calculate stack space in terms of required square footage.[2] The building's total size is based on these figures and the fact that a standard shelving bay is 36 inches center-to-center on the uprights. As described in chapter 3, a 30-foot building module will accommodate nine bays between columns lengthwise, and six ranges spaced at 39 inches. Thus, aisle widths that exceed ADA requirements can be provided. By taking care with this distribution, uniform aisle space can be assured between ranges. The columns should be incorporated within the shelving layout so that they do not obstruct travel within the stacks. Additionally, ranges of shelving should fill the space between columns, so that patrons cannot squeeze between the end of a range and an adjacent column.

When the architectural drawings are ready, an overlay superimposes the stack plan. Shelving will be installed according to this drawing. Numbering each of the bays represented on the stack layout will produce the stack map. This stack map serves, in turn, as the basis for the collection map, the purpose of which is to show how the collection and its expansion space are to be located in the new stacks. In other words, the stack map presents an aerial view of the shelving layout, while the collection map is a face-on representation of the collection as it appears in each bay. The former shows how much storage space is available; the latter, how it is filled. Both types of mapping are essential to the process of planning the size, layout, and use of new stack space. The degree of detail is largely dependent on whether the contracted mover has experience in moving a library. A collection cannot be moved, though, until it is known exactly how it will be placed in its new location and how room for future growth is programmed into the design.

Those libraries whose catalogs are already computerized can complete the first phase of collection mapping with relative ease. A volume count by LC classification is converted into linear feet by using a formula, such as six volumes per linear foot.[3] This calculation provides for expansion room. Assuming that either the top or bottom shelves are to remain vacant throughout the collection to accommodate future growth, the total linear footage of the existing book stock may then be placed on the shelving in a virtual sort of way. Nevertheless, to ensure that space requirements have indeed been met, it is a good idea to measure each classification.[4] Once the actual space to be occupied is known with certainty, the next phase of collection mapping can occur.

In the second stage, the location of expansion bays is established. A grid is created to represent a face-on view of the stacks, with each bay and its contents indicated. Because the linear-foot measurements are known with accuracy, distribution of expansion bays is a simple matter. An analysis of collection development over the past ten years is something most automated systems can produce. This information will reveal where provision for growth needs to be made and to what extent. Affixing a sign, saying This Bay to Remain Vacant, alerts the moving team to this fact and eases the supervision needed by the move coordinator. An appropriate number of bays or shelves is then inserted into the numbers of bays occupied by each classification.

To ensure that the collection is positioned according to the stack map, we recommend a scheme of color coding worked out in collaboration with the mover. Each LC classification is assigned a color so that both the origin and destination moving teams may easily match materials with location. In this way, books arrive at their proper destinations and can be reshelved in call-number order. If proper care is taken, the library's collections are being moved from several places within the LC classification simultaneously. With sufficient physical spacing, chaos and crowding may be kept to a minimum.

Some moves naturally are less complicated than others, such as those that occur indoors, under one roof. Others may involve shifting materials between different floors or from one building to another. If relabeling following reclassification of the collection is part of the scheme (as occurred when the University of Kentucky's library moved to a new building), the process becomes even more complex.[5] If subject libraries are being integrated into a general collection, material from two or more points may be converging on a particular location within the new stacks. A reliable map will prevent confusion and disorder at this stage of the proceedings. Ensuring that the books arrive at their final destination in as few steps as possible always is the goal.

Collection mapping is an exercise best undertaken without delay, because it is not a simple process even with the aid of a computer. The theoretical construct described here has to be refined by actual measurements and by a reliable estimate of the volume of material on hand at the time of mapping. Tables produced using a text-editor or spreadsheet application provide a neat representation of the stacks, but the data are laborious to enter. Results, however, will justify the effort involved. For one thing, professional movers appreciate having a workable moving strategy already in place, and are generally willing to reflect this advantage in their price quote.

Organizing a library move is a large task. Regardless of magnitude, planning takes a great deal of time, brainstorming, and energy, and cannot be done in isolation. Participation of key library staff is critical to the success of the operation. Utilizing the time in which others are involved in the design and construction of a new building also is crucial. On the day the doors open to the public, library users overwhelmed by new and unfamiliar surroundings deserve to have the library collection as well organized as possible. A move that is well planned and well executed should ease the distress of what otherwise may be a difficult adjustment. There are few times when a library is asked to plan for the future, particularly in terms of collection development or management. A spacious new library offers opportunities for collection development and ease of information access one cannot ignore.

Networks, Technology, and Special Facilities

Immediately following substantial completion, computer services staff and the cabling subcontractor begin testing the status of all network connections. With hundreds of study spaces suddenly added to the network, it is essential that all data pathways be functional. Print jobs destined for a high-speed machine elsewhere in the building, for example, should not arrive at a printer across campus. Server access must be tested, along with e-mail and online catalog links. Those workstations that require ATM bandwidth must have it. Every connection and each new machine have to be certified before opening day, when the network will be expected to perform flawlessly.

Part of the testing process involves solving ergonomic problems. Unless the architects and electrical engineers have been unusually diligent, study and work spaces are probably overilluminated. Ambient light levels may have to be adjusted, either by switching off rows of tubes or removing tubes altogether. Glare and computer-screen legibility may be serious concerns, even in contemporary libraries whose designers should have known better. Before staff and library users arrive in the building, as much as possible should be done to meliorate the effects of a poorly designed lighting system. We recommend that the owners do an independent analysis of UV-radiation and illumination levels, to determine whether corrective action is necessary. Until architects at last come to terms with computerized environments, this sort of post-facto remediation will be required.

Once cabling infrastructure and illumination problems are addressed, attention turns to such special facilities as the information commons and electronic classroom. Staff must have enough time to become thoroughly familiar with these complex environments, before their faculty and student users arrive in the library. Software should be installed and functioning; the same applies to all peripherals. In the classroom, projectors, monitors, cameras, and control systems need to be in perfect working order. Equally important is a high staff comfort level with the equipment and its operation. The technology is only as effective as those who use it. All this work can be proceeding while furniture installation and collection moving are under way. Someone, probably a library administrator with technical expertise, will have to certify compliance and readiness.

Implicit in this commissioning scenario is cooperation between the library and computer services. Several colleges and universities have already unified these two operations, or at least placed them in the same reporting structure. This sort of official collaboration facilitates the work of commissioning a new library building. Probably nowhere else on campus are computer services more closely involved in the educational mission than in an academic library suffused with information technology. In fact, it is highly advisable to have several computer-services staff members based in the library, where there will be continuous demand for technical assistance from both staff and users.

Gateway libraries, with their sophisticated networking infrastructure, are complex and delicate creations. Almost certainly, technical problems will arise during the year-long shakedown period. A few that may readily be anticipated are:

- faulty connectors
- misrouted data lines
- slow network response
- vandalism
- wire-management mishaps
- sluggish catalog terminals

Such challenges are to be expected, not only because of installation errors, but also because the technology is eternally in transition. Network architecture changes as bandwidth demands increase. New applications enter the experimental stage. There is, by its nature, no such thing as a stable network. Unpredictability and uncertainty easily upset a library environment, where people want information on demand. How should the library respond?

In a later section, we describe the commissioning process that aims to win maximum benefit from the investment in a new library building. It is not just the building that is being commissioned, however, but also its technological infrastructure and computer systems. They require as much attention as the building itself receives. The strategy is to complete a functional analysis of all systems and equipment, identify and correct faults, and strive to achieve network stability. Success depends on close collaboration between librarians and computer-services technicians, the kind that produces both technical functionality and reliable delivery of information.

Testing the Building

Testing and commissioning are complementary processes intended to deliver a quality building that meets its planners' expectations. Testing ensures that all systems (i.e., electrical, mechanical, networking) operate correctly. Commissioning has a larger purpose: to make certain that the building is able to fulfill its mission, as set forth in the original planning documents, and is likely to go on doing so as long as regular maintenance is performed. If this is to happen, all faults identified during testing need to be remedied. It is helpful to involve as many eyes as possible, including those of off-campus colleagues, in this exercise. There is no point in pretending that a new building, however admired it may be, is perfect. Better in the long run to search out the deficiencies and correct them early.

The testing process may be divided into three categories: (1) psychological, (2) physical, and (3) environmental. One might even devise a rating scheme to evaluate the building's performance under each of these headings. Some observations have general application to future campus development, and this information certainly will be useful to those who plan other projects. Formal and informal testing procedures, therefore, should be carried out during the year following substantial completion of the building.

Psychological Factors

Human reactions to new surroundings are never predictable, nor are they uniform. Design features that please one individual may well annoy another. What is important here is the general attitude. Is there a consensus that the building has met its planners' expectations and that it is capable of fulfilling its potential as a teaching instrument? When searching for this consensus, the trick is not to inhibit spontaneity. If you intended to create an interior design that would be inviting yet unobtrusive, you should keep this information to yourself while showing people around. Let them reach their own conclusions. Unsolicited praise that validates your original conception is worth far more than compliments teased out of a visitor. Should a critical opinion be expressed, then it is legitimate to explain what you had hoped to achieve. Agreement on aesthetic matters is always heartening, but it is not essential to a building's overall success.

Another psychological dimension, one that intrudes into the physical realm, is the general reaction to illumination levels in the building. One way of assessing this aspect is to walk people through the stacks and invite them to inspect the contents of the shelves. This is an opportunity to show how expansion room has been incorporated in the scheme of things. It is also a chance to note whether anyone has difficulty reading spine labels at any level. Illumination need be no more intense than is necessary to allow spine labels to be read. Lighting that is too intense, or that produces glare, is a misfortune that is all too common. Daylight will exacerbate the problem, unless window glass has been treated to reduce glare as well as heat gain and UV radiation. Meter readings can be taken to provide objective data. Remedial action may have to be considered after the fact.

Because the aim has been to create a building that is convenient to use as well as attractive, traffic flows demand close scrutiny. Are photocopiers located near all points of need? Is the signage system working? Can people entering the building for the first time locate the rest rooms without asking for directions? Library users are at ease in a building that not only is comfortable, but also is easy to understand. The more quickly it makes itself familiar, the more successful it is likely to be. By observing how people go about finding their way around, librarians can discover ways to improve accessibility. The idea, of course, is to have a library that encourages study and research.

There is no substitute for an effective system of signage. The architect will coordinate this aspect of the project, which is best undertaken after shelving and furniture are in place. Optimum signage placement is obvious when all sight lines are established. Company representatives will work with the architect to devise a system clear enough to curtail the simple directional questions asked of library staff. Legibility and compatibility with the interior design are two of the main criteria with respect to signage. Vendors will prepare a supplementary package if, on the basis of experience, additional signage is warranted.

During the year of testing, library staff should be prepared to make certain changes in response to users' comments. Furniture may have to be shifted or equipment relocated to fit patterns of demand. Lighting may require augmentation if illumination levels are too low in certain areas. Signage may need minor revisions if staff members find that they are regularly answering the same directional questions. Adjustments in white noise, temperature, and humidity levels may be advisable. Even intelligent buildings perform only in response to instructions from their human overseers.

Library staff members, who care deeply about their own working conditions, will offer plenty of advice. Much of it will have to do with ergonomics, for example, lighting, air quality, furniture design, placement of computer terminals, and so on. Staff suggestions should be accepted whenever possible so as to preserve and enhance morale. As daily operations resume in new space, old routines, habits, and relationships are transformed. Tensions always accompany change and, if allowed to fester, may grow into serious problems. It is best to confront and resolve issues as they arise, because most of them can be sorted out before they become quagmires.

A helpful, knowledgeable library staff is the key to consolidating a new building's role on campus. If the library has defined itself as a "teaching instrument," the staff is obliged to promote electronic research services and to assist those who lack the requisite skills. However attractive and functional the building itself may be, its effectiveness depends on relationships between staff and the university community. Libraries that offer an electronic information environment logically must assume an active teaching role. More productive relationships between librarians and faculty are likely to result.

Physical Factors

A full year is required for new buildings to reveal themselves. Some construction defects appear over time, particularly those involving foundations, moisture barriers, and mechanical systems. Air-handling systems must be able to cope with seasonal variations in outside temperature and humidity, and they have to run through a complete annual cycle before being pronounced fit. Library staff and technicians from the physical plant will need to work together during the shakedown to get optimal performance from the mechanical systems. Carpets, upholstery, and furniture need to be wear-tested and, if found to be defective, repaired or replaced. Time is also needed to work through the deficiency list ("punch list") that was prepared in cooperation with the architect and general contractor at the time of substantial completion. All fits and finishes have to be judged satisfactory before the contractor receives final payment. Thereafter, the library takes its chances with the university's maintenance department.

"Punching down" a new building is another time-consuming job that, in the end, repays the effort. Every room, area, and piece of furniture must be examined for defects and claims submitted. It is the owner's responsibility to make sure that deficiencies are remedied within applicable warranty periods. Librarians, maintenance personnel, the campus facilities office, architects, and the owner's representative all are involved in the process of punching down. This is the conventional way of bringing a new building online. We suggest a different approach here, one that has the potential to achieve more satisfactory results.

Intelligent buildings share with less-clever structures the same construction features: roofs, windows, vapor barriers, floor coverings, paintwork, plumbing fixtures, and so on. During the warranty year, it is a good idea to keep a close eye on all physical aspects of the building so as to carry out timely repairs and adjustments. Buildings that are expected to last for several generations deserve careful maintenance. In carpeted libraries, for example, it is essential to schedule regular steam cleaning. Once every fifteen to twenty years is a sufficient interval for carpet replacement, and poor maintenance should not be allowed to reduce the carpet's life span.

Furniture and equipment also should be evaluated for their ability to withstand wear and tear during the warranty period. If wooden items are vandalized, they should be refinished immediately so as not to encourage further depredations. Some chairs inevitably will fail and have to be replaced. When a building is obviously being allowed to run down, some people may take this as an invitation to hasten the process. No building is vandal-proof, but it is unwise to let defacers set the tone. A new building will retain its splendor longer if it is well cared for by its owners. Maintenance is often neglected, because "doing it is a pain" or because of shortstaffing in the physical plant. "Every building is potentially immortal," laments Stewart Brand, "but very few last half the life of a human."[6]

Environmental Factors

Modern library buildings typically are sealed environments to protect their contents from dirt, pollution, and seasonal variations in temperature and humidity. Costly air-handling systems are installed to ensure that proper conditions are maintained. Digital controls monitor the environment and create a proper mix of heated and cooled air. Fans and dampers within the ductwork deliver the air mixture to assorted micro-environments throughout the building. In an intelligent building, staff members are able to select the conditions that they prefer in their work areas.

Human reaction to the internal environment also determines a building's fate. An attractive, efficient library that turns out to be a sick building is tragic indeed. Many new structures suffer from "sick-building syndrome," defined as "general, non-specific symptoms of malaise which are experienced by people when they are in a particular building and which cease shortly after they leave it."[7] Numerous airborne pollutants, capable of creating sick-building syndrome, can be widely distributed by faulty or ill-maintained HVAC systems. Carbon monoxide, carbon dioxide, formaldehyde, bacteria, and radon gas are a few contaminants that may be injected into a building's environment. High absenteeism and low productivity are signs that employees are being adversely affected. Sick-building syndrome can be prevented if care is taken to ensure that HVAC systems do not draw pollutants inside, and if the chemical composition of various building materials is considered as they are being selected for use. Other design considerations are the building envelope, which should exclude radon gas if this is present in the site, and the use of low heat-gain filtered window glass. Of great value would be information on the contaminant-emission qualities of such building materials as carpets, fabrics, paints, sealants, furniture-core materials, plastics, and so on. When this sort of database becomes available, computers will acquire another role in the design process, one that will help to ensure that an aesthetically pleasing and functional library also offers a healthy interior environment.[8]

The performance of HVAC systems depends on several factors. One is how well they were balanced in the first place. Air balancing is a lengthy process whereby the intake and exhaust fans that exchange air within the building are adjusted to produce slight positive pressure. If the intake fan, which normally is the more powerful one, is too strong, internal pressure may be so high that doors fail to close and heated air is forced through the building envelope during cool months. Damage may then occur to the building's outer skin because of condensation on its inside surface. A second factor is the temperature and humidity sensors that control airflow through the ducts. If these are defective or improperly installed, the HVAC systems will not work. The same applies to thermostats, valves, and automated monitors. Proper evaluation of the air-handling mechanisms, therefore, takes time and demands cooperation from the building's users, designers, contractors, and maintenance staff.

Library administrators should possess some knowledge of how the mechanical systems are supposed to operate, if only to be able to explain potential problems to the technicians. The architect should be able to provide a written explanation prepared by the engineering consultant, who is the designer of the system, or the system's manufacturer. Those who live in the building every day are best able to spot any deterioration in the environment. Malfunctions must be repaired immediately to prevent damage to library materials and computer equipment.

Some environmental problems result from defective or poorly maintained mechanical equipment. Others stem from design faults that become obvious only after the concrete has been poured. Thermostats placed so close together that they fight each other are commonly identified during the warranty period. Relocation of a thermostat is, however, a minor matter in comparison with the incorrect siting of intake fans and exhaust vents, or of a loading dock. Fans that suck vented air or diesel fumes back into the building are certainly not unknown. Prevention is the only cure for architectural blunders that should have appeared during a review of the drawings. Librarians bear as much responsibility for spotting errors as do other members of the design team, such as architects and other project consultants.

Physical plant personnel assume responsibility for operating the building's mechanical systems. Everything else—security, lights, computer facilities, networks, and so on—belongs to other campus personnel and the library staff. Having draft policies and procedures in place well before opening day can alleviate confusion. As staff gain experience with the new building, revisions can be made. The important thing is to remain pragmatic and flexible during the shakedown. New routines will emerge as the environment becomes more familiar. These procedures typically evolve as one aspect of the commissioning process.

Commissioning the Building

"Commissioning" and building "shakedown" used to be treated as synonyms for a post-construction process intended to ensure "that you are getting the building you are paying for."[9] As HVAC and electrical systems have become more complex in recent years, a more exhaustive process than the traditional building punch-down is now required to assure that owners get their money's worth. Renewed emphasis on quality has produced, in turn, a more rigorous definition of commissioning. It is one that we wholeheartedly support, because the meek acceptance of buildings that architects, engineers, and contractors turn over to their new owners is no longer adequate. A different approach, which gained widespread support after 1995, parallels the rigorous quality-control evaluation of new warships before the navy places them in service.

An excellent definition of *commissioning* is this:

> [A] systematic process—beginning in the design phase, lasting at least one year after construction, and including the preparation of operating staff—of ensuring, through document verification, that all building systems perform interactively according to the documented design intent and the owner's operational needs.[10]

As part of a team approach to project design and construction, commissioning can lead to buildings of higher quality. This is one way to involve all parties in creating buildings that owners want, not necessarily ones that design professionals choose to give them. Some of the steps to be followed are: formulation of clear design criteria, documentation of all construction activities, testing of subsystems and their electronic controls, training for maintenance staff, and attention to all applicable warranties.[11] In a library, special consideration must be given to environmental controls and to the computer infrastructure, because optimal performance is an absolute requirement.

Experts in building commissioning advise that the project engineer, in collaboration with the owner's representative, is the best person to act as "commissioning authority." The critical nature of HVAC systems points toward the mechanical engineer as primary commissioner, who then must work closely with the company that tests and balances the air-handling systems.[12] The purpose of focusing on the mechanical systems is to avoid sick-building syndrome, which afflicts many modern structures. We suggest that the owner's representative, who is probably a seasoned construction professional, is a suitable commissioning agent. This individual's broad mandate to secure a satisfactory building gives her or him a strong vested interest in the outcome. In 1998, an approximate commissioning budget was in the range of 1.5 to 3 percent of the construction contract.[13]

The commissioning process aims to produce a building that, above all, satisfies the expectations of its owners. This can happen only if the professional designers insist on, and then respect, a clear and comprehensive building program. Too often, a poorly drafted or incomplete program obliges designers to second-guess their clients, with unfortunate results. Just as frequently, architects may ignore the owner's wishes, even written instructions, and forge blithely ahead to disaster. Commissioning, as figure 46 illustrates, enforces communication that may avert unlucky consequences. It follows, therefore, that architects who find the

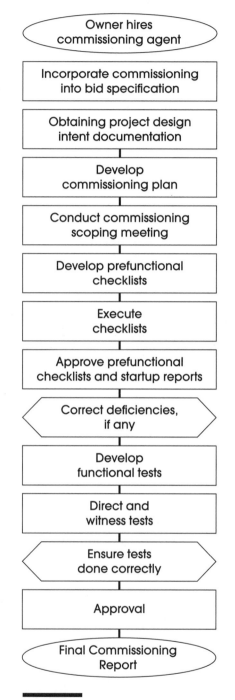

FIGURE 46
Typical commissioning process

process uncongenial should be rejected or should not bid a project in the first place. Communication must remain open throughout construction, so that suggestions and good ideas can be implemented without the need for a stream of change orders. Everyone knows from the outset what is expected and how it is to be achieved. The main vehicle for this collaboration is the design intent document, which spells out in detail exactly those building features that will satisfy the owner upon completion. It "sets the operational goals that form the basis for commissioning, whereas the construction documents set the requirements for the correct supply and installation of the building components."[14] Once all parties know the project's expected outcome, they can work as a team toward the common goal. There is nothing new in this process: just "the marginal additional effort" needed to produce satisfactory results. The process itself extends one year beyond building occupancy, so that systems can be monitored across all the seasons.[15]

Commissioning can go far toward achieving a building that functions properly and serves its owner's needs. There remains, however, the interface between the building and all the furnishings and equipment located therein. A library, in many ways, is a special case. Modern academic libraries are a complex of interlocking systems, the components of which all have separate warranties. Physical plant personnel are responsible for inspecting mechanical, electrical, and construction subsystems; librarians need to do the same for furnishings and equipment in regular use. Warranties are useless if allowed to expire before claims are filed.

Punch lists have a role to play in commissioning. They contain all matters that require attention from the contractor, any subcontractors, and all vendors who have supplied the project. Close inspection, conducted during building walk-throughs, always reveals chips, dents, surface damage, and operational failures to be corrected under warranty. Other deficiencies will emerge during the first year of operation, after which repairs are handled by local staff or under service contracts.

Inspection is a rigorous process that involves testing each power and data connection and every piece of attached equipment. Several university departments are likely to be involved, their efforts coordinated either by the library director or the owner's representative. Haphazard or intermittent inspections produce unsatisfactory results. Nothing is worse than having library users discover problems that the professionals should have caught. Furniture installations require frequent inspections while in progress, so as to focus immediate attention on defects. It is much easier to obtain instant satisfaction than to persuade a vendor to return to the site later. Once suppliers have packed up and left the building, service is much more difficult to obtain.

Experience gained in several building projects suggests that the library director or designate should be involved in every aspect of the shakedown and certification process. If HVAC systems are not providing appropriate temperature and humidity control, the director has a vested interest in rectifying the situation. Security (emergency exits, cameras, circulation control, and the like) is an ongoing concern; so are lighting levels, network speed, and clean electric power. All staff should be encouraged to report anomalies, however trivial they may seem at the time. Left unaddressed, they can add up to severe headaches after applicable warranties have expired. Worth keeping in mind is the futility of pursuing the architects for anything less than structural collapse. Their aesthetic judgments and functional arrangements, though they profoundly affect the new environment, carry no warranties. If you accepted their designs and recommendations before preparation of construction documents, do not expect any sort of compensation if things fail to work out as hoped, not even an apology. Many architects are adept at deflecting criticism to client or contractor, preferring to remain above the fray and to avoid debates over functionality or lack thereof.

Operational Policies and Procedures

New policies and procedures now replace old routines left behind after the move. They represent a consensus on how the building should operate, and cover several matters:

> opening and closing the building
>
> hours of operation and building access
>
> handling security breaches at the emergency exits
>
> administering new facilities, e.g., electronic classroom, group studies, information gallery
>
> appropriate use of visual surveillance and public-address systems
>
> appropriate use of library computing and networking resources
>
> reporting of problems related to the building or its furnishings and equipment
>
> handling of library materials in various formats
>
> food, drink, and tobacco use in the building

As is true of other aspects of planning for a new building, operational issues should be addressed early. Obviously it is impossible to foresee all contingencies, but guidelines can be put in place initially and revised later. The discussion gets everyone involved in thinking about how roles will change in the new situation, thus easing the transition. Every library staff will devise its own approach to policy matters. The main consideration has to be improved service to library users in a building that has been designed to enhance efficiency.

Library staff may generate operating policies in the process of reorganizing library services in the new building. Such policies should emerge, in any case, from a dialog with the library administration so that everybody has ownership. Experience will show where revisions need to be made. It is a good strategy, however, to have some idea how the library will operate before opening day. Policies and procedures can be revisited as part of the commissioning process, which continues during the warranty year.

Once architects have obtained their portfolio-enhancing photographs of a new building, their interest in the structure may rapidly wane. During the commissioning year, it is the owner's representative (OR) who leads the debugging team. He or she pays regular visits, collects data on all kinds of malfunctions, and coordinates warranty work. Another task is to oversee the spending-out of contingency budgets, so that the project shows neither a surplus nor a deficit when its books are finally closed. Finally, the OR can help local maintenance staff to become comfortable with the building's systems and upkeep schedules. This makes it easier to integrate the new library into the overall physical plant. By the time the shakedown year ends, the OR has created a complete performance review that can assist building managers in the future. For some time to come, the OR can be a valuable resource person when problems arise.

Change: Political Dynamics in a New Building

To this point, we have considered new library buildings primarily from the standpoints of facilities planning, the changing role of librarians in the age of information technology, and reactions of users to a new building. There is, in addition, an important political dimension that can disrupt the best-laid organizational plans if not addressed as an integral part of the planning process. A library filled with new furnishings and equipment will still be staffed by people socialized in the old premises and potentially resentful of change. Do not assume that the prospect of a modern building delights everyone on the staff. Initial expressions of enthusiasm for change in fact may mask serious misgivings about relinquishing familiar surroundings, routines, and relationships. Opposition to change, if not anticipated, can blight the transition from traditional ways to the different set of opportunities that a new building offers.

The psychology of change and transition offers some relevant insights having to do with those who advocate and manage change and those whose self-appointed mission is to oppose it. The dichotomy easily arises in library moves, when time-honored organization and associated routines disappear. Ways have to be found to mitigate disruption so that reorganization seems less threatening to those who must navigate the transition. One of the best strategies is to involve the entire staff in reorganizing services to fit a changed environment. If everyone owns a portion of change, things will go more smoothly. Almost invariably, however, there will be holdouts and naysayers who decry what others see as progress. This is where politics comes in, as proponents of change confront their adversaries in a contest of wills.

A "change agent" is "any individual seeking to reconfigure an organization's roles, responsibilities, structures, outputs, processes, systems, technology, or other resources."[16] This description fits any library director who seizes the opportunity presented by a new building to do things differently and, perhaps, better. Politics, in this situation, is the art of enlisting those who might be tempted to man the barricades. As a result, according to David Buchanan and Richard Badham, "the change agent becomes engaged . . . in the exercise of power, politics, and interpersonal influence."[17] The point is not to manipulate, but rather to articulate a realistic vision of positive change and win support for it. This can happen only by converting doubters to the ranks of the change agents.

A large part of planning a building is anticipating how to operate it when eventually it is completed. The design-development phase is not too early to begin this process. Considerable discussion will precede any degree of reorganization. Roles and responsibilities will change, preferably with the consent of those affected. A bit of persuasion from the change-agent-in-chief may be needed, but nothing at all can be accomplished from the top down. If the interaction of peers can produce results, then that is the best strategy. The desire to "get it right the first time" in every detail will impede progress, unless people realize that they are creating a work-in-progress. No one can foresee every contingency, so there should be agreement that everything will be reexamined a year after the move and revised as necessary. The main thing is to engage everyone in constructive debate and resolution.

Fortunately for today's library designers, they live in an era of transformation that forces them to grapple with such questions as: How does the Web cause us to change what is meant by a library?[18] Librarians, by now, are used to thinking about technology as a catalyst to institutional change. No librarian can escape technology's pervasive influence; it is part of the professional ambience. For technical-services librarians, this has been the case for many years. Now everyone is affected. Technology centers, information galleries, ubiquitous data connections, electronic classrooms, and so on have a place in every new library. The whole library environment is forever changed.

So much emphasis on change causes justifiable consternation among some older hands. Yet, if the way has been suitably prepared, the transition to a new working environment may well be smoother than anticipated. Change often proves more disturbing in anticipation than in reality. Comforting as that probability is for library planners, there also may be notable exceptions. That is why early consultations with the institution's Employee Assistance Program provider are a wise precaution. Expect the best, according to the old saying, but by all means prepare for the worst. Machiavelli's warning remains pertinent: "There is nothing more difficult and dangerous, or more doubtful of success, than an attempt to introduce a new order of things. . . ." *(The Prince)*.

A New Library and the Campus Culture

Construction of a new library captures the attention of everyone on campus, because the benefits accrue to all. As the building takes shape, interest grows and there is much speculation about how the final result will look. Thus, as soon as the basic structure is in place, small tours may be run—nothing elaborate, because owners have no inherent right to get in the contractor's way. Word rapidly spreads that a vital facility is taking shape. Tours may become more formalized as construction debris is cleared out and the finishing work proceeds. All this is in aid of creating a sense of anticipation, to which a variety of other activities also can contribute.

Scheduling a ceremonial book-passing is another means of focusing attention on the library. Several weeks before the move occurs, but after shelving is installed, a few hundred volumes may be passed along a human chain from the old library to the new. Local celebrities can be involved, thus capturing media attention. This is especially helpful if the occasion is to be used to promote fund-raising activities associated with the library, for example, an endowment campaign in support of the acquisitions budget. Disingenuous suggestions to use volunteers to move the entire collection can be diplomatically turned aside. A large move is best left to professionals who are equipped to handle it within a give time frame, perhaps a semester break.

There is so much uninformed talk about "the end of libraries as we know them" that no occasion should be missed on which to counter such nonsense. Obviously, campus authorities, legislators, or donors believed in the library's future, or else it would not have been built. Yet, it does not hurt to seize a chance to proclaim that libraries remain strong and to explain the reason why this is so. Nothing is so convincing as the experience of using a new library, with its electronic infrastructure and its inviting atmosphere. Before the day arrives to dedicate the building, it probably will have been open to the public for several weeks and been toured by thousands of visitors.

Library personnel will spend a great deal of time during the first year of operation conducting tours of the building. This is a potentially worthwhile effort, particularly if spaces within the library are to be the focus of a fund-raising effort. Alumni are always grateful for the personal attention they receive. Media tours are a good way to get the word out, by advertising the library's facilities and services.

Integration of a new library into the campus culture is symbolically recognized on dedication day, when the building officially comes into service. This is a ceremonial occasion, which recognizes the contribution of all who helped bring the project to fruition. Music, speeches, and revelry are the order of the day. Everyone basks in the aura of a job well done. The festivities concluded, work continues on the job of shaking down and commissioning the building.

Notes

1. Philip Leighton and David C. Weber, *Planning Academic and Research Library Buildings*, 3d ed. (Chicago: American Library Association, 1999), 177–184.

2. Ibid.

3. Recommended by Leighton and Weber, *Planning Academic and Research Library Buildings*, 180.

4. See Donna Lee Keerkul, "The planning, implementation, and movement of an academic library collection," *College & Research Libraries* 44 (4): 220–234 (July 1983).

5. See Adam Bruns, "Moving day: An exercise in mind and matter," *American Libraries* 30 (4): 48–50 (April 1999), for further detail on the move at the University of Kentucky.

6. Stewart Brand, *How Buildings Learn: What Happens After They're Built* (New York: Viking Press, 1994), 110–111.

7. Mark Tyler, "Sick buildings: Carrying the can," *Architect's Journal* 194 (August 1991): 48.

8. Laura J. Lonowski, "Indoor air quality: The role of building design, materials, and construction," *Construction Specifier* 44 (5): 144–153 (May 1, 1991).

9. Daniel L. Moberley, "Commissioning new buildings," *American School and University* 71 (6): 49 (February 1999).

10. Paul C. Tseng, "Building commissioning: Benefits and costs," *HPAC: Heating, Piping, Air Conditioning* 70 (4): 53 (April 1998).

11. Ibid., 54.

12. See Elia M. Sterling and Christopher W. Collett, "The building commissioning quality assurance process in North America," *ASHRAE Journal* 36 (10): 32–36 (October 1994).

13. Tseng, "Building commissioning," 59.

14. Ronald J. Wilkinson, "The commissioning design intent narrative," *ASHRAE Journal* 41 (4): 32 (April 1999).

15. Nancy B. Solomon, "Building commissioning," *Architecture* 84 (6): 126 (June 1995).

16. David Buchanan and Richard Badham, "Politics and organizational change: The lived experience," *Human Relations* 52 (5): 610 (May 1999).

17. Ibid., 611.

18. Brian Kroeker, "Changing roles in information dissemination and education," *Social Science Computer Review* 17 (2): 178 (summer 1999).

The Library as a "Teaching and Learning Instrument"

For many college students, the ubiquitous computer has become the number-two pencil on campus. . . . The campus has gone from the printed page to print-outs.[1]

The Evolving Library

Academic library design, in essence, is the process of creating a teaching and learning instrument: a building that is wired and equipped to facilitate the acquisition of electronic research skills. Over twenty years ago, Ralph Ellsworth related "the instructional role library buildings can play in the academic scene" to "the research services aspects of the libraries [that have] grown very extensively."[2] Now that information sources are converting to electronic format, accessibility is a serious concern. Electronic search systems are nonstandard and are not self-evident to the uninitiated. Such systems have to be learned, preferably in the context of courses in which faculty require their students to become reasonably adept at searching out literature in the field. We assume that electronic research skills will become indispensable to survival in university studies. Library buildings therefore should contribute to the education of students by offering them (1) easy access to information networks and digitized information, and (2) course-specific instruction in the techniques of electronic research. Surroundings are an important consideration in making a teaching instrument of the library. "An attractive and inviting environment which provides clear signage and an appearance of usability," writes James Rice, "will go a long way toward overcoming user resistance to library instruction."[3]

Changes now reshaping the publishing world and the role of librarians are manifesting themselves in library architecture. Buildings are being designed as teaching instruments in order to assist students to acquire the electronic research skills demanded by their academic programs and, later, in the job market. Once students achieve a basic level of comfort and competence with the technology, they are equipped to become independent learners able to assimilate changes as they occur. Teaching faculty and librarians share responsibility for producing university graduates with the ability to survive and prosper in new information environments. There is more to this educational process than refining the surfing skills of succeeding "Internet generations," to whom the Net is just another entertainment medium. Information retrieval on the Web is a skill-based activity that must be learned.

The technology that created a new information universe in less than a decade is not transparent to those who use it. A primary role being assigned to librarians for the immediate future is that of "navigator" in the electronic maze of the Internet. Also comprising this "digital soup" is a vast array of electronic sources, such as online library catalogs, CD-ROM databases, multimedia streams, campus information networks, program software, and full-text resources.[4] This teaching role is best fulfilled in a library building that is designed to support it. Features that distinguish a "teaching and learning library" are:

> extensive power and communications grids that are part of the building's fabric

> an electronic classroom in which library staff may teach electronic research skills in the context of specific courses

> an information desk located close to the main entrance with online access to the campus information network and access both to networked and Web-based resources

> study spaces wired for access to the campus information network by means of users' own notebook computers

> networked printing services that allow work to be sent to any printer on campus that is accessible to the public

> an interior environment that accurately controls temperature and humidity levels, offers an appropriate level of ambient illumination, and provides a comfortable place for study and research

> study furniture that takes account of ergonomic design for computer use

> group study space and computer workstations for library users, provided according to local decision and philosophy of library service

an information arcade or commons in which students may work on multimedia, full-text projects under the guidance of librarians, subject specialists, and technical-support people

Philip Tompkins, who helped to design the Leavey Library at the University of Southern California, describes his vision of a "teaching library":

> The challenge of reconceptualizing the library is to invent an integrated environment, replete with information specialists working in concert with teaching faculty and rich in courseware and information resources—a facility in which text, animation, graphics, sound, and video (and professional support) are configured to meet the needs of the independent learner, which is, after all, the primary goal of an information-literate society. Clearly, the design imperatives for such a facility would deviate significantly from the accepted concepts for planning American academic and research libraries.[5]

New buildings, as we have described them, are hybrids that combine a warehousing and an electronic-gateway function. Coexistence of a variety of information sources characterizes libraries designed to help teach the electronic research techniques required by university students. Digitized materials, without question, will assume a larger role as time goes on. They must be as easily accessible as are shelved books and periodicals in traditional academic libraries.

Locating full-text information sources, in either print or electronic format, is a large part of the battle. Then comes the creation of a finished piece of research. Word processors, statistical packages, Webpage creation software, and so on are the tools used at this stage. "Text processing," as Brian L. Hawkins points out, "has . . . caus[ed] students and faculty to do far more revision on their manuscripts than would heretofore have been possible."[6] Because computers facilitate research, writing, and incorporation of multimedia, students require a broad range of electronic research skills (ERS). Webpage creation and computer conferencing are common activities. Librarians will find themselves teaching broadly defined ERS in support of faculty who wish to build information technology into their courses. Not only will ERS benefit students after graduation, but courses with electronic components also are more adaptable to distance delivery. Distance education is a growth industry, which libraries will be required by their parent institutions to support.

Faculty are creating Web-enhanced courses for their on-campus teaching by using relatively simple software, such as Microsoft's FrontPage. "Lectures," reading materials, audio and video files, and graphics are integral to Web-enhanced courses, which also may be offered to distance-education students. A great deal of asynchronous learning will occur in libraries, where other source materials and electronic facilities are available. Easy access to the expertise of librarians is an added benefit. Academic libraries therefore will support this need by offering an integrated learning environment intended to inspire these activities as well as provide additional and enhanced resources.

Librarians fortunate enough to be involved in a building project have several models to consider. One is the 86,000-square-foot Leavey Library at the University of Southern California, opened in 1994 and designed "to provide maximum flexibility and enhanced power, data, and communications distribution throughout the building without sacrificing the ambience of an inviting environment."[7] A comfortable and attractive building, the Leavey Library is a mecca for students (fig. 47). Librarians and computer personnel staff the Information Commons, where expert assistance is available to those using on- or off-campus electronic sources. A number of "collaborative workrooms" offer group-study space. Two "learning rooms" and an auditorium comprise Leavey's teaching facilities. Also housed in Leavey is USC's Center for Scholarly Technology, which develops new applications in library, information, and instructional technology. Amy Ciccone, then acting assistant university librarian for Public Services, described Leavey as "a focal point for partnerships with faculty in developing and evaluating information technologies for teaching."

FIGURE 47
Leavey Library at the University of Southern California

The library at Indiana University–Purdue University at Indianapolis, also opened in 1994, is a second example (fig. 48). Built at a cost of $32 million, with $6 million invested in information technology, the library occupies 256,800 square feet, net assignable and has a seating capacity of 1,740. Although data transmission initially was over Category 3 UTP, fiber optic to the desktop looked more promising. (Today, full-motion video files can be transmitted over Category 5 UTP.) Study carrels contain network connectors that accommodate both present and future needs.

A third example is the library at Middle Tennessee State University in Murfreesboro, which opened early in 1999 (fig. 49). Gross square footage is 250,000 at a total cost of $32.75 million. The building is attractive and functional and is equipped with networked technology to encourage the use of portable computers. Twelve hundred data connections are active, with provision for a total of 2,400.

Winona State University applied these models to its new 108,000-square-foot library building, which opened in June 1999 (fig. 50). Winona State is a midsized, publicly funded university located in southeastern Minnesota. With 7,000 students and a faculty of 300, it is just the right size to support technological initiatives. In the fall of 2000, all first-year students will be required to participate in the university's Laptop Universal Access (LUNIAC) leasing program. A series of faculty Web Camps

FIGURE 48
Indiana University–Purdue University at Indianapolis

FIGURE 49
Middle Tennessee State University

FIGURE 50
Winona State University

has prepared the way for the integration of student laptops into the educational process. Winona State has experimented with the Lotus Notes Domino system, which will "allow WSU to develop a core of services: messaging, calendar, resource management, Web application, e-commerce, Web-enhanced learning and an e-business environment."[8] Library planners and designers anticipated that campus use of information technology would mature quickly, foresight that turned out to be accurate. The new library therefore has become an integral part of the campus's technology plan, which describes the infrastructure that will support teaching and learning.

Consciously designed to be a teaching instrument, this library has an information gallery strategically located in the center of its main floor. Equipped with high-end machines and a variety of peripherals, the gallery resembles a forty-eight-seat open computer lab, but there is a difference. Technical assistance and advice are easily available from the gallery manager, his staff, and reference librarians. "Surfing" is actively discouraged, because the gallery is defined as teaching/learning space. The gallery's faculty complement is the Academic Technologies Center, located on the second floor, where assistance is available on all matters relating to the educational applications of information technology. Over the past decade, a clear trend toward the inclusion of such facilities in new academic libraries has developed. There is every reason to believe that it will continue.

The teaching and learning libraries evolving at USC, IUPUI, Middle Tennessee State, Winona State, and elsewhere share the goal of making information technology accessible to users. By assuming an active teaching role, librarians can expand the classroom experience. This is the direction being followed by the Leavey Library, where the emphasis is on "training students and faculty to acquire information and knowledge from both traditional and very advanced information technology–based national and regional sources."[9] IUPUI librarians refer to their "learning library" as a place designed to "lead the novice users from a lower-level of expertise to the complex scholarly functions in a systematic, incremental manner."[10] Both libraries seek to cultivate electronic research skills, though IUPUI places greater reliance on independent learning. Whatever the focus, the important thing is that access be as transparent and straightforward as possible. Complex, opaque systems are difficult to teach and defy efforts at self-instruction.

The main reason to install innovative technologies in new buildings is to support changes in instructional programs and course-delivery modes. Recent developments in distance-education technology, such as Web-based and Web-enhanced courses, are enticing more universities into this enterprise. Interactive video signals transmitted along high-speed fiber-optic lines, controlled by ATM (asynchronous transfer mode) switches and routers, permit one site to link with several remote locations simultaneously. With this technology in place, distance education leaps from videotape or "talking heads" to online interaction between instructor and students. When distance education joins the mainstream, demands on libraries will increase. This will happen because it is unacceptable to offer distance learners inferior library service or a less rigorous program than on-campus students receive. Before online access to academic libraries became routine, instructors often omitted research papers because sources were inaccessible. Now distance learners may search the catalog of their home institution and order materials by e-mail or other electronic means. Access via proxy server to electronic full-text is now commonplace.

Emphasis within the academic world may shift toward distance learning, yet the library as a physical entity is not about to disappear. Proponents of the teaching library, such as Philip Tompkins, formerly of the University of Southern California, argue that the library will remain "a campus center and retreat for faculty and students" who find there the technology required for their work. Peter Lyman, now at Berkeley, suggests that "the library of tomorrow will be the home of the core curriculum of the future . . . and the place where students of any age will return to renew their knowledge." [11] Other advocates of information technology are less sanguine about the library's chances for survival as a physical entity. Escalating construction costs, according to Brian Hawkins, are causing universities to cease building libraries and "to consider alternatives to the present model." [12] Construction statistics, in fact, demonstrate a healthy social commitment to building new libraries; yet, at the same time, there is great interest in electronic solutions to space problems.

We shall return to the "electronic library" of Hawkins and others in the final chapter. For now, we predict that the physical library will remain a central place on campus, that it will house print collections, and that it will combine traditional functions with the teaching of electronic research skills. In addition, it will be the focus of support to distance-education courses. The library of the future, which will reside in buildings being planned and built today, is described thus in a 1993 study commissioned by the Council on Library Resources:

> The authors believe that libraries will continue to be associated with buildings. Although physical collections of books, journals, and other materials will no longer consume valuable space in these buildings, we can envision the need for work spaces where users consult library resources on state-of-the-art computer workstations; study spaces where users demand quiet for contemplation and reflection; large, medium, and small sharing spaces

equipped with state-of-the-art equipment to enable groups to incorporate technology into their gatherings.[13]

Although library buildings will continue to be built, the activities within them certainly will be transformed by information technology. That same technology, with equal certainty, will alter the university's mission and the nature of its clientele. Resident undergraduates and faculty will share library facilities and staff expertise with members of the community at large who are enrolled in distance-education courses. The self-contained, sometimes geographically isolated campus now finds the world at its doorstep, metaphorically and in reality. Computer linkages to worldwide information sources, by means of the Internet and the World Wide Web, already have permanently changed the role of libraries and those who work in them.

Underlying our ideas on library design in a digital world is a commitment to liberal education. Libraries, both traditional and electronic, exist to provide information sources to those who create knowledge. As the balance shifts from ownership of sources toward facilitating access to them, librarians acquire the vital role of navigators, guides, and teachers of electronic research skills (ERS). IBM's chief scientist pointed out early in the 1980s that "librarians must again become teachers and innovators, and not custodians, lest the treasures in their custody are made obsolete by alternative services that fail to serve humanity as imaginatively and profoundly as they could."[14] This role, now as in the past, is best exercised in collaboration with teaching faculty who are the subject-matter experts. The library, as a building and as an institution, can foster this partnership if suitably designed, equipped, and operated. Teaching and learning space is a basic requirement in all newly built libraries.

An electronic classroom is an integral part of any academic library that has been designed as a teaching instrument (see Appendix B). Appropriate furnishings and equipment include: seating for at least twenty students, but no more than thirty; desks that allow computer monitors to be recessed; one or more ceiling-mounted LCD projectors; and an instructor station, with network connection from which student computers and ambient lighting can be controlled. Videoconferencing or ITV capability also may be present; if so, the classroom should be acoustically isolated to prevent noise intrusion. This is the facility by means of which the library can reach students both on campus and off. All in all, a properly equipped instruction room is the most important feature of the library as a teaching and learning instrument.

A new library has the opportunity to develop innovative ERS teaching programs and to become an integral part of the university's teaching mission. ERS instruction offers to librarians a means of cultivating information literacy within the context of specific courses in which "the faculty member in effect becomes a collaborator in learning. . . ."[15] Evidence is accumulating that university undergraduates who do not acquire ERS during their studies will be less employable upon graduation. Apparently students and their parents are persuaded: Although Winona State requires incoming students to lease laptop computers beginning in 2000, over 75 percent of entering freshmen in 1999 chose to join the leasing program *voluntarily.* There is no conflict between the acquisition of research skills and the goals of a liberal education. The two are, in fact, mutually reinforcing, because critical evaluation of information is clearly part of the educational process. In the course of a four-year degree program, for example, students will subject hundreds of Websites to scrutiny as they separate valid information sources from dross. Critical-thinking skills are thereby enhanced.

With proper facilities at their disposal, librarians can assume an active role in the teaching of ERS. Liaison with faculty members is crucial, because nothing much will happen without their commitment to implementing information technology. With their encouragement it may be possible for academic librarians "to remove ourselves from the static environments of our libraries today" and to "work with . . . user communities more directly than ever before."[16] Despite the promise conjured by information technology, not everyone in the university is persuaded of the value of electronic research skills.

Librarians who see their building as a teaching instrument, and wonder why faculty sometimes fail to appreciate their interest in ERS, need to recall that universities are among society's most conservative institutions. Teaching methods have changed little since the Renaissance, and "five centuries of the printed book," as Sir Eric Ashby wrote some years ago, "have not diminished the need for the lecture, seminar, and tutorial."[17] Web-enhanced instruction will not, of course, supplant traditional methods of teaching in the short term. The lecture still dominates, and older faculty, in particular, remain suspicious of electronic gadgetry. Many are convinced of the medium's ability to muddle the message. Although there is no substitute for human contact between instructor and student, the relationship is typically an exclusive one: Learning is what occurs between teacher and student in a classroom. Libraries often are seen as service providers and as unwelcome interlopers in the teaching process. Scholars frequently seek information through their personal networks, not in the library. "When I need to find articles on a topic in an unfamiliar field," writes Steven Pinker, "I don't use the library computer; I send e-mail to a pal in the field."[18] Library avoidance is not the rule, however. There are a few examples (Earlham College is one of them) of close collaboration between teaching faculty and librarians, either on wired campuses or elsewhere. Increasing faculty attendance at such major annual conferences as EDUCAUSE, Syllabus, and the Mid-South Instructional Technology Conference indicates that the winds of change are gathering strength.

Faculty resistance to information technology, and to the library's teaching role, can be reduced by persuasion and compelling example. A success story from Winona State University is a series of Web Camps, first offered to faculty in the summer of 1998. Their purpose was to acquaint faculty with the pedagogical/"andragogical" advantages of Web-enhanced teaching and learning. Faculty learned, first, FrontPage software; then the emphasis shifted to ways and means of using technology to improve student learning. The impetus for this effort was Winona State's decision, made in 1999, to offer students universal access to laptop computers. Completion of a new library building coincided with the laptop initiative and found many faculty prepared to use technology in creative ways. Systematic renovation of classrooms to accommodate laptop-computer use paralleled these other ventures, thus making the introduction of information technology a campuswide project. Having a new library designed to support the use of electronic resources both stimulated the process of change and gave it focus.

New or renovated facilities are integral to the incorporation of teaching and learning technology. A library built to serve the needs of a networked campus can be the symbol, catalyst, and focal point of a different educational environment. With the advent of full-text databases of scholarly literature, librarians and teaching faculty have become partners in the academic enterprise. One group helps the other to ensure that students have access to the complete range of information sources held by the library or available on electronic networks. Libraries, therefore, should be designed to promote this partnership. With properly equipped instructional space available, the library plays a central role in teaching electronic research skills.

Teaching Electronic Research Skills

Philosophy

Since the beginning, libraries have classified and cataloged their contents in order to make their resources accessible. The emphasis in recent decades has focused on developing independent research skills among students who are learning to use an academic library. According to Joan Bechtel,

> what libraries do is "collect people and ideas" and "facilitate conversation among people": the primary task . . . of the academic library is to introduce students to the world of scholarly dialogue that spans both space and time and to provide students with the knowledge and skills they need to tap into conversations on an infinite variety of topics and to participate in the . . . debate on those issues.[19]

The desired outcome is a student who has learned to think critically: to locate, evaluate, and synthesize information in the process of coming to a rational conclusion about particular issues.[20] Graduates who possess the requisite skills, according to the designers of the Leavey Library, "will have a competitive edge in the rapidly growing information based economy." The same premise underlies laptop-computer-access programs at a number of universities around the country. Education's goal is to develop the ability to evaluate an array of sources so as to judge their relevance to a particular research topic. How to locate and analyze those sources is a skill that librarians can help to develop.

Although a wide range of full-text articles is currently available, formats, licensing agreements, and search protocols are a barrier to effective research. High access charges can exclude smaller academic libraries that do not belong to consortia, such as Minnesota's MINITEX, but the migration of scholarly publication to an electronic format demands that all libraries find a way to gain access. The California State University system, for example, is using its considerable buying power to secure favorable terms from the vendors of electronic-journal collections. Smaller colleges may be able to "kite-tail" on such contracts. Once that goal is reached, the challenge is to bring researchers and sources together.

The foundation of ERS belongs to what is traditionally called bibliographic instruction. Attention has shifted from the use of paper indexes, abstracts, and bibliographies to the electronic skill-set. The strategies needed to conduct research in electronic sources are generic, so once good basic skills are learned they can be applied in any discipline. A subject search in several citation databases, for example, CARL UnCover or *Historical Abstracts*, will elicit abstracts that can be used to develop a thesis that can guide further research. The topic may be narrowed or broadened in response to the availability of information. Thus an extensive literature search may result in a clearly focused set of references, all of them germane to the topic. This approach applies equally well to all academic disciplines and can be taught in the context of many different courses. Both the teaching and the conduct of electronic research require a knowledge of computers, search systems, and the galaxy of resources on the Internet.

Familiarizing students with the use of personal computers is a first step in the teaching of information literacy, one important aspect of which is "confidence and self-reliance" in the use of computers.[21] Most library users obtain some computer experience with OPACs, but require coaching to obtain proficiency with text-editing software or Webpage-creation, Internet access, and Web research. Campuses that have laptop-computer-access programs are finding willingness on the part of both students and faculty to assume responsibility for their own learning, but formal training also needs to occur. Electronic research skills should in fact be added to the basic curriculum offered to undergraduate students, so that they can function effectively in the information society in which they will work after graduation. Through an understanding of "the role, power, and uses of information," they will gain appreciation for retrieval, evaluation, organization, and manipulation of that information.[22] The teaching of ERS aims "to produce university graduates who are familiar with online systems, who use computers to research and write assignments, and who eventually will take valuable skills from the classroom to the workplace."[23] After all, "a library that supports and encourages electronic research offers its users access to information sources in the world at large."[24]

The electronic environment requires students to acquire basic critical-thinking skills. This ability, combined with ERS, will permit both experienced and novice researchers to gather appropriate information. In the electronic "environment it is imperative that students face the choices on the 'shelves' with ability to discern which of the available products are appropriate."[25] Librarians will help to devise "approaches to information, helping users shape search strategies, sort their information, and evaluate their sources."[26] The job of the librarian is to teach the use of electronic sources in such a way "that users become self-sufficient in finding information in the [electronic] library. That goal is most easily realized in a library which is designed for maximum user convenience."[27] By helping users to understand the function of online catalogs, to formulate search commands, to prepare search strategies, and to evaluate the results of their research, librarians assume their proper role in the information society. In the twenty-first-century library, this, however, is not the whole story; new roles for librarians with technical and teaching skills are emerging.

The position of "electronic resources specialist" (or variations on this theme) is appearing in academic libraries. Responsibilities may focus either on assisting the library's student or faculty clientele or on helping to integrate technology into the teaching and learning process. At Winona State, for example, one librarian manages the student-centered Information Gallery. Another librarian (a coauthor of this book), who holds a graduate degree in technical communication management, managed the Academic Technologies Center and worked closely with faculty who applied technology to course development. As librarians discovered at the University of Iowa, where they assist faculty in the use of information technology, "substantial face-to-face interaction between trusted colleagues" promotes effective transfer of expertise.[28] A gateway library is a natural agent of change, as the following example demonstrates. Among the most successful means of transferring technological expertise are periodic Web Camps in which faculty learn the techniques of producing courses for electronic presentation.

Faculty Web Camps

Web Camps are learning and development events that focus on providing interested teaching faculty with opportunities to enhance their curricula through creating Webpages, organizing and displayng of information, considering new and different teaching strategies, and trying out various means of electronic communication. To that end, the basic outline of a Website is provided for each faculty participant, who works on and develops the site over a period of eight days. Through a series of tutorials and lessons, the "campers" are introduced to and learn software applications that enable them to develop Websites they can use to improve their courses. Several guests are invited to stimulate discussion about Internet searching, the characteristics of a good Website, issues related to copyright and electronic resources, campus Web policies, and new technologies. An underlying theme throughout the Web Camps is a philosophical and practical discussion about how a subject-specific course Website might (or might not) provide a valuable enhancement to more traditional classroom teaching.

Web Camps take place in a studio classroom (located in the library's Academic Technologies Center) in which computers are positioned around the perimeter of the room, leaving the center of the room open for easy transit and communication. Novice computer users sit next to and between those with more experience. This kind of arrangement enables participants to call on their neighbors for peer teaching and collaborative learning. If additional help is needed, and it often is, one or the other of the consultants is asked to lend assistance or provide an answer. The schedule contains plenty of practice and development time following each tutorial and lesson, so that participants have the opportunity to apply their newly acquired skills. Consultants, who demonstrate the tutorials and lessons, are available throughout the eight days of each Web Camp to offer one-on-one coaching, answers, suggestions, recommendations, and other assistance. Planning for and hosting the Web Camps follow a modified version of the "let's learn together" approach more typical of music and other fine arts.

Purpose and Value of Web Camps

The most obvious purpose of the Web Camps is to provide faculty with an opportunity for concentrated and intense development of a Website devoted to one or more courses. A second purpose could be described as making the effort to "encourage and foster the development of social connections between and among individuals and groups." [29] To that end, Web Camps feature demonstrations of and discussions on

- specific parts of software and hardware applications
- incorporating technology into student curricular and cocurricular experiences
- humanistic social activities
- access to extensive resources
- informative, accurate Webpages
- interesting, interactive multimedia components
- easy navigation

Concentrating on these features means that faculty participants learn that "the key to enhancing learning and personal development is not simply for faculty to teach more and better, but also to create conditions that motivate and inspire students to devote time and energy to educationally purposeful activities, both in and outside the classroom." [30]

The main value in Web Camps is the fact that dedicated time (seven hours a day for eight days) is set aside for developmental purposes with consultants available to provide whatever support is necessary. Faculty participants become familiar with new teaching/learning approaches and technology integration as quickly as possible. Obtaining a reasonable comfort level is critical because "it is the faculty, finally, who will design and manage how technically mediated instruction will occur, ideally in a way that introduces new power and responsibility to the learner. This is an exciting but novel role for faculty and students alike, and one that is not without its share of risk." [31] By assuming this role, faculty participants gain experience in teaching with and through technology while simultaneously redefining and enlarging the scope of the pedagogies they endorse.

Web Camp Program

Throughout the eight days of Web Camp, participants gain experience by designing a Website around a stated curricular goal. Web Camps are hosted by several consultants well versed in Webpage creation, image-editing software, useful technologies, and how pedagogical activities can be developed. Consultants are available throughout the eight-day camp and after to provide assistance to campers.

The main software applications used during Web Camp are Microsoft's FrontPage and PaintShop Pro. FrontPage is a very powerful program that requires little experience beyond understanding basic word-processing concepts and electronic mail as well as having some knowledge of the Internet and its capabilities. Because familiar concepts are used, little time has to be devoted to teaching software; rather, time is spent using the software to create a learning environment. FrontPage is integrated in such a way that working with tables, forms, and hyperlinks as well as inserting images and multimedia files can be done with one software package.

Campers use PaintShop Pro during Web Camp to create their own graphics or edit the graphical creations of others. Adding images to Webpages greatly enhances their attractiveness to viewers. Although used by many professionals, PaintShop Pro is easily accessible for those with little experience in graphics production. This software offers easy and reliable ways to edit and tidy the image files that result from using the digital still cameras and flatbed and slide scanners that are available during Web Camp.

Web Camps are busy and intense for both consultants and participants. High levels of enthusiasm and cooperation mean that the challenge of getting through the curriculum is easily met. At Web Camp, participants

identify instructional goals

determine the appropriateness of technology for achieving those goals

design a good Website

receive assistance with assessment and evaluation

learn that technical and instructional support is available

work with digital cameras and scanners

add audio and video clips to Webpages

work with graphics, stills, and animations

create and use frames

develop forms

explore online testing

gain understanding of copyright and campus Web policies

experiment with discussion groups

become familiar with other technologies: streaming media, NetMeeting, WebCompass

Web Camp projects integrate the World Wide Web into the curriculum in such a way that learning is enhanced. Projects are expected to include at least some of the following: Web syllabi and commentaries, Web assignments, discussion forums, a collection of Internet links that are appropriate to a particular field of study, relevant diagrams and annotations, graphics, and animations, along with audio and video. Campers are expected to bring with them the basic outline for a Web project. In general, projects should fit into a course that is scheduled for the upcoming academic year. With word-processed files on floppy diskettes, faculty participants are able to use the copy-and-paste function to greatly ease the transition to Webpage creation. Because it is expected that the project will take more than the allotted eight days to complete, support is available to anyone after camp ends.

Continued Support and Development

Given the number of converging technologies now in view, and those that are just over the horizon (e.g., software shells for creating Web-enhanced courses, teaching/learning modules, broadband digital multimedia), it is essential to have a place in which research and development can occur, and in which faculty can find the assistance they need with their own projects. Here faculty may obtain the assistance necessary to gain expertise as they integrate technologies into their teaching.

The Academic Technologies Center will supply technical support and design specialists for faculty members' educational needs. The following components are contained within the ATC:

a development area in which faculty can work in collaboration with professional staff whose job is to stay current with effective educational technologies

a studio classroom where Web Camps and other similar events will occur

access to the university's electronic portfolio program for students

technical support office, with staff who are trained to maintain the hardware and the network throughout the campus

electronic resources and course design assistance

access to high-end multimedia computers, scanners, digital cameras, and other peripherals and software as required to reflect faculty use

Why is the library a natural home for this important faculty-support service? Most important is the library's long-standing interest in information technology, which originated in the MARC project of the 1960s. Today's new academic libraries are information hubs on campus networks, and thus contain a large technological infrastructure intended to support research. It therefore makes sense to build from strength by concentrating teaching and learning technologies in a central location. Once these technologies have achieved widespread acceptance, faculty support can be dispersed to the college or department level. In the meantime, the library serves as a congenial host.

Considering the Effect on Students

The emerging information age demands a different learning environment than that associated with the industrial age model of higher education. Much larger amounts of information are being screened and assimilated. Greater numbers of students arriving on campus are older and bring with them significant experience and accomplishment. "To remain employed in an unpredictable job market," says Elizabeth Tebeaux, "students can no longer depend on the future relevance of today's technology, which is becoming outmoded by the growth in knowledge stemming from technology."[32] For this reason, universities are having to acknowledge that technology is gaining momentum and validity as learning is being transformed. As a result, synergy and collaboration become more prominent as technology is fully integrated into learning. Ten top trends have been observed by the American Society for Training and Development as universities seek enhancements or alternatives or both to traditional campus-based scenarios for learning:[33]

1. Skill requirements will continue to increase in response to rapid technological change.
2. The American workforce will be significantly more educated and more diverse.
3. Corporate restructuring will continue to reshape the business environment.
4. Corporate training departments will change dramatically in size and composition.
5. Advances in technology will revolutionize the way training is delivered.
6. Training departments will find new ways to deliver services.
7. Training professionals will focus more on how to improve performance.
8. Integrated high-performance work systems will proliferate.
9. Companies will transform into learning organizations.
10. Organizational emphasis on human performance management will accelerate.

Learning is no longer confined to classrooms, libraries, and laboratories on a university campus, but is now occurring in the workplace, public libraries, factories, hotel rooms, and anywhere else that information technology enables a connection to a network. Information technology is making changes in the learning environment both possible and desirable. The advent of ATM (asynchronous transfer mode) networking protocols offers the possibility of rich, interactive learning opportunities employing multimedia, streaming audio and video, and access to full text. Every day, new information resources become available that promote active and flexible learning. With all these possibilities, it seems wise to follow the trend to create "a technologically enhanced environment, geographically confined or otherwise, that permits people to transcend both distance and time barriers to the educational process."[34] An academic library, for reasons already noted, is perhaps the best place on campus to assemble all the resources demanded by technology-based learning systems.

What Kind of Collaboration Can Occur?

Instructional technology "is hailed as a time saver, a conduit to open the university as never before, and as a tool to improve learning for all."[35] These words apply to all campuses where universal access via laptop computers is growing with each passing day. Technology initiatives, anywhere, are complicated by lack of resources, doubts about functionality, entrenched organizational values, and narrow discipline-specific concerns. Nevertheless, enthusiasm for Web-based technology is energizing faculty in ways earlier technologies failed to achieve. Interest is beginning to grow in restructuring universities to make optimal use of new technologies. Libraries, as information centers, are coming under closer scrutiny.

In recent years, higher education has seen the convergence of libraries and computing services, which, in turn, has implications for all instructional activities hosted by the library.[36] Pressure is growing to expand information-technology service efforts. Many libraries are responding successfully to these demands by providing increased access to electronic information resources as well as assistance in using these resources, along with creating and developing instructional programs devoted to giving students good research skills that will serve them well throughout their lives.

Convergence is significant, in large part, because the collaboration that may occur can only benefit the students. Librarians can help students to gain skills that will enable them to take the best advantage of Web-enhanced courses created by faculty. With instructional technologists assisting faculty in their design efforts and librarians helping students gain an understanding of research, it seems that collaborative learning is here to stay. Working together, instructional technologists and teaching librarians can help to create an environment that may produce well-educated young people who also are excellent candidates for the job market.

Research Skills Instruction for Students

Until recently, a typical view has been that expert knowledge confers the ability to teach. Often, this association is unclear to students. With the advent of information technology, the connection between subject-matter expertise and effective teaching has become even looser. University teaching that is technologically enhanced is now much more complicated, thus "demanding entirely new thinking about the variety of roles teachers play and the diverse activities they perform in their knowledge transmission functions." [37] Relationships with the library and its teaching functions with respect to research skills are growing as part of a good strategy that emphasizes a process that combines commitment, imaginative implementation, and sensible planning. "Innovation in technology-based teaching," writes Sir John Daniel, vice-chancellor of Britain's Open University, "requires the same care and understanding as the development of knowledge in any other field." [38] Partnerships and alliances between faculty, students, the library, and other campus organizations promise the greatest success. Ensuring that students achieve technical competence in addition to their disciplinary studies will produce well-rounded graduates suitably prepared for careers in an information society. With constant advances in technology, graduating students will be able to work successfully in a constantly changing environment where the continuing advance of technology will radically change many of their professional roles.

When the library chooses to become an active participant in the learning organization, interesting things can happen in a student's academic career. A learning organization is concerned about the reciprocal relationship between individuals and their college or university. "A learning organization," says Jennifer Rowley, "is an organization that facilitates learning for all of its members, and thereby continuously transforms itself." [39] When put together with faculty truly interested in creating the best possible learning environment for their students, the university experience becomes both dynamic and exciting. The library plays a vital role in this educational process.

Evaluation

Frequent evaluation of library programs that teach electronic research skills is essential, so as to maintain a close association between skills development and academic performance. Unless students see that their extra effort will result in a fairly quick payoff, they may lose interest or treat the technology mainly as an entertainment medium. Some background on information technology, and its effects on society and the workplace, may help to persuade reluctant students to participate more eagerly in ERS training. The ERS section should be reasonably short so that students can make use of their newly learned skills during the same academic term. The tempo of these instruction sessions has to be upbeat, yet not so fast as to lose the participants. The Mann Library at Cornell University seems to concur with these observations, and adds several other points: (1) students' motivation to learn is rewarded by improved grades and satisfaction of immediate needs; (2) students require hands-on experience, with personalized instruction, when they are introduced to library systems and computer software; and (3) specific course-related instruction does not reach enough students.[40]

Teaching information technology in the context of specific courses, however, is one way to connect effort with reward: Research skills translate into better papers and, thus, higher grades. A practical difficulty is providing adequate hands-on experience during the teaching sessions. Computers situated in a library instruction room or in labs elsewhere on campus are one answer. A better one is for each student to own or lease a notebook computer, because network connections are easier and cheaper to provide than a host of desktop PCs. The real dilemma is how to reach an entire student population.

An institutional commitment to the integration of information technology into the curriculum is the essential first step. ERS instruction will remain peripheral unless it becomes the focus of academic policy, as is the case at Wake Forest, Seton Hall University, and other "laptop universities." Once that happens, faculty can become actively involved in the teaching of research skills within their own courses. Support and assistance come from librarians who are *au courant* with evolving information technology. An assumption underlying this hypothesis is that faculty are familiar enough with the resources in their disciplines to teach their use. A related premise is that faculty believe ERS is important. As long as courses emphasize the mastery of subject matter exclusively, nothing is likely to change. Winona State's successful faculty Web Camps demonstrate that new means of course delivery are welcome innovations.

Implications for Library Buildings

Just as digital networks are part of a building's fabric, support services for students and faculty legitimately claim a share of library space. Given the importance of electronic research skills within the curriculum, classrooms and other instructional facilities should be included in all new construction. It may well be that 10 percent or more of net assignable space is allocated to such enterprises. Their existence establishes the library as a significant partner in the teaching/learning process. When planning and designing a new building, educational space requires careful programing. The library's ability to support changing techniques of higher education depends on adequate instructional space of its own. Building flexibility and utility are thereby enhanced. It is safe to assume, moreover, that power and data network connections (hard-wired or wireless data transmission) must be ubiquitous. A library that serves as a teaching and learning instrument is truly an "intelligent building."

Two questions remain: (1) Will teaching faculty take advantage of the technology to enhance their courses? and (2) What are the implications for the design of new library buildings? With respect to the first question, librarians have to be persuasive. They are the ones who are most familiar with the power and the limitations of information technology, and perhaps the ones most concerned that students acquire research skills in the course of their education. Many faculty members remain to be convinced that research skills may well be the permanent legacy of a university education, one that remains long after specific course content has been forgotten. Yet, research studies show that "students forget 50 percent of the [course] content within a few months" and that they "carry away in their heads and in their notebooks not more than 42% of the lecture content."[41] This is a strong argument in favor of teaching information literacy. Even more persuasive is the experience faculty members gain, in training environments such as Web Camp, in migrating their courses to the Web.

The Teaching Library and Distance Education

Campus-centered universities are entering the distance-education market in growing numbers, inspired by the need to find a new clientele and by the success of such ventures as Britain's Open University and the University of Phoenix. EDUCAUSE statistics indicate that the number of campuses involved in distance learning grew by 62 percent from 1991 to 1994; 54 percent of institutions surveyed were so engaged.[42] A recent "in-depth report" by Merrill Lynch states that "[a]pproximately 84% of four-year colleges are expected to offer distance learning courses in 2002." [43] According to the same study, 43 percent of postsecondary students are twenty-five years old or older. [44] The potential market for distance education therefore is a large and growing one. New technologies are also a driving force, "with at least 25 states investing in two-way video." [45] Fiber-optic networks installed by telephone companies offer the bandwidth required for interactive video and multimedia data transmission. Data compression, moreover, enables acceptable transmission of video and audio over ordinary phone lines, using RealPlayer software and plug-ins. Teaching at a distance thus is now more than a talking head addressing a passive student audience. Remote access to information sources available on the Internet, such as academic libraries, CARL UnCover, FirstSearch, JStor, Project Muse, and a variety of electronic publications, means that students can be asked to do research assignments that could not have been demanded previously. The National Information Infrastructure, currently under development, will "help educational institutions to reach students where they are or prefer to be located." [46] Courses offered by distance teaching can be as rigorous in their writing requirements as those given on campus, where a library is easily accessible. In fact, the value of electronic research skills is even more apparent in distance learning, because of their immediate practical value.

Libraries have supported off-campus courses for years, by such means as mailing out research materials to registered students. Within the past decade, distance learners have acquired access to the host university's online catalog, and to many more such sources, as the Web has expanded. Information technology enables instructors to offer distance-education courses that rival on-campus offerings in quality and depth. In addition, as George Gilder advises, colleges should use technology to "[summon] the best from universities everywhere" instead of being completely self-contained. [47] It is entirely possible to develop electronic research skills at a distance, by using online sources in addition to e-mail, fax, interactive television, and the telephone. All that is required are a PC, a modem, and touch-tone service to the remote location. [48]

A sizable investment in full-text sources, such as JStor or FirstSearch, is needed to support distance-education courses adequately. Electronic access is most expeditious for students enrolled in Web-enhanced courses that are open to distance learners. Faculty need only select the journal material students are required to read, and a proxy server (by authenticating the user as a registered student or faculty member) gives access to licensed databases. There is no need to house special collections for distance learners on the home campus. The library's general collections offer the necessary support, supplemented by resources drawn from any ILL consortia to which the library may belong.

Distance-education students will need instruction in accessing and searching online resources. Written guides may be sent to those who register for courses, or instructions may be posted on the university's Web-site. E-mail offers a means of providing personalized assistance as required. The main thing is to have a librarian available to render timely help to those who request it. As video links proliferate, that assistance will become even more personal and effective.

From a building-design standpoint, emphasis on distance education requires space and equipment for the interlibrary-loan operation. Generous area is needed to handle the volume of materials destined for off-campus students, who may or may not have good electronic access. Reference service also should be easily accessible to distance learners, by telephone, e-mail, or the Web. To be an effective teaching instrument, academic libraries have to be available in a variety of ways, through several channels of communication.

As distance learning grows, academic libraries will see their ILL operations expand. Materials available only in print will have to be scanned-in (digitized) and transmitted by e-mail or photocopied and mailed to remote sites. Mediation by a librarian can help distance learners acquire relevant information from the physical collections. Advice on electronic searching will have to be readily available by telephone, e-mail, or video connection. Web-enhanced teaching encourages interaction among students and instructor; the same interactivity can occur between librarian and information seeker over the same media of e-mail or videoconference.

Web-enhanced distance education is likely to increase pressure not only on the teaching faculty, but also on library support services. These problems are not insoluble, but adequate resources will have to be in place. Librarians require technology of sufficient power. More of them will become involved in the process, because the workload will be too heavy for one "distance-education librarian" to handle. Everyone involved in public services has a part in supporting off-campus learners. The building's information network complements the library's membership in ILL consortia. All the components thus are in place to support the institution's distance-education efforts.

Every Web course produced by local faculty is potentially deliverable at a distance. Not every residential campus, of course, will "go global," but there could be substantial growth in regional, nontraditional markets. Degree programs that appeal to employed adults, such as nursing, education, and business, may transcend campus boundaries, if only in a limited way. The outcome is certain to be more business for the library, now that its resources are more easily accessible to off-campus students. Building planners and campus administrators need to ensure that the electronic infrastructure (servers, modem connections, bandwidth) is there to meet a higher demand for services. There is no choice in the matter, if residential colleges are not to lose their clientele to Web courses offered by prestigious institutions around the world.

The fact is, as Michael Dolence points out in his publications and speeches, that quality higher education is universally available online and that "many Information Age workers will need to spend at least 20 percent of their time engaged in learning." [49] Over one million people are currently enrolled in such programs. By 2002, some two million college students will be distance learners. [50] There are some seventy-six million adult learners in this distance-education market, most of whom are not served by traditional, campus-based institutions. Yet, there is no reason to abandon the field to profit-making vendors of educational services, such as the University of Phoenix and Jones International University. Regional markets can be well served by universities that offer library resources and research support to students enrolled in Web-based courses. Quality of service can almost match that available on campus, provided the technological infrastructure is in place. Greater reliance on electronic means of course delivery, therefore, should enhance contacts between librarians and teaching faculty to the benefit of all students.

Copyright and Distance Education

On many college campuses, the library is the repository of wisdom on all matters related to copyright. Gone are the days when a simple disavowal of responsibility for infringement, posted on photocopiers, settled most copyright issues; the rest could be handled with reference to Sections 107 and 108 of the Copyright Act of 1976. With the advent of Web-enhanced and Web-based courses, along with an upsurge in online distance education, conditions have changed rapidly. For several years now, the law has struggled to protect intellectual property on the Internet. Libraries have a large stake in the outcome of copyright-law revision, the most recent result of which is the Digital Millennium Copyright Act (DMCA) of 1998. In essence, the DMCA forbids the use of decryption to gain access to material protected by a "digital envelope." "Fair use" remains under debate, but there will be no "free use" of encrypted information, which is accessible only to those who pay the required fee.

The DMCA offered no relief to colleges and universities involved in distance education, which is a leading growth industry. Each time an instructor creates a Web-enhanced or Web-based course, a potential distance market opens; this is true even if the course is intended solely for on-campus offering. Once the face-to-face classroom no longer exists, the whole notion of "fair use" becomes moot. Thus, even though electronic reserve is possible, its legality is uncertain. Embedding links to streaming media and electronic information sources in a Web-enhanced course raises similar questions. Libraries, as information hubs on their respective campuses, face the challenge of choosing between the technologically possible and the possibly illegal in supporting Web-enhanced courses. Gradually, the rules of engagement for this conflict between information providers and users are becoming clearer. Their main purpose, exemplified in the DMCA, is to prevent "downstream" distribution of copyright materials by authorized (or licensed) users, such as faculty and students.

Copyright law (Sec. 512) now "provides greater certainty that educational institutions providing network access for faculty, staff, and students will not, merely by doing so, become liable for infringing material transmitted over the network."[51] Individuals, however, remain responsible for their use of network facilities; that is why the DMCA requires institutions to drop "repeat infringers" from their networks. This is a concession to copyright owners, who greatly prefer licensing agreements to expanding the exemption in Section 110 for "the performance or display of any work in the course of face-to-face teaching activities."[52] The *Report* of the Register of Copyrights (1999) recommends greater latitude for distance-education purposes. In return for a broader definition of what constitutes a "classroom" (i.e., a virtual space), copyright users will be expected to comply with the prohibition on downstream copying and distribution of copyrighted materials.

The Register of Copyrights further recommends that there be statutory language to the effect "that the performance or display must be made by or at the direction of an instructor to illustrate a point in, or as an integral part of, the equivalent of a class session in a particular course."[53] This is an attempt to force new information technologies into a traditional mold, the purpose of which is to defend the intellectual-property rights of copyright owners. Whether or not it works, the effort at least promises greater educational access to digital information sources, with the exception of multimedia. Access to audiovisual materials "represents a new policy question that has not yet been considered."[54] The Register, however, advises allowing "transient" copies of such material, provided that they remain accessible to students only for the duration of the course and that there be no further duplication. This approach would clear the way for legal use of multimedia already easily accessible from networked servers.

Of particular interest to libraries is network access to course readings in electronic format ("e-reserves"). Provided that appropriate safeguards are in place (i.e., proxy-server authentication, password protections,

Internet protocol group restrictions, firewalls), greater leniency appears to be forthcoming. Thus, for example, a library that subscribes to JStor or FirstSearch could make these resources available to "eligible students," whether on or off campus. One way of legally doing so is to grant access to hyperlinks only to those with a username and password. Others could view a portion of the Website not restricted in this manner. There would be anytime/anyplace access for students registered in a particular course. The institution's obligation is to ensure that safeguards are in place and that they remain effective. Under such guidelines, Web-enhanced education should be able to flourish. Portable computers, moreover, would reach their full potential as aids to the teaching and learning process.

The implications in all of this for academic libraries are great. In an environment of controlled access to many sources of digitized information, the library is both gateway and gatekeeper. Course and media servers can be located in the library, if qualified staff are present. It is the library that arranges access to commercial databases and provides many of the network connections available on campus. New libraries should contain space for servers and for support services needed by faculty and students. These service units, by extension, can be useful to distance learners who require help with the technology, with the software, or with the techniques of electronic research. With the advent of Web-enhanced education, on-campus and distance learning are converging, as are libraries and computer centers. The design of both buildings and services must take account of these developments. Housing the computer center in a new library building is an option planners need to consider, as they wrestle with the "transformational" issues raised by Michael Dolence and other diviners of higher education's future.

Notes

1. Ernest L. Boyer, *College: The Undergraduate Experience in America* (New York: Harper and Row, 1987), 167.

2. Ralph E. Ellsworth, "How buildings can contribute," in *Educating the Library User*, ed. John Lubans Jr. (New York: R. R. Bowker, 1974), 415–422.

3. James Rice Jr., *Teaching Library Use: A Guide for Library Instruction* (Westport, Conn.: Greenwood Press, 1981), 130.

4. Suzanne Douglas, "Digital soup: The ABCs of distance learning," *EDUCOM Review* 28 (4) (July/August 1993).

5. Philip Tompkins, "New structures for teaching libraries," *Library Administration and Management* 4 (2): 78 (spring 1990).

6. Brian L. Hawkins, "Preparing for the next wave of computing on campus," *Change: The Magazine of Higher Learning* 23 (1): 27 (January/February 1991).

7. Linda Demmers et al., "Envisioning tomorrow's library" (Los Angeles: Leavey Library, University of Southern California, June 1993), 4.

8. Dan Pecarina, "The technology effect: Winona State University's search for an e-mail system

evolved into a whole new technology direction," *Multiversity* (summer 1999): 20.

9. Tompkins, "New structures for teaching libraries," 78.

10. Internal library document at Indiana University–Purdue University of Indianapolis.

11. Peter Lyman, "The library of the (not-so-distant) future," *Change: The Magazine of Higher Learning* 23 (1): 40 (January/February 1991).

12. Brian L. Hawkins, "Creating the library of the future: Incrementalism won't get us there!" <http://www.virtualschool.edu/mon/Academia/Hawkins LibraryOfFuture.html>.

13. Karen M. Drabenstott, "Analytical review of the library of the future," Council on Library Resources, February 1993 <http://www.si.umich.edu/~ylime/clr/CLRRVW.pdf>.

14. Lewis M. Branscomb, "The electronic library," *Journal of Communication* 31 (1): 150 (winter 1981).

15. Patricia Senn Breivik and Dan L. Jones, "Information literacy: Liberal education for the information age," *Liberal Education* 79 (1): 28 (1993).

16. Colin Steele, "Millennial libraries: management changes in an electronic environment," *Electronic Library* 11 (6): 398, 399 (December 1993).

17. Quoted in Ernest Boyer, *College: The Undergraduate Experience in America* (New York: Harper and Row, 1987), 173.

18. Steven Pinker, *How the Mind Works* (New York: W. W. Norton, 1999), 142.

19. Joan M. Bechtel, "Conversation, a new paradigm for librarianship?" *College & Research Libraries* 47 (3): 221 (May 1986).

20. Sonia Bodi, "Critical thinking and bibliographic instruction: The relationship," *Journal of Academic Librarianship* 14 (3): 151 (July 1988).

21. Harold W. Tuckett, "Computer literacy, information literacy, and the role of the instruction librarian," in *Coping with Information Illiteracy: Bibliographic Instruction for the Information Age*, ed. Glenn E. Mensching and Teresa B. Mensching (Ann Arbor: Pierian Press, 1989), 24.

22. Jan Kennedy Olsen, "The electronic library and literacy," *New Directions for Higher Education* 20 (2): 94 (summer 1992).

23. Richard J. Bazillion and Connie Braun, "Academic library design: Building a 'teaching instrument,'" *Computers in Libraries* 14 (2): 12 (February 1994).

24. Ibid., 15.

25. Cerise Oberman, "Avoiding the cereal syndrome, or critical thinking in the electronic environment," *Library Trends* 39 (3): 200 (winter 1991); see also Hannelore B. Rader, "Information literacy: A revolution in the library," *RQ* 31 (1): 25–29 (fall 1991).

26. Evan Farber, "Reflections on library instruction," in *The LIRT Library Instruction Handbook*, ed. May Brottman and Mary Loe (Englewood, Colo.: Libraries Unlimited, 1990), 4.

27. James Rice Jr., *Teaching Library Use: A Guide for Library Instruction* (Westport, Conn.: Greenwood, 1981), 130.

28. Carol Ann Hughes, "'Facework': A new role for the next generation of library-based information technology centers," *Library Hi Tech* 16 (3/4): 35 (July/September 1998).

29. Paul Treuer and Linda Belote, "Current and emerging applications of technology to promote student involvement and learning," in *Using Technology to Promote Student Learning: Opportunities for Today and Tomorrow*, ed. Catherine McHugh Engstrom and Kevin W. Kruger (San Francisco: Jossey-Bass, 1997), 22.

30. "The student learning imperative: Implications for student affairs," *Journal of College Student Development* 37 (2): 118 (1996).

31. George Connick and Jane Russo, "Technology and the inevitability of education transformation," in *The Electronic Classroom: A Handbook for Education in the Electronic Environment*, ed. Erwin Boschmann (N.J.: Learned Information, 1995), 18.

32. Elizabeth Tebeaux, "The high-tech workplace: Implications for technical communication," in *Technical Writing and Practice*, ed. B. E. Fearing and W. K. Sparrow (New York: Modern Language Association, 1989), 137.

33. American Society for Training and Development, *Position Yourself for the Future: The Top Ten Trends*, 1996, <http://www.astd.org/industry/trends/bassi.htm>.

34. From the Virtual University, <http://www.avistar.com/education/education.html>.

35. Mathew L. Ouellett and Christine A. Stanley, "Instructional technology and diversity: Parallel challenges for our institutions," *Journal of Staff, Program and Organization Development* 15 (1): 5 (1997–1998).

36. Neil McLean, "Convergence of libraries and computing services: Implications for reference services," *LASIE* 28 (3): 5 (September 1997).

37. James L. Bess, "Teaching well: Do you have to be schizophrenic?" *Review of Higher Education* 22 (1): 4 (1998).

38. John S. Daniel, *Mega-Universities and Knowledge Media: Technology Strategies for Higher Education* (London: Kogan Page, 1996), 141.

39. Jennifer Rowley, "The library as a learning organization," *Library Management* 18 (2): 91 (1997).

40. Olsen, "The electronic library and literacy," 96.

41. American Library Association, Presidential Committee, *Final Report*, 7; see also Patricia Senn Breivik and Ward Shaw, "Libraries prepare for an information age," *Educational Record* 70 (1): 16 (winter 1989).

42. Information provided by EDUCAUSE via e-mail, July 28, 1994. "No-response" rates to the EDUCAUSE survey were 15 percent (1991/92), 12 percent (1993), and 6 percent (1994). Over four hundred institutions responded to each survey.

43. Michael T. Moe, Kathleen Bailey, and Rhoda Lau, *The Book of Knowledge: Investing in the Growing Education and Training Industry* (New York: Merrill Lynch, April 1999), 121.

44. Ibid., 9, 42.

45. *Chronicle of Higher Education* (July 6, 1994): A20.

46. NRENAISSANCE Committee of the National Academy of Sciences, *Realizing the Information Future* (Washington, D.C.: National Academy Press, 1994), chap. 3, par. 3.

47. "Talking with George Gilder," *EDUCOM Review* 29 (4): 37 (July/August 1994).

48. Richard J. Bazillion and Connie Braun, "Technology and library users: Automation and outreach: Library services to off-campus students," *Journal of Distance Education* 7 (2): 67–75 (fall 1992).

49. Michael G. Dolence and Donald M. Norris, *Transforming Higher Education: A Vision for Learning in the 21st Century* (Ann Arbor, Mich.: Society for College and University Planning, 1995), 9.

50. U.S. Copyright Office, *Report on Copyright and Digital Distance Education* (Washington, D.C.: U.S. Copyright Office, May 1999), 19.

51. Ibid., ix.

52. Ibid., vii.

53. Ibid., xvii.

54. Ibid., xx.

CHAPTER 7

Academic Libraries at the Millennium

The book is here to stay. What we're doing is symbolic of the peaceful coexistence of the book and the computer.[1]

The survival powers of the book notwithstanding, technological changes in the making could, *one day, profoundly alter the traditional operation of libraries—and their buildings.*[2]

Provosts and librarians share an image of the future of information resources on their campus. They all strongly prefer a future in which there is universal access by faculty and students to multiple information sources in all possible media via a single multifunctional workstation.[3]

How will academic libraries of the twenty-first century and beyond differ in form and function from their predecessors? As Niels Bohr once quipped "it's difficult to predict—especially the future." But if one extrapolates on the basis of current trends, it is likely that electronic information sources will explode in number and importance. Scholars in most academic fields already find an increasing amount of their research materials in electronic format.[4] Print media as means of knowledge transfer are declining as "Internet access enables libraries to leverage their resources so as to acquire more of the scholarly record, to own materials collectively and to share them between libraries and their end users."[5] These developments do not necessarily mean that libraries will lose their central place on the university campus. Scholars will always require a haven in which uninterrupted study and contemplation can occur in reasonably comfortable surroundings. Print collections will continue to grow, because no evidence exists that the presses are ceasing to roll. And as long as librarians are skilled in electronic techniques of scholarly research, they will have a place in the evolving university.

Technological innovation may accelerate in society at large, but will not conquer universities without a struggle. This is so because higher education is based on dynamic human interactions that machines cannot duplicate and sometimes cannot enhance. Uncritical adoption of any technology or teaching device does not happen in higher education, and innovations must prove themselves to skeptics who demand that they indeed contribute to the education of students. EDUCAUSE, which musters over five thousand attendees at its annual conferences, encourages and promotes intelligent applications of information technology. The organization believes that technology is never an end in itself, but rather a tool in the hands of skilled educators. Electronic means, whether applied in the library or the classroom, will be most successful where computers are least obtrusive. Buildings will incorporate networks and computers into their fabric and thus become, to use Heather Edwards's felicitous phrase, "instruments of education."

Several new library buildings in North America illustrate the symbiosis of information technology, architecture, and education. Notwithstanding the advance of electronic research, the library as a physical entity is holding its own. In 1997 and 1998, thirty-five academic-library projects reached completion; half of these were new buildings (with a total value of $234.5 million).[6] One reason for the library's survival is the need for institutional support of electronic access, which exceeds the financial means of individual scholars and students. As in the past, when colleges purchased book collections for general use, institutions will find ways to encourage faculty research. Consortial licensing of full-text databases is widespread, as is Web-enhanced teaching. Creative scholarship is finding new outlets and, in the process, is saving higher education from stagnation.

Presuming, then, that academic life goes on and that libraries survive as physical entities, what sorts of places will they be? Such universities as Cornell and the SUNY system are forecasting that central library space will reach a steady state by the time the new century is a decade old. After that, technology and remote storage will accommodate growth in the volume of scholarly publication. New buildings will not attempt to house the artifacts of a print culture, in whole or even in large part. This being the case, libraries built in the early years of the twenty-first century are destined for use in an epoch dominated by electronic publication. These buildings will begin life as hybrids, housing both print and electronic media. Librarians at Cornell University observe that "the availability of electronic resources has not lessened users' needs to consult the printed literature . . . , nor has it made print-based information and document delivery services obsolete."[7] Yet much of the twentieth-century's printed output is published on high-acid-content paper and therefore is perishable. As paper holdings decay and their contents are scanned into digital storage media, space occupied by shelving can find other uses. That is why building flexibility is the leading criterion of today's library construction.[8]

Assuming, furthermore, that faculty and students will always require a central place in which to study and broaden their access to sources of information, what sort of facility should be planned when a new library is needed? There are two models from which to choose, one proposed by Patricia Battin almost two decades ago and represented by several buildings constructed during the intervening years; the other is England's De Montfort University library. "I want to emphasize as strongly as I can," wrote Battin in 1984, "that in my view the personal computer does not mean an end to books—I think the printed word will be with us for a very long time."[9] She proposed a "scholarly information center" that draws on the resources of both the library and computer services. Libraries that have equipped themselves with electronic classrooms, information galleries, and academic technologies centers, while caring for the print materials in their custody, exemplify Battin's point.

The second model is more radical. At the 1992 Essen Symposium, the delegates from De Montfort University declared: "The *Electronic* Library implies that what we now recognize as a physically identifiable library has been taken to its ultimate form: a resource area comprising space, people and facilities but where there may not be a book in sight."[10] Though most planners will prefer to hedge their bets by selecting the hybrid model, the evolution of library services is tilting toward greater reliance on electronic information sources. De Montfort, a university built *de novo* during the 1990s, points the way toward a future in which the book may occupy a much smaller place in the constellation of library resources. The question for most of us is this: How do we get there from here? For those who plan to make the journey, a closer look at the British experience is instructive if not necessarily reassuring.

Higher education in Britain is government funded. Rising materials costs and large staffing complements absorb more money than the system provides. Full-service universities that support teaching and research across a broad spectrum of disciplines are under closer scrutiny by those who pay the bills. Financial pressures are threatening traditional library services that are based on the ownership of large collections of print materials. There is an incentive to find cost-effective means of delivering both higher education and the library and information services that it requires—hence the emphasis on electronic communications and networking. Any solution looks appealing that reduces the investment in bricks-and-mortar libraries. Just because it is possible to conceive of an electronic "library without walls," however, does not mean that society, in the end, will be well served if this model triumphs. There are significant risks in committing scientific knowledge to the digital realm, however enticing the electronic vision may be.

The prospect of an electronic library offering "universal access, by students and faculty, to information in all possible media via a single, multifunction workstation" is technologically sound.[11] Until quite recently there seemed to be no sense of urgency in the quest for electronic solutions to the problems of knowledge dissemination. During the early 1990s, a few pioneers published scholarly e-journals that struggled for academic respectability. Then Web-enhanced education accelerated, beginning in 1997, and networked access to information became essential. Brian Hawkins (now president of EDUCAUSE; then of Brown University) recognized the new library as "a collection of information, in many formats, stored electronically in locations throughout the world, but organized and collected and shared via a central networked organization."[12] This electronic library may not itself be a "place," but its information sources will be tapped by academic libraries around the world connected to "a ubiquitous and seamless web of interrelated networks."[13] And these libraries definitely will remain "places," because, "for a *community* of learning to function adequately, buildings and equipment are required."[14] Hawkins argues that "this new library needs to bring together scholars and information resources without necessarily bringing either one to a physical building."[15] Perhaps not "necessarily," but if learning is to survive amid the ferment of information technology, it needs its cathedrals and even its priesthood. Ideas need institutions to preserve and nurture them, even though those institutions may themselves be transformed by new technologies.

Although a comprehensive digital library will exist only a couple of decades into the new century, physical libraries will not thereby be rendered obsolete. Even the digital library will require institutional (that is, consortial) sponsorship to ensure its survival across generations of technological change. The servers that contain it require maintenance and replacement with new forms of technology. Some institution or consortium must be responsible for preserving the digital resource and for supervising technology migration. The greatest threat, from the standpoint of historical preservation, is the potential loss of digitized information. For this reason, the great research libraries (and many smaller ones) will maintain their traditional role as repositories of society's collective memory.

Libraries that serve a localized clientele, such as a college community, face a future that is less well defined.

These libraries certainly will operate in greatly changed circumstances in the years ahead. Ownership of materials will decline in importance, as the obligation to provide access to them becomes heavier. "Overall," predicts the NRENAISSANCE Committee, "the future role of libraries will evolve to reflect and interact with developments in individual, personal information retrieval systems and also developments in the publishing arena and other sources of supply for electronic information resources," at least as long as most research materials are in print format.[16] This trend implies, as we have pointed out, an expanding role for interlibrary loan in all libraries.[17] Emphasis on distance learning, moreover, will require that a variety of information forms (text, graphic, sound, video) be accessible over a broadband network. Eldred Smith and Peggy Johnson observe that ILL "must be transformed from a last resort to a primary activity."[18] Caroline R. Arms foresaw a library in which each researcher has "a workstation attached to the network" on which to retrieve information and use it as desired.[19] This workstation, we believe, is the notebook computer and its vastly more powerful successors. As considerable experience with universal-access programs demonstrates, portable computing is now an important part of the higher education process.

Unlimited access to bibliographic citations and abstracts already exists in libraries where the online catalog serves as a gateway to Internet resources worldwide. Gaining possession of the item itself remains a more difficult proposition. Articles and shorter pieces are easily scanned and then transmitted by fax; books will require physical delivery. The librarian's job, as always, will be to seek the "seamless integration" of all information media.[20] "The integration of multiple technologies," according to Pat Molholt, "is critical to the continued success and growth of the information industry and to our ability to offer services that truly address the needs of our users."[21]

Interlibrary loan departments will expand as their importance increases. High-speed Internet access is essential, along with the ability to digitize and transmit documents of all kinds. Thanks to scan-and-transmit technology (e.g., ARIEL), much faster and more-efficient communication among libraries now is possible. Interactive ILL allows patron-initiated transactions to occur without intermediation by the library.[22] Patrons still must have "status" at an institution that will guarantee the return or replacement of borrowed items. This is less an issue where electronic transmission is involved; yet, there must be a way to bill charges appropriately. It may well happen that ILL departments expand for a time, to meet demand generated by falling acquisitions budgets on most campuses, and then contract as interactive ILL is introduced. Eventually, at least in theory, they will disappear as the digital library swells. At any rate, it is electronic communications that will permit the resource-sharing on which academic research will rely in the years ahead.

Distance education also is poised to transform library service and the facilities through which it is offered in the new century. Regardless of how distance-education courses are delivered (whether by correspondence, television, or interactive video, or on the Web), many of them will have a research component. On-campus students, for their part, can obtain materials that have been digitized.

Copyright law is coming to grips with the issue of who controls the transformation of print into digital format, and vice versa. The technical as well as legal questions are these: How may documents be altered by recipients of electronic copies? How is the archival copy (the *Urtext*) to be preserved? Copyright statutes in the United States and Canada, for the moment at least, are largely products of a print culture. Issues raised by the electronic environment are receiving attention, but copyright law remains unrevised in substance. The only movement has been toward more restricted access to electronic information sources, thanks to the Digital Millennium Copyright Act. Access by means of license has become the norm, and only the buying power of large consortia is able to control licensing costs.[23] As matters stand, libraries are on shaky legal ground when they scan-in print materials, because this activity may not be covered by their license agreement with the national copyright collective. Although it is a simple matter to create an "electronic reserve," permission must be obtained for each item—a time-consuming and not always successful process. Similarly, licensing arrangements with vendors of such products as CD-ROM publications may prevent off-campus distribution, even when transmission capability exists. Yet, problems devised by human minds can be solved by the application of intelligence.[24] Therein lies reason for optimism, the DMCA notwithstanding. Both the U.S. Copyright Office and Congress are inclined to recognize the special needs of distance education by allowing copyrighted materials to be used by "a defined class of eligible students" present in cyberspace. Copyright law is likely to be revised to facilitate the expanding distance-education market.

One incentive to make an effort to broaden access is the burgeoning interest in distance education among campus-based universities. Once relegated to marginal status, distance learning is achieving new stature for several reasons:

the development of effective and accessible educational technologies

the emerging pattern of multiple careers, which forces workers to undergo retraining while simultaneously holding a job the constant need to update acquired skills

close ties between higher education and business, as a result of which rewards flow toward those who teach and learn practical skills, such as the techniques of electronic research

government demands that universities prove their accountability by making themselves accessible to a large proportion of the adult population[25]

Britain's Open University has inspired imitators throughout the world and, in 1998, formed an alliance with Western Governors' University. Two other examples are Canada's Athabasca University and New Zealand's Open Polytechnic. Institutions founded exclusively to offer distance education are now facing competition from traditional campuses eager to reform their mandates.[26] Numerous established universities in North America are offering distance-education courses on the Web. Evidence is mounting that global competition in educational services, fueled by information technology, is growing more intense. Another incentive is the struggle for public and corporate dollars in a climate of diminishing public resources. Distance education is one bone of contention, admittedly a very large one, in a worldwide arena where few universities can assume that they will survive unchanged indefinitely.

Today, there is a premium on flexibility and innovation—exactly the qualities that distinguish good library design. If the library is to remain a place and not become an abstraction (i.e., a "virtual library"), then it will have to be designed to serve an on- and off-campus clientele equally. Those who require sources from distant locations will find it convenient to search for and acquire them through a library. Distance learners will gain access to course and research materials from digital collections created and made available by a library. The library, in other words, is the social institution through which individuals borrow intellectual property owned by someone else. In the future, the library's role will be similar to its present one: to bring together researchers and their sources, regardless of distance. No matter in what form information is stored (paper, image, digitized text, and media), libraries very likely will mediate between the researcher and the object of his or her quest.

Because we have grown accustomed to expecting every sort of miracle from the "information revolution," the foregoing may seem more like a profession of faith than a description of unfolding reality. History generally is unkind to both prophets and conservatives. There are surprises in store for all of us. Every great value system assumes an institutional form: Religion has its cathedrals, Education its universities, Government its palaces and, yes, Learning its famous libraries. So far no one has proposed a "virtual state" or a "virtual church," though undoubtedly someone will. As for libraries, they are important because of their contents (irrespective of format) and because they symbolize humanity's defining virtue: intelligence. For that reason alone, libraries are likely to maintain their physical presence for some time to come.

That is not to say that the structures themselves are immutable. Social values, technological change, and financial reality all influence the design of library buildings to one degree or another. Grecian columns, stone lions, and soaring atria all have had their day and no longer mesmerize library designers. There is less interest in monumentality and little reverence for vanished civilizations and their architectural wonders. Functionality and operational economy are today's goals, although elaborate structures, such as the Stauffer Library at Queen's University in Canada or the San Francisco Public Library, are still built. Architects, for their part, will always insist on making their "statement," sometimes at the expense of functionality. Our library buildings, in their own ways, reflect our view of the human condition. The places we build to house and preserve our collected wisdom reveal our opinion of ourselves.

Whether the De Montfort model carries the day remains to be seen. Gregory J. E. Rawlins, who applauds the electronic book, concedes that "it will be many decades before another piece of technology called virtual reality . . . eclipses paper."[27] The notion of a bookless "resources area" still grates on those who cannot accept digitization as the total solution to preserving knowledge. "The bound book," declares Sven Birkert, "is the single most potent figure we have for the life of the mind, and we abandon it at our peril."[28] There is an abiding fondness for archaic forms: print on paper, bound volumes, even the aroma of roomfuls of books. The power of nostalgia is not to be denied. Recall, if you will, that bestsellers among audio CDs in the mid-1990s were recordings of Gregorian chant by Spanish Benedictines. Just because technology sometimes beckons us toward a spiritless world does not mean that we have to follow. Libraries designed and equipped to use information technology can serve for years to come as places where new knowledge is created.

New library buildings all receive formal or informal reviews when they are opened. Some projects, because of their scale or their innovativeness, capture the attention of librarians far and wide. More-modest or less-pretentious buildings nevertheless receive their due from those who appreciate the culture of libraries. The ultimate verdict is rendered by users who either come and feel at home, or else are repelled by the new surroundings. Why a new library succeeds or fails is perhaps not as mysterious a thing as, for instance, the acoustic properties of a new concert hall. Poor lighting, lack of functionality, environmental problems, or defective interior design can scuttle a library building, regardless of the virtues of its collections or service to users. If a library is to serve as the gateway to information sources beyond its own walls, as a place in which to create new knowledge, then it needs a proper form. Study space, arrangement of collections, network connectivity, lighting levels, and a variety of physical and psychological factors determine the reception accorded a new building. In the end, a building is judged by the company it keeps.

Contemporary library buildings need to incorporate information technology, just as they do the best construction materials. Technology is simply an element of the building's fabric, although one that potentially can make a teaching instrument of the building itself. A properly designed and equipped building, as we have tried to show in this book, can contribute to the educational process in significant ways. Libraries stand, above all, for the preservation of culture and learning by means of their custodial role. They also keep students and faculty in touch with the world of learning that pulsates through the Internet and the Web. And they can help students to acquire the research skills they will take with them into the workplace once their studies end. A library that promotes these goals justifies its own existence.

Notes

1. Vartan Gregorian, on the computerization of the New York Public Library card catalog, *Time,* February 25, 1985.

2. *Libraries at Large* (New York: R. R. Bowker, 1969), 274.

3. Richard M. Dougherty and Carol Hughes, *Preferred Futures for Libraries* (Mountain View, Calif.: Research Libraries Group, 1991), 3.

4. Stephen E. Wiberley Jr. and William G. Jones, "Humanists revisited: A longitudinal look at the adoption of information technology," *College & Research Libraries* 55 (6): 506–507 (November 1994).

5. NRENAISSANCE Committee, "Libraries and the broadening of public interest in networking," chap. 3 in *Realizing the Information Future* (Washington, D.C.: National Academy Press, 1994), par. 4.

6. Bette-Lee Fox with Emily J. Jones, "Library buildings: Another year, another $543 million," *Library Journal* 41 (1): 41–54 (December 1998).

7. Susan J. Barnes, "The electronic library and public services," *Library Hi Tech* 12 (3): 48–49 (1994).

8. Michael W. Matier and C. Clinton Sidle, "Developing a strategic plan for library space needs through 2010," paper presented at the annual spring conference of the Society for College and University Planning, Philadelphia, 8–10 April 1992), [21], ERIC, ED 349024.

9. Patricia Battin, "The electronic library—a vision for the future," *EDUCOM Review* 19 (2): 12 (summer 1984).

10. Mel W. Collier et al., "The electronic library —virtually a reality?" in *Opportunity 2000: Understanding and Serving Users in an Electronic Library*, ed. Ahmed H. Helal and Joachim W. Weiss (Essen: Universitätsbibliothek Essen, 1993) ERIC, ED 358863, 140.

11. Brian L. Hawkins, "Creating the library of the future: Incrementalism won't get us there!" <http://www.virtualschool.edu/mon/Academia/HawkinsLibraryOfFuture.html>.

12. Ibid.

13. NRENAISSANCE Committee, "Libraries and the broadening of public interest," par. 5.

14. Ernest L. Boyer, "Buildings reflect our priorities," *Educational Record* 70 (1): 25 (winter 1989).

15. Hawkins, "Creating the library of the future."

16. NRENAISSANCE Committee, "Libraries and the broadening of public interest," par. 11.

17. John H. Pollitz, "Libraries in the 21st century—what's in store for them," *Illinois Libraries* 74 (4): 297 (May 1992).

18. Eldred Smith and Peggy Johnson, "How to survive the present while preparing for the future: A research library strategy," *College & Research Libraries* 54 (5): 393 (September 1993).

19. Caroline R. Arms, "A new information infrastructure," *Online* 14 (5): 21 (September 1990).

20. Kenneth E. Marks, "Planning for technology in libraries," *North Carolina Libraries* 49 (fall 1991): 128.

21. Pat Molholt, "Libraries and the new technologies: Courting the Cheshire Cat," *Library Journal* 113 (19): 38 (November 15, 1988).

22. The Association of Research Libraries is working on this problem. See Shirley K. Baker and Mary E. Jackson, "Maximizing access, minimizing cost: A first step toward the information access future" (ARL Committee on Access to Information Resources, February 1993).

23. Lawrence Biemiller, "New model for journal subscriptions becomes a reality at Cal. State U.," *Chronicle of Higher Education* (July 16, 1999): A26.

24. See the Draft Statement by the Coalition for Networked Information, "Fair use in the electronic age: Serving the public interest," November 8, 1994, <http://www.cni.org>.

25. Erling Ljoså, "Distance education in a modern society," *Open Learning* 7 (2): 23–30 (June 1992).

26. Greville Rumble, "The competitive vulnerability of distance universities," *Open Learning* 7 (2): 31–45 (June 1992).

27. Gregory J. E. Rawlins, "Publishing over the next decade," *Journal of the American Society for Information Science* 44 (8): 476 (September 1993).

28. Sven Birkert, "The book as emblem: The besieged stronghold?" *Journal of Scholarly Publishing* 26 (1): 6 (October 1994).

ATM Networking and Building Design

ATM (asynchronous transfer mode) is a means of transmitting large quantities of data across an existing local area network (LAN). Applications that demand high bandwidth, such as full-motion video or computer videoconferencing, can be run on a LAN that consists of a fiber-optic backbone with at least Category 5E twisted-pair copper wire to the desktop. ATM can achieve speeds of 155 Mbps (scalable to 622 Mbps) through the network's switches.[1] Most "legacy" LANs satisfy these requirements, so upgrading to ATM standards is a matter of adding the proper switches, routers, and video servers. Though by no means inexpensive, this equipment is far less costly today than even a short time ago. With prices dropping as demand rises, ATM is quickly becoming a reasonable alternative to 10 BASE-T Ethernet or FDDI and FDDI II (fiber distributed data interface that handles up to 100 Mbps and is called Fast Ethernet). Only the ATM standard can support the demands of the "electronic academy," which will allow the introduction of multimedia, consisting of full-motion video, sound, and graphics, into classroom teaching and distance education. Another advantage is its ability to support library service to students by means of electronic reference (based on e-mail and computer conferencing) and provision of research materials.

At this stage in the evolution of networks, ATM has two competitors: Fast Ethernet (bandwidth of up to 100 Mbps) and Gigabit Ethernet, which is ten times faster still. Both are natural extensions of the familiar 10 BASE-T local area network, with the second promising to deliver the bandwidth needed by multimedia, imaging, and other massive applications over installed Category 5 UTP. Implementation lies somewhere in the future, while ATM is already here and is compatible with Gigabit Ethernet.[2] ATM is the technology of choice for those businesses and educational institutions that require desktop video now. An ATM-based network can handle mixed traffic (video, graphics, data, voice) without compromising the quality of video transmissions. For those desktops needing full-motion video, a 155 Mbps ATM network interface card for Category 5 UTP costs about $500.[3]

ATM's characteristics include scalability, low latency, and Quality of Service (QoS). That is, ATM offers bandwidth that expands to meet demand, transmission delays are indiscernible, and voice/video signals traverse the network without degradation. Bandwidth is assigned to users who need it, while narrow pipes easily accommodate data flows. An existing (legacy) network can be upgraded to ATM in two ways: Use LAN emulation software, which consumes only 10 percent of the 155 to 622 Mbps bandwidth; or install ATM switches that act like a PC motherboard and transfer information at multi-Gbps speeds. The second alternative is cheaper and easier to implement.

One way to unite full-motion video with real-time voice communication is to transmit compressed data over the network. A less-expensive solution for a LAN environment is to run parallel networks over the same Category 5 cable: One pair of wires is used to carry uncompressed audio-video signals and the other pair is used for ATM signals from a video server or public broadcaster. This approach will provide full-motion videoconferencing capability on campus. Connection to a remote site requires a codec and an ISDN or T-1 line in order to maintain quality. The advantages of having parallel networks are:

The ATM network is not saturated by high-priority compressed data packets.

Existing installed Category 5 or lower wiring can be used to deliver uncompressed audio-video signals.

A few words about the way in which ATM handles data flows will help to explain its superior performance as a network standard. ATM transmits voice, audio, text, and graphics in 53-byte packets or cells, each with a 5-byte header that enables randomly sent data cells to be reassembled into a complete "document" at the receiving end. In this header is information that establishes the cell's priority on the network; for example, voice receives a higher priority than data so that conversations can occur in full-duplex, allowing two people to speak and be heard simultaneously. ATM switches open "virtual circuits" of sufficient bandwidth within the fiber/copper wiring grid. Bandwidth appears on demand according to the requirements of specific users. Speeds of more than 2.5 Gbps can be reached over fiber. The disassembling and reassembling of ATM cells from LAN frames and back again occurs with a delay of only 10 microseconds. At a standard speed of 25 Mbps, an ATM switch can deliver a variety of video sources to the desktop: stored film clips, imported television signals (e.g., network newscasts), and digitized interactive television (ITV). Any other Windows-based application can also be delivered, along with computer videoconferencing.

Several applications can be present on-screen simultaneously, and this is the key to ATM's educational usefulness. If students at a remote site (home, dorm room, off-site classroom) can see their instructor, view images, hear both voice and music, and communicate interactively, course instruction assumes a dynamic quality even at a distance. Add to this mix electronic access to library materials and e-mail, and educators have powerful instructional tools at their disposal. Campus-based instruction also can benefit from the introduction of a variety of multimedia components into a classroom presentation. The potential of ATM-based networks to improve student learning is immense.

University administrators have to decide whether that potential justifies a substantial investment in equipment upgrades, network expansion, building retrofit, and new construction. Several years ago, only the wealthiest universities could consider a campuswide ATM network. Case Western Reserve, for example, committed $18 million to its fiber-optic grid at a time (1992) when the cost-per-port was $1,800.[4] Today the price tag is substantially lower, mainly because fiber-to-the-desktop is no longer needed to implement ATM. Conversion of electrical impulses to light waves now happens in switches located in each campus building. Ordinary RJ45 plugs connect the PC to the building's copper-wire network. There is no need for coders/decoders (codecs) at the desktop. Nevertheless, if full multimedia networking is to be achieved, special equipment is required. The components of an ATM network are described here, using trade names owned by Bay Networks (recently acquired by Nortel), which has over 20 percent of market share for ATM networks. The descriptions are based on recent product literature and technical articles on ATM.

Switch: This device provides an interface between ATM and the existing Ethernet or token-ring LAN. Through a series of ports, the switch delivers enhanced bandwidth to specific PCs or servers. It responds to the bandwidth requirements of the particular applications, such as voice or video transmission. Depending on demand, switches can be installed in campus buildings as required. This equipment enables broadband applications to be transmitted across an existing fiber/copper LAN. If such a network is already in place, there is no need to pull new wire. Because the switch can easily be added to an existing Ethernet, "the eventual move to ATM should be remarkably straightforward."[5]

Multimedia switch: This box brings several kinds of images to the PC. The switch can accommodate up to twenty ATM ports at 25 Mbps. Capacity can be increased as needed, and the equipment is easily stored in racks. If videoconferencing equipment, such as PictureTel, is being used, the switch provides a constant bitrate flow of 384 Kbps along a virtual circuit created especially for the purpose. The moving image, though technically not full-motion, is still reasonably smooth.

Media operating software: This software runs the multimedia switch and allows such uses as e-mail and Netscape. This software resides on adapter cards in the PC and therefore does not use the computer's own memory. It integrates several standards, including ISDN and H.320, which simplifies network management. Multimedia signals receive network priority so as not to degrade transmission quality.

When the preceding components are added to a legacy LAN, the network acquires ATM capability as needed by individual network users at a given time. In other words, the power of ATM is "scalable," which means that it responds to the demands of users who are connected to the switches' ports. Bandwidth is thus allotted only to those who need it, and only as it is required; virtual circuits come and go. Other network users, who are not consumers of multimedia, receive their normal, narrow bandwidth allocation. Recent fears of a "bandwidth crisis" on legacy networks have been laid to rest, thanks to scalable ATM.

Once the network has achieved ATM standards, what are the implications for teaching and learning? How much retrofitting will classrooms, libraries, and dorm rooms need in order to take advantage of networked multimedia and computer videoconferencing? The first of these questions is by far the more complex, but it has to be answered before a significant investment in new facilities can be justified. What follows is a sketch of desktop multimedia's contribution to the educational process.

A conspicuous benefit of ATM is the opportunity for direct interaction between instructor and students, and between students and the course material. Lectures and demonstrations can be augmented by video clips, direct broadcast feeds (e.g., network or cable television), Windows-based e-mail, or videoconferencing. A whiteboard is available for jotted notes or diagrams, illustrations, and mathematical computations. Instruction can occur in real time or be made available via modem at the student's convenience. If teaching occurs in a classroom setting, ATM allows the instructor to import multimedia on demand from a central server. Within restrictions imposed by copyright law, VHS tapes and other analog materials can be transferred to a media server and made available on the network. Access can be restricted to registered students in a given course, thus avoiding legal issues associated with the dissemination of copyrighted media. Supplementary course readings can be provided in the same way through electronic reserve. Any publicly available information, such as course syllabi and reading lists, can be published on a Webpage. Student research, it follows, will be submitted in electronic format, which simplifies the faculty member's task of providing advice and correction. Multimedia may be "viewed [as] an extension to the evolving electronic document," thus acquiring a status equivalent to that historically enjoyed by text.[6] Especially good work may be added to the student's evolving electronic portfolio. Portfolios then may be published on CD-ROM or as individual Websites. These portfolios become the basis for the electronic resumes of graduating students.

Portfolio-based teaching, which requires students to archive their best work in order to demonstrate progressive learning, depends on an ATM network that allows multimedia electronic documents to be created, shared, critiqued, revised, and saved. Portfolios themselves contain artifacts (e.g., projects, art, dance, chemistry experiments) produced by students over the course of their academic careers. Electronic portfolios may be submitted to potential employers or clients, and are constantly being revised and updated. They emerge from the educational process over time, a record of achievement that measures potential more accurately than does a paper transcript of grades. If an evolving portfolio becomes the focal point of a student's education, then information technology is its basis. Networked learning is the outcome of this technology.

ATM's ability to bring a bitstream of any size into the classroom or to a student's own desktop can change how learning occurs. Lecturing becomes only one teaching method, in some cases the least important one, because "only one-third of students leave lectures with most of the information units recorded."[7] Students learn through a process of interaction with the instructor (either directly or at a distance), course materials, and supplementary material procured from the library or the Internet. Even classroom geography changes, from the typical face-forward configuration to a "studio" setting of the sort pioneered at Rensselaer Polytechnic Institute.[8] Studio instructors do not typically lecture their students, but rather circulate among them in order to guide their work. Each student has a computer workstation located on the room's perimeter. The instructor has his or her own station from which to conduct demonstrations or deliver minilectures.

The physical arrangement of studio classrooms simplifies network connections, because power and communications plugs are most convenient when wall mounted. Some wire pulling will be necessary to make the fiber backbone universally accessible, but that chore is a fact of life in today's universities and colleges. Each building that requires 155 Mbps service will have its own ATM switch located at the fiber copper interface panel. Every ATM-enabled device is connected to this box via Category 5 UTP copper wire. Overall cost of the ATM upgrade depends on how many devices are to receive the service. One of the heaviest consumers of bandwidth, however, will be the library.

Academic libraries now being designed and built are best construed as teaching/learning instruments capable of direct involvement in the educational process.[9] Having outgrown the traditional role of warehouses for print materials, libraries are primary nodes on the campus information network. The advent of ATM only enhances their significance. Libraries are now able to collect materials to support their institutions' particular curriculum and research focus, and to make these materials easily accessible regardless of format. Electronic media thus become integral components of library collections, not a special format requiring separate treatment and handling. It follows that electronic research skills are essential to finding information stored in various formats, and that the library will be responsible for teaching them. Every library consequently needs an electronic classroom (perhaps more than one or two) with ATM capability at each workstation. Prominently located on the library's main floor should be an information gallery, equipped with high-end computers on which students create new electronic documents based on an array of digitized information sources.

A third feature of new library buildings is a constellation of group-study rooms, each linked to the ATM switch. Collaborative learning is a natural outgrowth of the studio classroom and the emphasis on electronic research skills. Learning results from an iterative process involving students, instructor, and classroom peers. Attempted mastery of a body of knowledge in isolation (e.g., cramming in the library or dorm room) is a superseded technique. Mastery always was an elusive prize, even for faculty. A more rational and attainable goal is skill at ferreting out information, applying it to either a broad or narrow research problem, and presenting the results in an appropriate format. Much of this work can be done collaboratively, because people have many ways of solving a research or analytical puzzle. Each student profits from insights contributed by others. Examples and solutions can be drawn from the network on demand. There is no formula for determining an optimum number of group studies. Demand is likely to increase with the spread of networked learning on campus. Most important is to ensure that all study spaces offer network access, so that students can connect their laptop computers.

A library designed around the technology it will deploy is likely to be more successful than one in which information technology is an add-on. The building's internal network should be scalable toward full ATM at each study space and workstation. The information gallery, classrooms, and group studies need ATM at the outset. Study spaces, each with its own network connection, can be upgraded incrementally. A legacy LAN (10 BASE-T or token-ring) will still serve perfectly well for such applications as e-mail, catalog searching, Web browsing, data exchange, and the like. As student laptop computers become more powerful, ATM can be expanded.

Within the library itself may be a media center, where digitized audio and video sources are collected and distributed campuswide. Direct access via the network to all media holdings is the goal. Robotic equipment can queue up a given title on demand, either for independent or group study or for projection in a classroom setting (as at the IUPUI library). Instructors locate a title in the library's online catalog and call it up. For copyright reasons, on-demand access will have to be limited to those who use the material for teaching or research purposes. Network management software handles that task, according to established guidelines on simultaneous access. Media center staff members develop collections, advise users, and ensure that equipment operates properly. They also may assist users of the information gallery in the selection and use of information sources. Staff will need to be well versed in copyright regulations, because digitized materials are especially sensitive in this respect. Though technically possible, it is legally risky to transfer analog materials (e.g., videotapes, sound cassettes) to digitized format for network distribution. Eventually the legal thickets will be cleared, but that will not happen soon. New media centers, in any case, should incorporate ATM technology without concern for the current legal climate, for copyright law will adapt to technological change in the end.

Despite ATM's obvious advantages, it is not yet a perfect solution. Full-motion video is not yet available, but it is imminent. In addition, there is a presumed absence of standards governing voice and video transmission over LANs. The ATM Forum/IETF (Internet Engineering Task Force) is now at work to resolve this issue. Less encouraging for the present is the status of ATM wide area networks (WANs). Various system vendors currently are trying to sort out routing tables so that ISDN phone lines can serve as the backbone for the ATM WAN. Telephone companies expect demand to precede investment, and will install ATM switches only in guaranteed market areas. Once ATM service is in place, the horizons for distance education expand greatly. Each student with a suitably equipped PC can have access to the same resources available on campus. Direct videoconferencing links with the course instructor can help overcome isolation and create a learning community of scattered students. Equally important, reading and research support can be of the same standard for on- and off-campus students.

ATM networking will influence building design, course design, and the educational process itself. Although computer communication, however efficient, cannot replace the experience of campus life, it can expand the university's horizons and bring high-quality education to distance learners. Given that potential, investment in ATM is critical to institutional survival in this new age of financial distress for universities. Because ATM can be implemented gradually on existing LANs, there is good reason to build toward it from this point on. Intermediate solutions, such as FDDI and FDDI II, may safely be ignored; they are evolutionary dead ends. A wiser investment is expansion of the campus fiber backbone and the copper-wire network in each building. As new buildings are planned and constructed, especially libraries, it is essential to design them around ATM LANs. Equally important is curricular redesign to take advantage of the capacities of ATM. Studio teaching, at least in some disciplines such as mathematics, may entirely replace standard lecture methods, and will require extensive use of networked resources. This agenda will keep higher education busy for some time to come.

Research is under way to find means of routing IP traffic over switched ATM networks. The advantage will be higher-quality multimedia transmissions; a drawback is more complicated network architecture. The enterprise involves many vendors, and standardization is some distance away. Yet the goal of integration is an important one for network engineers, who are seeking the best means of moving huge quantities of data. "[B]y 2003, the Internet will be more than 90% of the bandwidth [in the world] and by 2004, more than 99%."[10] Thus, an alliance between IP and ATM appears likely. One strategy is to use ATM's high-speed switches for IP routing, thus "combin[ing] the simplicity and robustness of IP with the speed and capacity of ATM."[11] Work is under way to resolve interface problems that must be overcome before ATM and IP can be linked to create the high-speed networking demanded by today's Internet.[12]

Notes

1. Zeitnet, "ATM LAN emulation in workgroup networks," 1996 <http://www.rahul.net/zeitnet/atm/intrpwp.html>.

2. For new developments in this technology, see the homepage of the Gigabit Ethernet Alliance at <http://www.gigabit-ethernet.org>.

3. Barbara Gengler, "Where cutting edge meets reality," *Internetwork* 7 (10): 31 (October 1996).

4. Raymond K. Neff and Peter J. Haigh, "CWRU-net—a case history of a campus-wide fiber-to-the-desktop network," *CAUSE/EFFECT* 15 (2): 26–38 (summer 1992).

5. Charles B. Darling, "Ethernet backbone switches: On the road to ATM," *Datamation* 42 (1): 65 (January 1, 1996).

6. Carl Frappaolo, "Moving to multimedia," *Inform* 10 (April 1996): 10.

7. Diana G. Oblinger and Mark K. Maruyama, *Distributed Learning* (CAUSE Professional Paper #14, 1996), p. 3 <http://www.educause.edu/asp/doclib>.

8. For information on studio classes, see "The Rensselaer Studio Courses" at <http://ciue.rpi.edu/studioteaching.html>.

9. The following principles apply to the library-building project just completed at Winona State University. They are explained in the authors' *Academic Libraries as High-Tech Gateways: A Guide to Design and Space Decisions* (Chicago: American Library Association, 1995).

10. S. A. Karim and P. Hovell, "Everything over IP—an overview of the strategic change in voice and data networks," *BT Technology Journal* 17 (2): 26 (April 1999).

11. Peter Newman et al., "IP switching—ATM under IP," *IEEE/ACM Transactions on Networking* 6 (2): 128 (April 1998).

12. Chin-Tau Lea et al., "A/I net: A network that integrates ATM and IP," *IEEE Network* 13 (1): 48–55 (January/February 1999); and David Passmore, "Choices multiply for converging ATM and IP in the WAN," *Business Communications Review* 28 (11): 20 (November 1998).

Electronic Teaching and Learning Facilities

An academic library that aspires to be a teaching instrument, in the sense discussed in this book, should house certain teaching and learning facilities dedicated to exploiting information technology. Three such spaces are:

the electronic classroom

the information gallery or commons

the academic technologies center (or similar terminology)

These rather expensive installations support the increasing use of technology on campus, specifically the growth of Web-enhanced courses and widespread student use of portable computers. A library that is wired to provide almost universal access to power and data connections is one that, in addition, should serve as the central place on campus for the application of educational technologies.

We describe here the philosophy and practical considerations that Winona State University applied to its design and space decisions as planners integrated these spaces into the new library. A few models already existed, such as the Information Arcade at the University of Iowa or the Information Commons in the Leavey Library at the University of Southern California, but we did not attempt to re-create any particular precedent. Instead, we defined a set of principles and sought to put them into practice. These principles were:

1. Application of the "Seven Principles for Good Practice in Undergraduate Education," as set forth by Arthur Chickering and Zelda Gamson in 1987. Each of these principles, to some degree, is reinforced by the application of information technology.[1]
2. Universal student access to laptop computers will enhance both teaching and learning. In the spring of 1999, the faculty senate of Winona State University decided that all incoming first-year students will be required to lease a laptop through a university-sponsored program, beginning with the 2000 academic year.
3. Faculty will require considerable support as they migrate their teaching from time-honored lecture methods to a more interactive approach.

4. Students will need an equal amount of support, both technical and instructional, as they produce their course assignments in electronic format.

5. No university campus is an island. Using the Internet and interactive television, campuses will reach out to their hinterlands and become regional educational centers.

6. Notwithstanding the emphasis on technology in higher education, the library still serves as a gateway to traditional resources and as a guide to the entire research process. It therefore will remain a central place on campus and one, moreover, that provides an inviting environment.

These ideas found their way into a building program that anticipated a rather more traditional facility than the one that opened in June 1999. We have now had about twelve months of experience with the new library. The electronic learning spaces are in constant use, as are the wired tables and carrels. Critical comments are very few and almost always constructive in nature. The most serious problem involves power and data connections between study tables and floor boxes: Plugs are not recessed and are easily dislodged; engineers are working on a solution. The entire university community seems to be satisfied with the new building. We consequently offer this model to others who wish to include similar facilities in their new buildings. Detailed descriptions, along with photographs, follow.

The Electronic Classroom

Winona State University is a heavy user of interactive television (ITV) and beams more than three hundred classes a year to its campus in Rochester, Minnesota. Any new classroom, we decided, should be ITV capable (fig. 51). The classroom is also an instruction room for librarians teaching electronic research skills. We thought it best to provide for two possible Internet connections, each channeled through a high-end LCD projector onto either a conventional screen or a SmartBoard (fig. 52). When an image is present, the SmartBoard becomes an interactive screen by means of which an instructor can navigate the Internet. Each student is seated at a PC; between each pair of students is a 13-inch television monitor for the remote-site television image. Four large monitors, one facing the instructor and the others facing the class, also show the remote site. ITV operations are instructor controlled, using the DL Navigator system. Web-enhanced courses thus may be offered by a live instructor to a remote site, at which students also have access to Web resources.

FIGURE 51
Electronic classroom at WSU, showing ITV configuration

FIGURE 52
Electronic classroom from the rear

Face-to-face classroom teaching is combined with elements of distance learning.

By using the SmartBoard as an electronic whiteboard, instructors can introduce a large component of interactivity into their teaching, and can provide students with downloadable notes and annotations. Instructors also can focus on individual students, even at remote sites, and offer personal attention mediated by the technology. Because the electronic classroom is entirely controlled by the instructor, she or he can try many different techniques. We purchased a system that, rather than creating a technological straitjacket, encourages interactive learning. That, at least, is the spirit in which we hope the faculty will use this classroom.

The Information Gallery

This forty-eight-seat facility (which can be expanded) occupies the center of the library's main floor. It is neither an afterthought, nor is it hidden away. It is front and center, and very obvious to everyone entering the library. When the doors first opened, on June 7, 1999, a line of students headed directly for the Information Gallery (IG). Since that day, there has rarely been a vacant seat. In essence, the IG is an open computer lab, supported by the technology fee that all students pay. The main difference is that students can obtain both technical and research assistance from a convenient service area. Thus, the IG is a learning space, not just a place to surf the Net or to check e-mail. As faculty assign more electronically produced course work, the IG grows in importance. It offers scanners and other peripherals unavailable elsewhere on campus, and its computers are far more powerful than are the students' laptops.

In treating the IG as an open, easily accessible area, Winona State University is taking the position that computer resources are available to all comers. The inevitable competition for space will diminish as more and more students join the laptop-leasing program. General-purpose computer labs should disappear, leaving such facilities as the IG and advanced labs in computer science and engineering. From an educational standpoint, the important thing is that the IG promotes universal acquisition of electronic research skills.

The Academic Technologies Center

Early in the design phase, technology planners concluded that the library was a natural location for the campus's main faculty-support service. It had become clear by then that information technology belonged in the mainstream of the curriculum. We therefore decided to create an Academic Technologies Center (ATC) and to situate it in space originally assigned to the university's media center (fig. 53). This change in plan gave tacit recognition that digital technology represented the future at Winona State. The ATC's purpose is to investigate and apply new means of electronic course enhancement and delivery, and to educate faculty in the implications of these applications for teaching and learning. Rather than designing courses for faculty members, the ATC staff show them how to do the job themselves. This strategy causes subject-matter specialists to come to grips with the best means of integrating technology into their teaching.

The ATC contains office space for staff, a development area with individual workstations (fig. 54) where faculty have access to high-end computers and peripherals (including scanners and digital still and video cameras), and a studio classroom that seats eleven people. Connie Braun, coauthor of this book, developed and offered a series of Web Camps, intended to acquaint faculty with the techniques and educational implications of Web-enhanced teaching. Almost sixty faculty members graduated from Web Camp, and all found the experience valuable.

Emphasis in the ATC is on the use of cross-platform software, because faculty use both PCs and Macs. Platform independence is an important criterion of software selection. The ATC also experiments with hardware integration, including SmartBoards and LCD projectors. Faculty members learned techniques for using such hardware in Web Camp. Individual assistance is available to faculty, as they put into practice the principles learned in Web Camp.

Also located in the ATC are the servers that support all electronic teaching and learning. There are, for example, several course servers for faculty use, as well as a RealPlayer server that provides access to streaming multimedia over the campus information network. We are experimenting with an ATM/IP network in order to combine bandwidth, quality of service, and ease of access to Web-based resources. The ATC acts as the hub of the academic network, where faculty can obtain both technical and course-design assistance when they need it. In the ATC, the service ethic traditionally associated with libraries should prevail. Faculty reaction has been positive, which is not especially surprising: A recent survey by the *Chronicle of Higher Education* indicated that, for 67.2 percent of faculty, the main source of stress during the past two years was information technology.[2]

We expect that the library, with its various student and faculty support services, will help to develop a culture of collaboration on this campus. Everyone uses information technology as an education tool, not as

FIGURE 53
Academic Technologies Center at WSU

FIGURE 54
Faculty workstation in the Academic Technologies Center

an end in itself. The library both symbolizes and promotes the integration of technology. It also preserves the culture of print, which coexists peacefully with emerging technologies.

Notes

1. Arthur W. Chickering and Zelda F. Gamson, "Seven principles for good practice in undergraduate education," *AAHE Bulletin* 39 (7): 3–7 (1987).

2. *Chronicle of Higher Education* (September 3, 1999): A21.

Academic Planning Board, The University of California, Berkeley. "Toward electronic scholarly information: The IST five-year vision (1993–1998)." Draft report at <http://ist.berkeley.edu/IST5>.

Adams, Judith A. "The computer catalog: A democratic or authoritarian technology?" *Library Journal* 113 (2): 31–36 (February 1, 1988).

Allen, Matthew, and Lothar Retzlaff. "Libraries and information technology: Towards the twenty-first century," *Australian Library Journal* 47 (1): 91–98 (February 1998).

American Library Association, Presidential Committee on Information Literacy. *Final Report.* Chicago: American Library Association, 1989. ERIC, ED 315074.

American Society for Training and Development. *Position Yourself for the Future: The Top Ten Trends* <http://www. astd.org/industry/trends/bassi.htm>.

Arms, Caroline R. "A new information infrastructure." *Online* 14 (5): 15–22 (September 1990).

_____. "The technological context." In: *Campus Strategies for Libraries and Electronic Information,* ed. Caroline R. Arms. Bedford, Mass.: Digital Press, 1990.

Arms, William Y. "The design of the Mercury Electronic Library." *EDUCOM Review* 27 (6): 38–41 (November 1992).

_____. "The institutional implications of electronic information." Paper presented at a conference on Technology, Scholarship, and the Humanities: The Implications of Electronic Information, 1992 <http://www. cni.org/docs/tech.schol.human/Arms.html>.

Arnold, Kathryn, Mel Collier, and Anne Ramsden. "ELINOR: The Electronic Library project at De Montfort University Milton Keynes." *Aslib Proceedings* 45 (1): 3–6 (January 1993).

Ashdown, Ian. "Visual reality: Computer techniques for lighting design" <http:// www.ledalite.com/library-/ldp.htm>.

Auster, Ethel. *Retrenchment in Canadian Academic Libraries.* Ottawa: Canadian Library Association, 1991.

Bailey, J. Russell. "Mr. Architect, listen." *Library Journal* 90 (21): 5147–5151 (December 1, 1965).

Baker, Shirley K., and Mary E. Jackson. "Maximizing access, minimizing cost: A first step toward the information access future." ARL Committee on Access to Information Resources, February 1993.

Bakken, Frode. "The possible role of libraries in the digital future." *Libri* 48 (2): 81–87 (1998).

Bankes, Steve, and Carl Builder. "Seizing the moment: Harnessing the information technologies." *Information Society* 8 (1): 1–59 (1992).

Barna, Peter. "The light of color." *Interiors* 149 (2): 62, 66 (September 1989).

Barnes, Susan J. "The electronic library and public services." *Library Hi Tech* 12 (3): 44–62 (1994).

Barzun, Jacques, and Henry Graff. *The Modern Researcher.* 5th ed. Boston: Houghton-Mifflin, 1992.

Battin, Patricia. "The electronic library—a vision for the future." *EDUCOM Review* 19 (2): 12–17, 34 (summer 1984).

———. "The library: Center of the restructured university." *College & Research Libraries* 45 (3): 170–176 (May 1984).

Bauer, Claude J. "Technology trends for the intelligent building." *Construction Specifier* 46 (1): 45–57 (January 1993).

Bazillion, Richard J. "Personal computing and academic library design in the 1990s." *Computers in Libraries* 12 (3): 10–12 (March 1992).

Bazillion, Richard J., and Connie Braun. "Academic library design: Building a 'teaching instrument.'" *Computers in Libraries* 14 (2): 12–16 (February 1994).

———. "Technology and library users: Automation and outreach: Library services to off-campus students." *Journal of Distance Education* 7 (2): 67–75 (fall 1992).

Bazillion, Richard J., and Susan Scott. "Building a high-tech library in a period of austerity." *Canadian Library Journal* 48 (6): 393–397 (December 1991).

Bechtel, Joan M. "Conversation, a new paradigm for librarianship?" *College & Research Libraries* 47 (3): 219–224 (May 1986).

Beckman, Margaret. "Cost 'avoidance' in library building planning: What, where, when, why, who?" *Canadian Library Journal* 47 (6): 405–409 (December 1990).

———. "Interaction of building, functions, and management." *Canadian Library Journal* 39 (4): 203–205 (August 1982).

———. "Library buildings in the network environment." *Journal of Academic Librarianship* 9 (5): 281–284 (November 1983).

Beiser, Karl. "CD-ROM—middle-aged crazy after all these years." *Database* 16 (6): 91–95 (December 1993).

———. "Specs for a CD-ROM workstation." *Online* 17 (4): 101–104 (July 1993).

Bennett, Philip M. "Users come first in design: Physiological, psychological, and sociological factors." *Wisconsin Library Bulletin* 74 (March 1978): 51–58.

Bennett, Scott. "Copyright and innovation in electronic publishing: A commentary." *Journal of Academic Librarianship* 19 (2): 87–91 (May 1993).

Bess, James L. "Teaching well: Do you have to be schizophrenic?" *Review of Higher Education* 22 (1): 1–15 (fall 1998).

Biemiller, Lawrence. "New model for journal subscriptions becomes a reality at Cal. State U." *Chronicle of Higher Education* (July 16, 1999): A26.

Birkert, Sven. "The book as emblem: The besieged stronghold?" *Journal of Scholarly Publishing* 26 (1): 3–7 (October 1994).

Blair, Joan. "The library in the information revolution." *Library Administration and Management* 6 (2): 71–76 (spring 1992).

Blumenstyk, Goldie, and Vincent Kiernan. "Idea of online archives of papers sparks debate on future of journals." *Chronicle of Higher Education* (July 9, 1999): A25–A26.

Bodi, Sonia. "Critical thinking and bibliographic instruction: The relationship." *Journal of Academic Librarianship* 14 (3): 150–153 (July 1988).

Bomberg, Mark, and William Brown. "Building envelope and environmental control: Issues of system integration." *Journal of Thermal Insulation and Building Envelopes* 17 (July 1993): 5–12.

———. "Building envelope: Heat, air, and moisture interactions." *Journal of Thermal Insulation and Building Environments* 16 (April 1993): 306–311.

Boschmann, Erwin, ed. *The Electronic Classroom: A Handbook for Education in the Electronic Environment.* Medford, N.J.: Learned Information, 1995.

Boss, Richard W. *Information Technologies and Space Planning for Libraries and Information Centers.* Boston: G. K. Hall, 1987.

Bostwick, Arthur E. "The librarian's ideas of library design." *Architectural Forum* 47 (6): 507–528 (December 1927).

Bowers, C. A. "Teaching a nineteenth-century mode of thinking through a twentieth-century machine," *Educational Theory* 38 (1): 41–46 (winter 1988).

Boyer, Ernest L. "Buildings reflect our priorities." *Educational Record* 70 (1): 25–27 (winter 1989).

———. *College: The Undergraduate Experience in America.* New York: Harper and Row, 1987.

Brakel, Pieter van. "Education and training for information professionals in the face of the Internet and the World Wide Web." In *Libraries for the New Millennium: Implications for New Managers*, ed. David L. Raitt, 240–282. London: Library Association Publishing, 1997.

Brand, Stewart. *How Buildings Learn: What Happens After They're Built.* New York: Viking Press, 1994.

Brandston, Howard. "A design process for lighting," *Interior Design* (New York) 60 (7): 126–129 (May 1989).

Branscomb, Anne W. "Common law for the electronic frontier." *Scientific American* 265 (3): 154–157 (September 1991).

Branscomb, Lewis M. "The electronic library." *Journal of Communication* 31 (1): 143–150 (winter 1981).

Braun, Eric. *The Internet Directory.* New York: Fawcett Columbine, 1994.

Brett, George H., II. "Networked information retrieval tools in the academic environment." *Internet Research* 3 (3): 26–36 (fall 1993).

Brodie, Kent C., and Carla T. Garnham. "Online CD-ROM access in a DIGITAL environment." In *Managing Information Technology: Facing the Issues.* Proceedings of the 1989 CAUSE National Conference, Track VIII, November/December 1989.

Brottman, May and Mary Loe, eds. *The LIRT Library Instruction Handbook.* Englewood, Colo.: Libraries Unlimited, 1990.

Brown, Carol R. *Selecting Library Furniture: A Guide for Librarians, Designers, and Architects.* Phoenix: Oryx Press, 1989.

Brown, Peggy, ed. *Computer Literacy . . . Would Plato Understand?* Washington, D.C.: Association of American Colleges, 1983. ERIC, ED 231263.

Bruns, Adam. "Moving day: An exercise in mind and matter." *American Libraries* 30 (4): 48–50 (April 1999).

Buchanan, David, and Richard Badham. "Politics and organizational change: The lived experience." *Human Relations* 52 (5): 609–630 (May 1999).

Budd, John M., and Lisa K. Miller. "Teaching for technology: Current practice and future direction." *Information Technology and Libraries* 18 (2): 78–83 (June 1999).

Busa, Roberto, SJ. "Informatics and new philology." *Computers and the Humanities* 24 (5/6): 339–343 (December 1990).

Butler, Declan. "Briefing: The writing is on the Web for science journals in print." *Nature* 397 (6176): 1–2 (January 21, 1999).

Cahana, Michael Z. "The use of computers by lighting designers." *Lighting Design and Application* 19 (6): 2–9, 46 (June 1989).

Caplan, Priscilla. "You can't get there from here: E-prints and the library." *Public Access Computer Systems Review* 5 (1): 20–24 (1994) <http://info.lib.uh.edu/pr/v5/n1/caplan.5n1>.

Carey, David, and Jenine Strom. "Getting the point." *Canadian Datasystems* (May 1992): 29–32.

"CATaloguing and retrieval of information over network applications (CATRIONA)." Pilot study proposal, July 1994 <http://bubl.ac.uk/org/catriona/cat1rep.htm>.

"Category 5: Wire management." *EC and M: Electrical Construction and Maintenance* 92 (12): 58 (November 15, 1993).

"Category 9: Lighting." *EC and M: Electrical Construction and Maintenance* 92 (12): 92–96, 101–102 (November 15, 1993).

Chaney, Michael, and Alan F. MacDougal, eds. *Security and Crime Prevention in Libraries.* Brookfield, Vt.: Ashgate, 1992.

Chickering, Arthur W,. and Zelda F. Gamson. "Seven principles for good practice in undergraduate education." *AAHE Bulletin* 39 (7): 3–7 (1987).

Chodorow, Stanley, and Peter Lyman. "The responsibilities of universities in the new information environment." In *The Mirage of Continuity: Reconfiguring Academic Information Resources for the 21st Century*, ed. Brian L. Hawkins and Patricia Battin, 61–78. Washington, D.C.: Council on Library and Information Resources and Association of American Universities, 1998.

Chronicle of Higher Education (October 28, 1992): A22; (September 2, 1992): A19; (September 30, 1992): A17; (July 6, 1994): A20.

Cirillo, Susan E., and Robert E. Danford. *Library Buildings, Equipment, and the ADA: Compliance Issues and Solutions.* Chicago: American Library Association, 1996.

Clarkson, Mark. "All-terrain networking." *BYTE* 18 (9): 111–120 (August 1993).

Clement, Gail P. "Library without walls." *Internet World* 5 (6): 60–64 (September 1994).

Coalition for Networked Information. "Fair use in the electronic age: Serving the public interest." Draft statement. The Coalition, November 8, 1994.

Coates, Vary T. "The future of information technology." *Annals of the American Academy of Political and Social Science* 522 (July 1992): 45–56.

Cohen, Aaron, and Elaine Cohen. *Designing and Space Planning for Libraries: A Behavioral Guide.* New York: R. R. Bowker, 1979.

Cohen, Elaine. "Analyzing architectural and interior design plans." *Library Administration and Management* 1 (3): 91–93 (June 1987)

———. "The architectural and interior design process." *Library Trends* 42 (3): 547–563 (winter 1994).

Collier, Mel W., Anne Ramsden, and Zimin Wu. "The electronic library—virtually a reality?" In *Opportunity 2000: Understanding and Serving Users in an Electronic Library*, ed. Ahmed H. Helal and Joachim W. Weiss. Essen: Universitätsbibliothek Essen, 1993. ERIC, ED 358863.

Collins, Kelly L. K., and Sharon Nelson Takacs. "Information technology and the teaching role of the college librarian." *Reference Librarian* 18 (39): 41–51 (1993).

Connick, George, and Jane Russo. "Technology and the inevitability of education transformation." In *The Electronic Classroom: A Handbook for Education in the Electronic Environment*, ed. Erwin Boschmann, 14–20. Medford, N.J.: Learned Information, 1995.

"Construction management and the evolution of construction project delivery." *ENR: Engineering News Reports* 236 (23): C45–C46 (June 10, 1996).

Corey, James F. "A grant for Z39.50." *Library Hi Tech* 12 (1): 37–47 (1994).

Coy, Peter. "Invasion of the data shrinkers." *Business Week* (February 14, 1994): 115–116.

Crawford, David. "Meeting scholarly information needs in an automated environment: A humanist's perspective." *College & Research Libraries* 47 (6): 569–574 (November 1986).

Creth, Sheila D. "The Information Arcade: Playground for the mind." *Journal of Academic Librarianship* 20 (1): 22–23 (March 1994).

Crews, Kenneth D. "Copyright law, libraries, and universities: Overview, recent developments, and future issues." Working paper for presentation to the Association of Research Libraries, October 1992

<http://palimpsest.stanford.edu/bytopic/intprop/crews.html>.

Crouch, C. L. "Too much light is poor light." In *Reader on the Library Building,* ed. Hal B. Schell, 233–234. Englewood, Colo.: Microcard Edition Books, 1975.

Cummings, Anthony M., Marcia L. Witte, William G. Bowen, Laura O. Lazarus, and Richard H. Ekman. *University Libraries and Scholarly Communication: A Study Prepared for the Andrew W. Mellon Foundation.* Association of Research Libraries, November 1992.

"Current issues in higher education information technology." *CAUSE/EFFECT* 17 (1): (spring 1994). CAUSE Information Resources Library Document (CEM9412) <http://www.educause.edu/asp/doclib>.

Dakshinamurti, Ganga. "Automation's effect on library personnel." *Canadian Library Journal* 42 (6): 343–351 (December 1985).

Daniel, John S. *Mega-Universities and Knowledge Media: Technology Strategies for Higher Education.* London: Kogan Page, 1996.

Darling, Charles B. "Ethernet backbone switches: On the road to ATM," *Datamation* 42 (1): 64–65 (January 1996).

Darnton, Robert. "The new age of the book." *New York Review of Books* 46 (5): 5–7 (March 18, 1999).

Data Research Associates. "Open DRANet: Networking and automation services for library resource-sharing." St. Louis, 1994.

Davies, J. Eric. "Intellectual property." In *Security and Crime Prevention in Libraries,* ed. Michael Chaney and Alan MacDougall. Brookfield, Vt.: Ashgate, 1992.

De Gennaro, Richard. *Libraries, Technology, and the Information Marketplace: Selected Papers.* Boston: G. K. Hall, 1987.

de Klerk, Ann, and Joanne R. Euster. "Technology and organizational metamorphoses." *Library Trends* 37 (4): 457–468 (spring 1989).

Demas, Samuel. "Collection development for the electronic library: A conceptual and organization model." *Library Hi Tech* 12 (3): 71–80 (1994).

Demmers, Linda, Karen M. G. Howell, and Lucy Siefert Wegner, "Envisioning tomorrow's library." Leavey Library, University of Southern California, Los Angeles, 1993.

Detweiler, Richard A., William Beyer, Davis Conley, Ellen F. Falduto, and Reid Golden. "Opportunistic planning for information technologies: Upside down or downside up?" Paper presented at CAUSE92, Dallas, December 1992. CAUSE Information Resources Library Document (CNC9203).

Douglas, Suzanne. "Digital soup: The ABCs of distance learning." *EDUCOM Review* 28 (4): 22–30 (July/August 1993).

Dowler, Lawrence. "Gateways to knowledge: A new direction for the Harvard College Library." In *Gateways to Knowledge: The Role of Academic Libraries in Teaching, Learning, and Research,* ed. Lawrence Dowler, 95–107. Cambridge, Mass.: MIT Press, 1997.

———, ed. *Gateways to Knowledge: The Role of Academic Libraries in Teaching, Learning, and Research.* Cambridge, Mass.: MIT Press, 1997.

Dowler, Lawrence, and Laura Farwell. "The Gateway: A bridge to the library of the future." *RSR: Reference Services Review* 24 (2): 7–11 (1996).

Drabenstott, Karen M. "Analytical review of the library of the future." February 1993 <http://www.si.umich.edu/~ylime/Newfiles/morekmd.html#Anchor-Digital-4581>.

Dubin, Fred S. "Intelligent buildings: HVAC, lighting, and other design trends." *Construction Specifier* 43 (2): 51–57 (February 1990).

Edwards, Heather M. *University Library Building Planning.* Metuchen, N.J.: Scarecrow Press, 1990.

Ellsworth, Ralph E. "The college and university library as a building type."

American Institute of Architects Journal 43 (5): 69–72 (May 1965).

_____. "How buildings can contribute." In *Educating the Library User,* ed. John Lubans Jr. New York: R. R. Bowker, 1974.

_____. "Library architecture and buildings." *Library Quarterly* 25 (1/4): 66–75 (January/ October 1955).

Eshelman, Paul, and Kesia Tatchell. "How beneficial a tool is computer-aided design?" *Human Ecology Forum* 20 (1): 15–19 (fall 1991).

Farber, Evan. "Reflections on library instruction." In *The LIRT Library Instruction Handbook,* ed. May Brottman and Mary Loe. Englewood, Colo.: Libraries Unlimited, 1990.

Farrington, Gregory C. "Higher education in the information age." In *The Learning Revolution: The Challenge of Information Technology in the Academy,* ed. Diana G. Oblinger and Sean C. Rush, 54–71. Bolton, Mass.: Anchor Publishing, 1997.

Fazio, P., C. Bedard, and K. Gowri. "Knowledge-based system approach to building envelope design." *Computer Aided Design* 21 (8): 519–527 (October 1989).

Fearing, B. E., and W. K. Sparrow, eds. *Technical Writing and Practice.* New York: Modern Language Association, 1989.

Fisher, Thomas. "Electrifying floors." *Progressive Architecture* 67 (2): 116–121 (February 1986).

Fleming, Stephen. "Get ready for T3 networking." *Data Communications* 18 (11): 82–94 (September 1, 1989).

Focke, John W. "The new American library: Technological, educational, and social changes are redefining traditional roles: Implications for building design." *Texas Library Journal* 73 (3): 114–117 (fall 1997).

Foster, Clifton Dale. "A wireless future: College and university libraries unplugged." *Broadening Our Horizons:*

Information Services, Technology. Proceedings of the 1996 CAUSE Annual Conference <http://www.educause.edu/ir/library/text/ CNC9640.txt>.

Fox, Bette-Lee, with Emily J. Jones. "Library buildings: Another year, another $543 million." *Library Journal* 41 (1): 41–54 (December 1998).

Francis, Bob. "OCR comes down to the desktop." *Datamation* 37 (18): 44–45 (September 15, 1991).

Frappaolo, Carl. "Moving to multimedia." *Inform* 10 (April 1996): 10.

Freeman, Geoffrey T. "An architect's view: Libraries in the twenty-first century." *Harvard Library Bulletin* 4 (1): 32–37 (spring 1993).

Friedman, Rick. "Facility management software: Its uses." *Office* 115 (4): 12–13, 21 (April 1992).

Fritz, Joanne. "Playground for the mind." *Iowa Alumni Review* (spring 1993): 22–26.

Fuller, F. Jay, and William E. Post. "Library space management by computer." *Library Software Review* 10 (3): 170–173 (May/June 1991).

Gal, Cynthia A., et al. "Territoriality and the use of library study tables." *Perceptual and Motor Skills* 63 (2): 567–574 (1986).

Garcia, Lori. "Communication is key to efficient lighting controls." *Energy User News* 22 (4): 16, 28–29 (April 1997).

Garrett, John R., and Patrice A. Lyons. "Toward an electronic copyright management system." *Journal of the American Society for Information Science* 44 (8): 468–473 (September 1993).

Gasparro, Daniel M. "Putting wireless to work." *Data Communication* 23 (5): 57–58 (March 21, 1994).

Geake, Elisabeth. "Network set to put journals in the picture." *New Scientist* (November 21, 1992): 18.

Genge, G. R. "Roofing and waterproofing update." *Canadian Architect* 32 (7): 47–49 (July 1987).

Gengler, Barbara. "Where cutting edge meets reality." *Internetwork* (October 1996).

Gigabit Ethernet Alliance <http://www.gigabit-ethernet.org>.

Gorman, Michael. "The academic library in the year 2001: Dream or nightmare or something in between?" *Journal of Academic Librarianship* 17 (1): 4–9 (March 1991).

Graves, William H. "Toward a national learning infrastructure." *EDUCOM Review* 29 (2): 32–37 (March/April 1994).

Greenberg, Donald P. "Computers and architecture." *Scientific American* 264 (2): 104–109 (February 1991).

Gregorian, Vartan, Brian L. Hawkins, and Merrily Taylor. "Integrating information technologies: A research university perspective." *CAUSE/EFFECT* 15 (4): 5–12 (winter 1992).

Guernsey, Lisa. "A new career track combines teaching and academic computing." *Chronicle of Higher Education* (December 11, 1998): A35.

Gyorki, John R. "New deal for smart cards." *Machine Design* 65 (11): 38–44 (June 11, 1993).

Hacken, Richard D. "Tomorrow's research library: Vigor or rigor mortis?" *College & Research Libraries* 49 (6): 485–492 (November 1988).

Harnad, Stevan. "Implementing peer review on the Net: Scientific quality control in scholarly electronic journals." *Proceedings of the International Conference on Refereed Journals*. Winnipeg: University of Manitoba Libraries, 1994.

Hart, Jeffrey A., Robert R. Reed, and Francois Bar. "The building of the Internet: Implications for the future of broadband networks." *Telecommunications Policy* 16 (8): 666–689 (November 1992).

Hawkins, Brian L. "Creating the library of the future: Incrementalism won't get us there." 1993 <http://www.virtualschool.edu/mon/Academia/HawkinsLibraryOfFuture.html>.

———. "Planning for the national electronic library." *EDUCOM Review* 29 (3): 19–29 (May/June 1994).

———. "Preparing for the next wave of computing on campus." *Change: The Magazine of Higher Learning* 23 (1): 24–31 (January/February 1991).

———. "The unsustainability of the traditional library and the threat to higher education." In *The Mirage of Continuity: Reconfiguring Academic Information Resources for the 21st Century,* ed. Brian L. Hawkins and Patricia Battin, 129–153. Washington, D.C.: Council on Library and Information Resources and Association of American Universities, 1998.

Hawkins, Brian L., and Patricia Battin, eds. *The Mirage of Continuity: Reconfiguring Academic Information Resources for the 21st Century.* Washington, D.C.: Council on Library and Information Resources and Association of American Universities, 1998.

Heathcote, Denis, and Peter Stubley. "Building services and environmental needs for information technology in academic libraries." *Program* 20 (3): 26–38 (January 1986).

Hedge, Alan, William R. Sims Jr., and Franklin D. Becker. "Effects of lensed-indirect and parabolic lighting on the satisfaction, visual health, and productivity of office workers." *Ergonomics* 38 (2): 260–280 (1995).

Helal, Ahmed H., and Joachim W. Weiss, eds. *Opportunity 2000: Understanding and Serving Users in an Electronic Library.* Essen: Universitätsbibliothek Essen, 1993.

Helander, Martin G., and Thiagarajan Palanivel. "Ergonomics of human-computer interaction." *Impact of Science on Society* 42 (1): 65–74 (1992).

Helping Employers Comply with the ADA: An Assessment of How the United States Equal Employment Opportunity Commission Is Enforcing Title I of the Americans with Disabilities Act. A Report of the United States Commission on Civil Rights. Washington, D.C.: The Commission, September 1998.

Heterick, Robert C. "The shoemaker's children." *EDUCOM Review* 29 (3): 60 (May/June 1994).

Hills, Alex. "Terrestrial wireless networks." *Scientific American* 278 (4): 86–91 (April 1998).

Hine, David. "Integrating fire-safety systems." *Canadian Architect* 38 (8): 25 (August 1, 1993).

Hisle, W. Lee. "Roles for a digital age." In *Creating the Future: Essays on Librarianship in an Age of Great Change*, ed. Sally Gardner Reed, 29–41. Jefferson, N.C.: McFarland, 1996.

Hlava, Marjorie. "A vision for ASIS: 1993 inaugural address." *Bulletin of the American Society for Information Science* 20 (3): 2–4 (August/September 1994).

Hoffert, Barbara. "Books into bytes." *Library Journal* 117 (14): 130–135 (September 1, 1992).

Hoffman, Nicholas von. "Checking out electronic libraries: Repackaging information for the next millennium." *Architectural Digest* 53 (10): 130, 134, 138 (October 1996).

Horny, Karen. "Digital technology: Implications for library planning." In *Advances in Librarianship*, ed. Irene P. Godden, 107–126. New York: Academic Press, (1992).

"How many footcandles do I really need?" SDGE, An Enova Company <http://espsun3.esp-net.com/sdge/ bull8.htm>.

Hughes, Carol Ann. "'Facework': A new role for the next generation of library-based

information technology centers." *Library Hi Tech* 16 (3/4): 27–35 (July/September 1998).

Hulser, Richard P. "Prepare today for the digital library of tomorrow." In *The Future Compatible Campus: Planning, Designing, and Implementing Information Technology in the Academy*, ed. Diana G. Oblinger and Sean C. Rush, 218–229. Bolton, Mass.: Anker, 1998.

Hurt, Charlene S. "A vision of the library for the 21st century." *Journal of Library Administration* 15 (3/4): 7–19 (1991).

Huston, Dryver R., and Peter L. Fuhr. "Intelligent materials for intelligent structures." *IEEE Communications Magazine* 31 (10): 40–45 (October 1993).

Illuminating Engineering Society. "Recommended practice of library lighting, RP-4." Reprinted from *Journal of the Illuminating Engineering Society* (April 1974).

Isbell, Dennis, and Carol Hammond. "Information literacy competencies." *College and Research Libraries News* 54 (6): 325–327 (June 1993).

Jackson, Mary E. "Library to library: Copyright and ILL." *Wilson Library Bulletin* 66 (April 1991): 84–87.

Jain, Raj. "FDDI: Current issues and future plans." *IEEE Communications Magazine* 39 (1): 98–105 (September 1993).

Johnson, Dell. *The Future of Electronic Educational Networks: Some Ethical Issues.* Texas, 1991. ERIC, ED 332689.

Jones, David J. "Staying smart: Challenges of library design in the 1990s." *Australian Library Journal* 42 (3): 214–227 (August 1993).

Jones, Frederic H. *Architectural Lighting Design.* Los Altos, Calif.: Crisp Publications, 1989.

Kahin, Brian. "The copyright law: How it works and new issues in electronic settings." *Serials Librarian* 24 (3/4): 163–172 (1994).

_____. "Scholarly communication in the network environment: Issues of principle, policy, and practice." *Electronic Library* 10 (5): 275–286 (October 1992).

Karim, S. A., and P. Hovell. "Everything over IP—an overview of the strategic change in voice and data networks." *BT Technology Journal* 17 (2): 24–30 (April 1999).

Kaser, David. "Twenty-five years of academic library building planning." *College & Research Libraries* 45 (4): 268–281 (July 1984).

Katzev, Richard. "The impact of energy-efficient office lighting strategies on employee satisfaction and productivity." *Environment and Behavior* 24 (6): 759–778 (November 1992).

Kaufman, Paula T., and Tamara Miller. "Scholarly communications: New realities, old values." *Library Hi Tech* 10 (3): 61–78 (1992).

Keerkul, Donna Lee. "The planning, implementation, and movement of an academic library collection." *College & Research Libraries* 44 (4): 220–234 (July 1983).

Kehoe, Brendan P. *Zen and the Art of the Internet: A Beginner's Guide to the Internet.* Englewood Cliffs, N.J.: Prentice Hall, 1993.

Kemper Littman, Marilyn. "Wireless technologies in the learning environment: Prospects and challenges." *International Journal of Educational Telecommunications* 41 (1): 3–30 (June 1998).

Kennan, Mary Anne. "The impact of electronic scholarly publishing." *LASIE* 28 (3): 24–33 (September 1997).

Kessler, Helen J. "In the right light." *Journal of Property Management* 63 (5): 52–57 (September/October 1998).

Klobas, Jane E. "Information services for new millennium organizations: Librarians and knowledge management." In *Libraries for the New Millennium: Implications for Managers*, ed. David L. Raitt, 39–64. London: Library Association Publishing, 1997.

Korshin, Paul J. "The idea of an academic press at the *fin de siècle.*" *Scholarly Publishing* 22 (2): 67–77 (January 1991).

Kovacs, Robert. "The overselling of fiber optics? Cable planning for educational technology." *Tech Trends* 38 (5): 15–17 (October 1993).

Kroeker, Brian. "Changing roles in information dissemination and education." *Social Science Computer Review* 17 (2): 176–188 (summer 1999).

Krol, Ed. *The Whole Internet: User's Guide and Catalog.* Sebastopol, Calif.: O'Reilly and Associates, 1992.

Kurzweil, Raymond. "The future of libraries part 1: The technology of the book." *Library Journal* 117 (1): 80–82 (January 1992).

_____. "The future of libraries part 2: The end of books." *Library Journal* 117 (3): 140–141 (February 15, 1992).

_____. "The future of libraries part 3: The virtual library." *Library Journal* 117 (5): 63–64 (March 15, 1992).

Ladner, Sharyn J., and Hope N. Tillman. "How special librarians really use the Internet." *Canadian Library Journal* 49 (3): 211–215 (June 1992).

Laiserin, Jerry. "Meeting client expectations." *Architecture* 86 (5): 188–190 (May 1997).

Lancaster, F. W. "Electronic publishing." *Library Trends* 37 (3): 316–325 (winter 1989).

_____, ed. *Libraries and the Future: Essays on the Library in the Twenty-first Century.* New York: Haworth Press, 1993.

Lande, Nathaniel. "Toward the electronic book." *Publishers Weekly* 238 (42): 28–30 (September 20, 1991).

Landow, George P. "Twenty minutes into the future, or How are we moving beyond the book?" In *The Future of the Book*, ed. Geoffrey Nunberg, 209–237. Berkeley: University of California Press, 1996.

Lanham, Richard A. *The Electronic Word: Democracy, Technology, and the Arts.* Chicago: University of Chicago Press, 1993.

Langmead, Stephen, and Margaret Beckman. *New Library Design: Guide Lines to Planning Academic Library Buildings.* Toronto: J. Wiley and Sons Canada, 1970.

Lea, Chin-Tau, et al. "A/I net: A network that integrates ATM and IP." *IEEE Network* 13 (1): 48–55 (January/February 1999).

Learn, Larry L. "Asynchronous transfer mode (ATM): Containerized shipping for electronic information." *Library Hi Tech News* 101 (April 1993): 16–19.

_____. "The role of telecommunications in library automation: Past, present, and future perspectives." *Library Technology Reports* 26 (4): 503–515 (July/ August 1990).

Leighton, Philip D., and David C. Weber. "The influence of computer technology on academic library buildings: A slice of recent history." In *Academic Librarianship Past, Present, and Future: A Festschrift in Honor of David Kaser,* ed. John Richardson Jr. and Jinnie Y. Davis. Englewood, Colo.: Libraries Unlimited, 1989.

_____. *Planning Academic and Research Library Buildings.* 3d ed. Chicago: American Library Association, 1999.

Leonard, Milt. "FDDI rides twisted pair to the top." *Electronic Design* 41 (19): 85–88 (September 16, 1993).

Les, Michael. "How can we get high-quality electronic journals?" *IEEE Intelligent Systems* 13 (1): 12 (January/February 1998).

Leslie, Jacques. "Good-bye, Gutenberg." *Wired* 2 (10): 68–71 (October 1994).

Lester, June. "Library and information studies education." In *Creating the Future: Essays on Librarianship in an Age of Great Change,* ed. Sally Gardner Reed, 162–188. Jefferson, N.C.: McFarland, 1996.

Lewis, David W. "Inventing the electronic university." *College & Research Libraries* 49 (4): 291–304 (July 1988).

Licklider, J. C. R. *Libraries of the Future.* Cambridge, Mass.: MIT Press, 1965.

Ljoså, Erling. "Distance education in a modern society." *Open Learning* 7 (2): 23–30 (June 1992).

Lonowski, Laura J. "Indoor air quality: The role of building designs, materials, and construction." *Construction Specifier* 44 (5): 144–153 (May 1, 1991).

Lord, David. "Computer aided lighting." *Progressive Architecture* 71 (11): 126–129 (November 1990).

_____. "Simulation of lighting designs." *Architecture: The AIA Journal* (June 1988): 106–108.

Lowry, Anita. "The Information Arcade: A library and electronic learning facility for 2000 and beyond." Paper presented at the 1993 CAUSE Conference, San Diego, December 1993 <http://www.educause. edu/asp/doclib>.

_____. "The Information Arcade at the University of Iowa." *CAUSE/EFFECT* 17 (3): 38–44 (fall 1994).

Lubans, John, Jr., ed. *Educating the Library User.* New York: R. R. Bowker, 1974.

Lyman, Peter. "The library of the (not-so-distant) future." *Change: The Magazine of Higher Learning* 23 (1): 34–41 (January/ February 1991).

_____. "What is computer literacy and what is its place in liberal education?" *Liberal Education* 81 (3): 4–15 (summer 1995).

_____. "What is a digital library? Technology, intellectual property, and the public interest." *Daedalus* 125 (4): 1–33 (fall 1996).

Lynch, Clifford A. "Networked information: A revolution in progress." In *Networks, Open Access, and Virtual Libraries: Implications for the Research Library,* ed. Brett Sutton and

Charles H. Davis, 12–39. Urbana-Champaign: University of Illinois Graduate School of Library and Information Science, 1992.

_____. "Rethinking the integrity of the scholarly record in the networked information age." *EDUCOM Review* 29 (2): 38–40 (March/April 1994).

Lynch, Clifford A., and Cecilia M. Preston. "Internet access to information sources." In *Annual Review of Information Science and Technology,* ed. Martha E. Williams, 263–312. Washington, D.C.: American Society for Information Science, 1990.

Macdonald, Angus Snead. "A library of the future, part I," *Library Journal* 58 (21): 971–975 (December 1933).

Malinconico, S. Michael. "Electronic documents and research libraries." *IFLA Journal* 22 (3): 211–225 (1996).

_____. "Technology and the academic workplace." *Library Administration and Management* 5 (1): 25–28 (winter 1991).

_____. "What librarians need to know to survive in an age of technology." *Journal of Education for Library and Information Science* 33 (3): 226–240 (summer 1992).

Mann, Thomas. "Reference service, human nature, and copyright—in a digital age." *Reference Service in a Digital Age: A Library of Congress Institute* (June 29–30, 1998) <http://.cweb.loc.gov/rr/digiref/mann.html>.

Margolis, Michael. "Brave new universities." *FirstMonday* 3 (5) (1998) <http://www.firstmonday.org/issues/issue3_5/margolis/index.html>.

Marks, Kenneth E. "Planning for technology in libraries." *North Carolina Libraries* 49 (fall 1991): 128–131.

Martin, Jean. "Planning a library: An interview with architect Hugh Hardy." *Wilson Library Bulletin* 67 (9): 38–40 (May 1993).

Marvin, Carolyn, and Mark Winther. "Computer-ease: A twentieth-century literacy emergent." *Journal of Communication* 33 (1): 92–108 (winter 1983).

Mason, Ellsworth. "The development of library lighting: The evolution of the lighting problems we are facing today." *Advances in Library Administration and Organization* 10 (1992): 129–144.

_____. *Ellsworth Mason on Library Buildings.* Metuchen, N.J.: Scarecrow Press, 1980.

_____. "A guide to the librarian's responsibility in achieving quality in . . . lighting and ventilation." *Library Journal* 92 (2): 201–206 (January 15, 1967).

_____. "Lighting and mechanical progress in universities." *Library Trends* 18 (2): 246–261 (October 1969).

Matier, Michael W., and C. Clinton Sidle. "What size libraries for 2010?" *Planning for Higher Education* 21 (4): 9–15 (summer 1993).

Mays, Vernon. "P/A technics: Light for the site." *Progressive Architecture* 69 (November 1988): 108–113.

McClure, Polley Ann. "Organizing information technology—integration or disintegration?" *CAUSE/EFFECT* 15 (3): 3–5, 11 (fall 1992).

McCusker, Tom. "Credit card modems now do fax, too." *Datamation* 39 (16): 65–67 (August 15, 1993).

McHugh Engstrom, Catherine, and Kevin W. Kruger, eds. *Using Technology to Promote Student Learning: Opportunities for Today and Tomorrow.* San Francisco: Jossey-Bass, 1997.

McKnight, Cliff. "Electronic journals—past, present . . . and future?" *Aslib Proceedings* 45 (1): 7–10 (January 1993).

McLean, Neil. "Convergence of libraries and computing services: Implications for reference services." *LASIE* 28 (3): 5–9 (September 1997).

McMillan, Gail, Paul Metz, James Powell, and Maggie Zarnosky. *Report of the Scholarly Communications Task Force.* Report presented to the Library Administrative Council, University Libraries, Virginia Polytechnic Institute and State University, May 1994 <http://scholar.lib.vt.edu/reports/task-force.html>.

Mensching, Glenn E., and Teresa B. Mensching, eds. *Coping with Information Illiteracy: Bibliographic Instruction for the Information Age.* Ann Arbor: Pierian Press, 1989.

Merrill, M. David. "Instructional strategies that teach." *CBT Solutions* (November 1997) <http://www.cbtsolutions.com/cbtsolutions/html/9711_mer.htm>.

Metcalf, Keyes D. *Library Lighting.* Washington, D.C.: Association of Research Libraries, 1970.

_____. "Library lighting." In *Reader on the Library Building,* ed. Hal B. Schell, 223–227. Englewood, Colo.: Microcard Edition Books, 1975.

Metz, Paul, and Paul M. Gherman. "Serials pricing and the role of the electronic journal." *College & Research Libraries* 52 (4): 315–327 (July 1991).

Michaels, Andrea, and David Michaels. "Designing for technology in today's libraries." *Computers in Libraries* 12 (10): 8–15 (November 1992).

Michaels, David Leroy. "Technology's impact on library interior planning." *Library Hi Tech* 5 (4): 59–63 (winter 1987).

Miller, Arthur. "From here to ATM." *IEEE Spectrum* 31 (6): 20–24 (June 1994).

Minick, Evelyn, J. Thomas Becker, and Stacia Brokaw. "Carpeting your library." *College & Research Libraries News* 55 (7): 410–412 (July/August 1994).

Mintz, Anne P. "Availability of electronic full-text sources: A look behind the scenes." *Database* 16 (5): 24–31 (October 1993).

Moberly, Daniel L. "Commissioning new buildings." *American School and University* 71 (6): 48–49 (February 1999).

Moe, Michael T., Kathleen Bailey, and Rhoda Lau. *The Book of Knowledge: Investing in the Growing Education and Training Industry.* New York: Merrill Lynch, April 1999.

Moen, William. "The ANSI/NISO Z39.50 protocol: Information retrieval in the information infrastructure" <http://www.cni.org/pub/NISO/docs/Z39.50-brochure>.

Mogge, Dru. "ARL directory tracks growth in e-publishing" <http://www.arl.org/newsltr/196/dej.html>.

Molholt, Pat. "Libraries and campus information: Redrawing the boundaries." *Academic Computing* 4 (5): 20–21, 42–43 (February 1990).

_____. "Libraries and the new technologies: Courting the Cheshire Cat." *Library Journal* 113 (19): 37–41 (November 15, 1988).

Morris, William T., and Tony E. Beam. "How to install fiber-optic cable." *LAN Technology* 6 (12): 71–77 (December 1990).

Mulvey, Dennis L. "Project delivery trends: A contractor's assessment." *Journal of Management in Engineering* 14 (6): 51–54 (November/December 1998).

Murphy, Peter. "Making libraries more people friendly: Lighting for a computerized world." *Journal of Academic Librarianship* 22 (1): 56–57 (January 1996).

"Navigating the networks: The training hurdle." *Bulletin of the American Society for Information Science* 20 (3): 15–24 (February/March 1994).

Naylor, Bernard. "The future of the scholarly journal: Clearing the ground." Paper delivered to the general meeting, LIBER, July 7, 1994. *LIBER Quarterly* 4 (1994): 283ff.

Neavill, Gordon B. "Electronic publishing, libraries, and the survival of information."

Library Resources and Technical Services 28 (1): 76–89 (January/March 1984).

Neff, Raymond K. "Campus nets for the nineties." *EDUCOM Review* 29 (2): 41–44 (March/April 1994).

Neff, Raymond K., and Peter J. Haigh. "CWRUnet—case history of a campus-wide fiber-to-the-desktop network," *CAUSE/EFFECT* 15 (2): 26–38 (summer 1992).

Nevison, John M. *Computing as a Matter of Course: The Instructional Use of Computers at Dartmouth College.* Hanover, N.H.: Dartmouth College, Kiewit Computation Center, 1976. ERIC, ED 160061.

Newman, Peter, et al. "IP switching—ATM under IP." *IEEE/ACM Transactions on Networking* 6 (2): 117–129 (April 1998).

Noam, Eli M., and Caterina Alvarez. "The future of the library." *Business and Finance Bulletin*, no. 107 (winter 1998): 29–32.

Novitski, B. J. "Architect-client design collaboration." *Architecture* 83 (6): 131–133 (June 1994).

NRENAISSANCE Committee of the National Academy of Sciences. *Realizing the Information Future.* Washington, D.C.: National Academy Press, 1994.

Nunberg, Geoffrey, ed. *The Future of the Book.* Berkeley: University of California Press, 1996.

_____. "Will libraries survive?" *American Prospect* 41 (November–December, 1998): 16–23 <http://epn.org/prospect/41/41nunb.html>.

Oakley, Robert L. "Copyright issues for the creators and users of information in the electronic environment." *Electronic Networking* 1 (1): 23–30 (fall 1991).

Oberman, Cerise. "Avoiding the cereal syndrome or critical thinking in the electronic environment." *Library Trends* 39 (3): 189–202 (winter 1991).

Oblinger, Diana G., and Mark K. Maruyama. *Distributed Learning.* CAUSE Professional Paper 14, 1996 <http://www.educause.edu/asp/doclib>.

Oblinger, Diana G., and Sean C. Rush, eds. *The Future Compatible Campus: Planning, Designing, and Implementing Information Technology in the Academy.* Bolton, Mass.: Anker, 1998.

_____. *The Learning Revolution: The Challenge of Information Technology in the Academy.* Bolton, Mass.: Anker, 1997.

Odlyzko, Andrew. "The economics of electronic journals," 1997 <http://www.press.umich.edu/jep/04-01/odlyzko.html>.

_____. "The slow evolution of electronic publishing." Preliminary version, September 10, 1997 <http://www.research.att.com/~amo/doc/slow.evolution.txt>.

_____. "Tragic loss or good riddance? The impending demise of traditional scholarly journals."<http://www.research.att.com/~amo/doc/tragic.loss.txt>.

O'Donnell, James J. *Avatars of the Word: From Papyrus to Cyberspace.* Cambridge, Mass.: Harvard University Press, 1998.

Olsen, Jan Kennedy. "The electronic library and literacy." *New Directions for Higher Education* 20 (2): 91–102 (summer 1992).

Ouellet, Mathew L., and Christine A. Stanley. "Instructional technology and diversity: Parallel challenges for our institutions." *Journal of Staff, Program, and Organization Development* 15 (1): 5–10 (1997–1998).

Parkhurst, Carol A. *Library Perspectives on NREN: The National Research and Education Network.* Chicago: Library and Information Technology Association, 1990.

Passmore, David. "Choices multiply for converging ATM and IP in the WAN." *Business Communications Review* 28 (11): 20 (November 1998).

Pecarina, Dan. "The technology effect: Winona State University's search for an e-mail system evolved into a whole new technology direction." *Multiversity* (summer 1999): 19–21.

Peck, Calvin H. "A systematic approach simplifies design." *American School and University* 62 (11): 46–49 (July 1, 1990).

Phelan, William S. "Guide for concrete floor and slab construction." *ACI Materials Journal* 86 (3): 252–296 (May/June 1989).

Pichler, Manfred. "The right time for intelligent lighting control." *Electrical Engineer* (February 1991): 46–50.

Pinker, Steven. *How the Mind Works.* New York: W. W. Norton, 1999.

Piternick, Anne B. "Serials and new technology: The state of the 'electronic journal.'" *Canadian Library Journal* 46 (2): 93–97 (April 1989).

Pollitz, John H. "Libraries in the 21st century—what's in store for them." *Illinois Libraries* 74 (4): 296–298 (May 1992).

Pool, Robert. "Turning an info-glut into a library." *Science* 266 (October 7, 1994): 20–22.

Potter, William G. "Libraries, computing centers, and freedom of access." *Journal of Academic Librarianship* 13 (5): 299–302 (November 1987).

Proceedings of the NREN Workshop. Library Information Technology Association. Monterey, Calif., September 16–18, 1992. EDUCOM, 1992.

"Project SCAN: University of California seeks trailblazers for electronic frontier." <http://www.ucpress.edu/scan>.

Quinn, Frank. "Consequences of electronic publication in theoretical physics." In *Scholarly Publication at the Crossroads: A Subversive Proposal for Electronic Publishing,* ed. A. Okerson and J. O'Donnell, 170–174. Washington, D.C.: Association of Research Libraries, 1995.

Quinnell, Richard A. "ATM networking." *EDN* 39 (5): 67–68, 78–84 (March 3, 1994).

Rader, Hannelore B. "Information literacy: A revolution in the library." *RQ* 31 (1): 25–29 (fall 1991).

Raitt, David L., ed. *Libraries for the New Millennium: Implications for Managers.* London: Library Association Publishing, 1997.

Ramsden, Anne, Zimin Wu, and Dianguo Zhao. "Piloting the ELINOR electronic library." Paper presented at Computers in Libraries International 94, London, 17 February 1994. E-mail communication with Connie Braun.

Randel, Mark. "PC accessories can ease the PC blues." *Office* 113 (5): 10–13 (May 1991).

Rapple, Brendan A. "A new model of libarian education for the networked environment" <http://www.ala.org/acrl/paperhtm/d37.html>.

Rawlins, Gregory J. E. "The new publishing: Technology's impact on the publishing industry over the next decade." *Public-Access Computer Systems Review* 3 (8): 5–63 (1992).

_____. "Publishing over the next decade." *Journal of the American Society for Information Science* 44 (8): 474–479 (September 1993).

Reed, Sally Gardner, ed. *Creating the Future: Essays on Librarianship.* Jefferson, N.C.: McFarland, 1996.

Report of the Joint Funding Council's Libraries Review Group (the Follett Report), December 1993 <http://www.niss.ac.uk/education/hefc/follett/report>.

Rice, James, Jr. *Teaching Library Use: A Guide for Library Instruction.* Westport, Conn.: Greenwood Press, 1981.

Richardson, John, Jr., and Jinnie Y. Davis, eds. *Academic Librarianship Past, Present, and Future: A Festschrift in Honor of David Kaser.* Englewood, Colo.: Libraries Unlimited, 1989.

Robb, Sam. "Pass to compliance." *American School and University* 70 (11): 36–43 (July 1998).

Rockwell, Eric. "The seven deadly sins of architects." *American Libraries* 20 (4): 307, 341–342 (April 1989).

Rockwell, Richard C. "Using electronic social science data in the age of the Internet." In *Gateways to Knowledge: The Role of Academic Libraries in Teaching, Learning, and Research*, ed. Lawrence Dowler, 59–80. Cambridge, Mass.: MIT Press, 1997.

Rohlf, Robert H. "Library design: What *not* to do." *American Libraries* 17 (2): 100–104 (February 1986).

Rosedale, Jeff. "Transforming the reserve function—developing new partnerships to provide instructional support in an electronic age." Preliminary summary of a workshop on electronic reserves issues, sponsored by the Association of Research Libraries, June 1994.

Rosenblatt, Susan. "Information technology investments in research libraries." *Educom Review* 34 (4): 28–33 (July/August 1999).

Roszak, Theodore. *The Cult of Information: The Folklore of Computers and the True Art of Thinking*. New York: Pantheon Press, 1986.

Rowley, Jennifer. "The library as a learning organization." *Library Management* 18 (2): 88–91 (1997).

Roy, G .G., and J. Owen. "SR: A PC-based CAD system for shadow and reflection studies in the built environment." *Computer-Aided Design* 21 (8): 497–504 (October 1989).

Rumble, Greville. "The competitive vulnerability of distance universities." *Open Learning* 7 (2): 31–45 (June 1992).

Russell, Albert R. "Avoiding building failures: The role of the owner's representative." *Construction Specifier* 47 (11): 143–144 (November 1994).

Samaras, Pete. "Lighting basics for computerized work environments." *Interior Design* 68 (10): 169–170, 184 (August 1997).

Sandler, Mark. "Transforming library staff roles." *Library Issues: Briefings for Faculty and Administrators* 17 (1) (September 1996) <http://www.libraryissues.com/pub/LI9609.html>.

Saunders, Laverna M. "The virtual library today." *Library Administration and Management* 6 (2): 66–70 (spring 1992).

Schell, Hall B., ed. *Reader on the Library Building*. Englewood, Colo.: Microcara, 1975.

Schill, Harold B. "Bibliographic instruction: Planning for the electronic information environment." *College & Research Libraries* 48 (5): 433–453 (September 1987).

Schneiderman, R. Anders. "Why librarians should rule the Net." *E-Node* 1 (4) (September 5, 1996) <http://www.igc.org/e-node/1996/enode0104a.htm>.

Schogel, Jane. "Lighting advances offer new options to designers." *Energy User News* 22 (4): 18–19 (April 1997).

Scully, Vincent. *Architecture: The Natural and the Manmade*. New York: St. Martin's Press, 1991.

Seaman, Scott. "Copyright and the electronic library." *DIGIT* (May/June 1994) <http://www.colorado.edu/CNS/Digit/mayjune94/copyright.html>.

Senn Breivik, Patricia, and Dan L. Jones. "Information literacy: Liberal education for the information age." *Liberal Education* 79 (1): 24–28 (1993).

Senn Breivik, Patricia, and Ward Shaw. "Libraries prepare for an information age." *Educational Record* 70 (1): 13–19 (winter 1989).

Shedlock, James, and Faith Ross. "A library for the twenty-first century: The Galter Health Sciences Library's renovation and expansion project." *Bulletin of the Medical Library Association* 85 (2): 176–186 (April 1997).

Simpson, Antony E. "Information-finding and the education of scholars: Teaching electronic access in disciplinary context." *Behavioral and Social Sciences Librarian* 16 (2): 1–18 (May/June 1998).

Smith, Eldred. *The Librarian, the Scholar, and the Future of the Research Library.* New York: Greenwood Press, 1990.

_____. "A partnership for the future." *Scholarly Publishing* 22 (2): 83–92 (January 1991).

_____. "The print prison." *Library Journal* 117 (3): 48–51 (February 1, 1992).

Smith, Eldred, and Peggy Johnson. "How to survive the present while preparing for the future: A research library strategy." *College & Research Libraries* 54 (5): 389–396 (September 1993).

Smith, Lester K. "Lighting and air-conditioning in libraries." In *Planning Library Buildings: From Decision to Design,* ed. Lester K. Smith. Chicago: American Library Association, 1986.

Smith, Lester K., ed. *Planning Library Buildings: From Decision to Design.* Chicago: American Library Association, 1986.

Smith, Roger A. "Purchasing computer-aided design software." *Technology Teacher* 52 (2): 7–9 (November 1992).

Solomon, Nancy B. "Building commissioning." *Architecture* 84 (6): 123–128 (June 1995).

Soule, Charles C. *How to Plan a Library Building for Library Work.* Boston: Boston Book Company, 1912.

Spiers, Joseph. "Let there be light." *Architectural Record (Lighting)* (August 1990): 21–25.

Stahl, Bil. "Networked information resources: Not just a library challenge." CAUSE Information Resources Library Document (CEM9239), 1992 <http://www.educause.edu/asp/doclib>.

Stallings, William. "Under the hood: FDDI speaks." *BYTE* 18 (4): 197–200 (April 1993).

"Standards for college libraries, 1995 edition, draft," *College & Research Libraries News* 55 (5): 261–272, 294 (May 1994).

Steele, Colin. "Millennial libraries: Management changes in an electronic environment." *Electronic Library* 11 (6): 393–402 (December 1993).

Sterling, Elia M., and Christopher W. Collett. "The building commissioning quality assurance process in North America." *ASHRAE Journal* 36 (10): 32–36 (October 1994).

Stevens, Norman D. "Research libraries: Past, present, and future." *Advances in Librarianship* 17 (1993): 79–109.

Stone, P. T. "Fluorescent lighting and health." *Lighting Research and Technology* 24 (2): 55–61 (1992).

"The student learning imperative: Implications for student affairs." *Journal of College Student Development* 37 (2): 118–122 (1996).

Studt, Tim. "PC cards nearly do it all." *R & D Magazine* 36 (4): 45–46 (March 1994).

Suprenant, Bruce A. "Vapor barriers under concrete slabs." *Concrete Construction* 37 (4): 292–294 (April 1992).

Sutton, Brett, and Charles H. Davis, eds. *Networks, Open Access, and Virtual Libraries: Implications for the Research Library.* Urbana-Champaign: University of Illinois Graduate School of Library and Information Science, 1991.

Sweetland, James H. "Humanists, libraries, electronic publishing, and the future." *Library Trends* 40 (4): 781–803 (spring 1992).

"Talking with George Gilder." *EDUCOM Review* 29 (4): 32–37 (July/August 1994).

Tebeaux, Elizabeth. "The high-tech workplace: Implications for technical communication." In *Technical Writing and Practice,* ed. B. E. Fearing and W. K. Sparrow, 136–144. New York: Modern Language Association, 1989.

Tenopir, Carol, and Lisa Ennis. "The digital reference world of academic libraries." *Online* 22 (4): 22–28 (July/August 1998).

Tesler, Lawrence G. "Networked computing in the 1990s." *Scientific American* 265 (3): 86–93 (September 1991).

Thatcher, Sanford G. "Towards the year 2001." *Scholarly Publishing* 24 (1): 25–37 (October 1992).

Thompson, Godfrey. *Planning and Design of Library Buildings.* New York: Architectural Press, 1977.

Thorin, Suzanne E., and Virginia D. Sorkin. "The library of the future." In *The Learning Revolution: The Challenge of Information Technology in the Academy,* ed. Diana G. Oblinger and Sean C. Rush, 164–179. Bolton, Mass.: Anchor Publishing, 1997.

Tompkins, Philip. "New structures for teaching libraries." *Library Administration and Management* 4 (2): 77–81 (spring 1990).

Toombs, Kenneth E. "The evolution of academic library architecture: A summary." *Journal of Library Administration* 17 (4): 25–36 (1992).

Treuer, Paul, and Linda Belote. "Current and emerging applications of technology to promote student involvement and learning." In *Using Technology to Promote Student Learning: Opportunities for Today and Tomorrow,* ed. Catherine McHugh Engstrom and Kevin W. Kruger, 17–30. San Francisco: Jossey-Bass, 1997.

Trinkley, Michael. *Preservation Concerns in Construction and Remodeling of Libraries: Planning for Preservation* (September 1992). ERIC, ED 355959.

Troll, Denise A. "Information technologies at Carnegie-Mellon." *Library Administration and Management* 6 (2): 91–99 (spring 1992).

Tseng, Paul C. "Building commissioning: Benefits and costs." *HPAC: Heating, Piping, Air Conditioning* 70 (4): 51–60 (April 1998).

Tucker, Marc S. "The 'Star Wars' universities: Carnegie-Mellon, Brown, and M.I.T." In *Computers on Campus: Working Papers: Current Issues in Higher Education,* ed. Marc S. Tucker. Washington, D.C.: American Association for Higher Education, 1993. ERIC, ED 240947.

Tuckett, Harold W. "Computer literacy, information literacy, and the role of the instruction librarian." In *Coping with Information Illiteracy: Bibliographic Instruction for the Information Age,* ed. Glenn E. Mensching and Teresa B. Mensching. Ann Arbor: Pierian Press, 1989.

Tuller, Charlie, and Diana Oblinger. "Information technology as a transformation agent." *CAUSE/EFFECT* 20 (4): 33, 38–45 (winter 1997–1998).

Twigg, Carol A. "The changing definition of learning." *EDUCOM Review* 29 (4): 22–25 (July/August 1994).

Tyler, Mark. "Sick buildings: Carrying the can." *Architect's Journal* 194 (August 1991): 48–50.

Uhler, Scott F., and Philippe R. Weiss. "Library building alterations under the Americans with Disabilities Act." *Illinois Libraries* 78 (1): 5–7 (winter 1996).

U.S. Copyright Office. *Report on Copyright and Digital Distance Education.* Washington, D.C.: U.S. Copyright Office, May 1999.

Vasi, John. "Trends in staff furnishings for libraries," *Library Trends* 36 (2): 377–390 (fall 1987).

Veaner, Allan B. "1985–1995: The next decade in academic librarianship, part I." *College & Research Libraries* 46 (3): 209–229 (May 1985).

Ward, Maribeth. "Expanding access to information with Z39.50." *American Libraries* 25 (7): 639–641 (July/August 1994).

Waters, Donald J. *Electronic Technologies and Preservation.* Washington, D.C.: Commission on Preservation and Access, 1992. ERIC, ED 351037.

Weber, David C. "The future capital funding of university library buildings." *IFLA Journal* 16 (3): 309–326 (1990).

Wegner, Lucy Siefert. "The research library and emerging information technology." *New Directions for Teaching and Learning* 51 (fall 1992): 83–90.

Weiser, Mark. "The computer for the 21st century." *Scientific American* 265 (3): 94–104 (September 1991).

Wiberley, Stephen E., Jr., and William G. Jones. "Humanists revisited: A longitudinal look at the adoption of information technology." *College & Research Libraries* 55 (6): 499–509 (November 1994).

Wielhorski, Karen. "Teaching remote users how to use electronic information resources." *Public-Access Computer Systems Review* 5 (4): 5–20 (1994).

Wilkinson, Ronald J. "The commissioning design intent narrative." *ASHRAE Journal* 41 (4): 31–36 (April 1999).

Wills, Mathew, and Gordon Wills. "The ins and outs of electronic publishing." [n.d.] <http://www.mcb.co.uk/literati/articles/insandouts.htm>.

Wilson, Alex. "Achieving energy efficient lighting." *Architecture: The AIA Journal* (June 1988): 109–113.

_____. "Glass: Window developments: An improved outlook." *Architecture: The AIA Journal* (August 1990): 95–98.

Wilson, Linda J. "Education for the electronic reference environment." *Journal of Academic Librarianship* 15 (2): 96c–96d (May 1989).

Winstead, Elizabeth B. "Staff reactions to automation." *Computers in Libraries* 14 (4): 18–21 (April 1994).

Wood, Damon. "The elements of quality lighting." In *Lighting Upgrades: A Guide for Facility Managers*. New York: UpWord Publishing, 1996.

Wright, Gordon. "A civic success." *Building Design and Construction* 36 (5): 58–60 (May 1995).

Ylvisaker, Peter N. "Underfloor air delivery: An ergonomic frontier?" *Buildings* 84 (November 1990): 56–58.

Young, Arthur P. "Information technology and libraries: a virtual convergence." *CAUSE/EFFECT* 17 (3): 5–7 (fall 1994).

Young, Jeffrey R. "Superfast Canadian network opens without much to carry." *Chronicle of Higher Education* (July 1, 1999) <http://www.chronicle.com/search97cgi/s97_cgi>.

Young, Lucie. "Natural light at work." *Metropolis* 12 (8): 51–55, 68–71 (April 1993).

Young, Peter R. "Periodical prices, 1988–1990." *Serials Librarian* 18 (3/4): 1–21 (1990).

Young, Philip H. "Visions of academic libraries in a brave new future." In *Libraries and the Future: Essays on the Library in the Twenty-first Century*, ed. F. W. Lancaster, 45–57. New York: Haworth Press, 1993.

Zeeman, Joe. "The Z39.50 standard—almost a reality." *Canadian Library Journal* 49 (4): 273–276 (August 1992).

Zeitnet. "ATM LAN emulation in workgroup networks" (1996) <http://www.rahul.net/zeitnet/atm/intrpwp.html>.

Page numbers in *italics* refer to figures.

Richard J. Bazillion is dean of library and information services, and professor of history, at Winona State University in Minnesota. His experience in library-construction projects includes three new buildings, two in Canada and one in the United States. Each library uses recent networking and communication technologies to enhance its teaching mission within the university.

Connie L. Braun has worked on two full-scale library-building projects, specializing in interior layouts, furniture selection, and move planning and orchestration. She has also been involved in smaller projects, designing and organizing library spaces at remote campuses that are part of a larger college or university organization. She is College Librarian/ Instructional Technology Specialist at Minnesota State College–Southeast Technical.